THE LEGACY OF COLONIALISM:
GENDER AND CULTURAL IDENTITY IN POSTCOLONIAL SOCIETIES

Máire ní Fhlathúin

GALWAY UNIVERSITY PRESS
1998

First published in 1998 by
Galway University Press Ltd

ISBN 1 901421 15 5

Printed by ColourBooks Ltd, Dublin

CONTENTS

Contents

INTRODUCTION

Colonial Histories and Postcolonial Texts

Máire ní Fhlathúin

Colonial discourse theory, especially in its earlier incarnations, developed a view of the postcolonial subject as unable to escape from the colonial encounter, as reacting to a world shaped by the colonizer, and responding to the experience of colonialism rather than initiating a discourse of the decolonized. Edward Said and Homi K. Bhabha—who form, together with Gayatri Chakravorty Spivak, the trio described by Robert Young as the 'Holy Trinity' of colonial-discourse analysis (163)—have at the centre of their theoretical frameworks a series of moments of entrapment, where colonizer and colonized are fixed in a relationship of dependency and inequality. Said's *Orientalism* accepts the success of the West's Orientalist strategies of the past: 'So impressive have the descriptive and textual successes of Orientalism been that entire periods of the Orient's cultural, political and social history are considered mere responses to the West. The West is the actor, the Orient a passive reactor. The West is the spectator, the judge and jury, of every facet of Oriental behavior' (109). Mimicry, identified by Bhabha as the colonized's strategy of resistance, takes place on the colonizer's ground: 'the words of the master become the site of hybridity—the warlike, subaltern sign of the native' (121)—but they are still, recognizably, the master's words. Spivak sees even more recent academic study as replicating this pattern, claiming that 'much so-called cross-cultural disciplinary practice, even when "feminist", reproduces and forecloses colonialist structures' (237).

This theoretical model of postcolonial analysis has recently been extended, as issues of gender, ethnicity and social class, relatively neglected in the early days of postcolonial theory, have moved centre-stage. Whether informed by or in opposition to colonial discourse theory, critical and historical inquiry has begun to focus on the material fabric of postcolonial societies, in which the memory and the legacy of the colonial encounter interact with other elements. These include, for example, a pre-colonial heritage imperfectly recovered, the contemporary geo-political and economic landscape, the increasing hegemony of English as a world language which was once forced on and then appropriated by de-colonized states. Postcolonial theory is no longer homogenous, if ever it was so: the range of essays in this book demonstrates the variety of approaches required to analyze these different aspects of contemporary postcolonial societies.

1

Some of the developments in theories of postcolonialism are illustrated by the first essay, on 'Gender and Colonial Space', in which Sara Mills takes the dyad of public (male) and private (female) space and explores the ways in which this set of categories is complicated and compromised by the interaction of gender and colonial spatial relationships. The essay also moves towards outlining a framework for further study which draws on readings of the material conditions of colonial space rather than 'the psychoanalytical models developed within postcolonial cultural theory which polarize and essentialize gender and racial divisions'.

In the rest of this collection, fourteen essays consider aspects of history, fiction and art in societies where colonialism has shaped cultural and national forms. They comprise three main sections. The first explores episodes in the history of the Caribbean and of aboriginal Australia—two regions where the legacy of colonialism is a long history of white domination and racial oppression—together with modern expressions of that history in Aboriginal literature and in the fiction of Toni Morrison. The second, on Ireland, deals with a different case: a region where the lines of demarcation between colonizer and colonized have sometimes become blurred in the course of a relationship encompassing the mutual expression of violence, racism and complicity. The third section considers aspects of contemporary culture where the modern world has been formed by its colonial past, in essays dealing with the cultural status and consumption of images and objects of art.

In the USA and the Caribbean, the defining element of these societies was their experience of slavery, something addressed in this book by two essays on different aspects of the legacy of slavery. In '"Lost Daughters of Afrik"?: Caribbean Women, Identity and Cultural Struggles from Slavery to Freedom', Barbara Bush examines the dynamic process of identity-formation undergone by black women during and after slavery. Constrained first by the narrow field of self-hood permitted by a slave-owning society, and later by the identities generated by the versions of black femininity supplied by black men, white men and white women; black women look towards their own history in an effort to fashion a self independent of these imposed masks. Deirdre Reddington's study of the work of Toni Morrison examines a literary instance of this attempt to recover an individual history. Analyzing Morrison's use of magic realist motifs and devices, the essay finds her novels to constitute a 'fabulous reality' where the past and the present are held in creative tension, co-existing in a narrative which records the disruption of individual and family relationships in a society fragmented by an unassimilatable history.

Lee A. Talley, writing on Jamaica Kincaid's novel *Lucy*, argues that Kincaid is engaged in a different re-writing of history, incorporating the 'Lucys' of Charlotte Bronte and William Wordsworth in an act of revisionism which questions the power to define which is normally associated with canonical texts. Through a careful analysis of the intricate connections between Kincaid's *Lucy* and Wordsworth's Lucy poems, the essay describes Lucy Potter's drive to free herself of the image created for her, expressed in her wish to re-name herself. But the name she chooses is Enid, after Enid Blyton—indicative of 'the insidious ways in which colonial ideology is globally consumed'. In the poetry of Derek Walcott, Paula Burnett finds an instance of a more positive fusion of Western canonical structures and Caribbean heritage in 'a distinctively Caribbean cultural synthesis'. Drawing on theories of psychoanalysis, language and postcolonialism, she explains how Walcott's work re-casts postcolonial alienation into 'a plural identity, of fragments tightly knit into a new whole': creating a subject for whom the term 'postcolonial' becomes a description, not a prison.

The narratives of postcolonialism incorporate the fantasies, delusions, knowledge and experience of two cultures—something which is too often overlooked in work which concentrates on colonizer *or* colonized, one to the exclusion of the other. Kay Schaffer, writing on the genesis and development of a preoccupation with cannibalism in the story of Eliza Fraser, describes the interaction of these two mindsets, and the resulting representation of Aboriginal behaviour in the popular discourse of the time. Her essay, 'Whose Cannibalism?: Consumption, Incorporation and the Colonial Body', also goes beyond this seminal event—tracing the resonances of the cannibalism motif in modern Australia, and the different approaches taken to such issues in contemporary academic research—in a study combining both historical research and theoretical analysis. Another aspect of the same historical picture is discussed in Chris Weedon's 'Gender, History and Identity in Writing by Australians of Aboriginal Descent', which examines the deployment of fiction and poetry as weapons in the Aboriginal resistance to the racism which is the legacy of colonialism in Australia. As in the case of Toni Morrison's use of the history of slavery, this essay finds that Aboriginal story-telling 'acts to reclaim…a history not only of oppression but of resistance to it'.

———————

Elleke Boehmer, writing in a recent survey of postcolonial literature, characterizes Ireland, compared to other postcolonial nations, as 'a different case because its history has been so closely and so long linked to that of

Britain'. At the same time, she observes that 'its resistance struggle was in certain other colonies taken as talismanic by nationalist movements...' (4). Within Ireland itself, academics associated with the Field Day group have engaged in an overtly postcolonial reclaiming of Irish literature and Irish writers, most notably in the volumes of the *Field Day Anthology of Irish Writing*. The essays in the second section of this book address the question of the nature of identity in pre-twentieth-century Ireland—formed by discourses of colonialism very different to those which shaped Australia or the Caribbean—and the modern literature which grows out of this history.

Eoin Bourke's 'Poor Green Erin' casts an unusual sidelight on the links between the histories of Ireland and Britain, in an account of 'German Perspectives of the "Irish Question" in the mid-19th Century'. While Germany was, at the time, 'neither an interested party in the binary colonial relationship nor involved in a colonizing project of its own', the commentators described in this essay are influenced by their own positions on questions of religion, race and politics (as well as being, in a few cases, apparently preoccupied by the Irish love-affair with the pig); their variety provides an insight into the complexity, and sometimes the complicity, of apparently neutral interventions in the colonial and postcolonial debate. Theories of race are explored from another angle by Penny Boumelha, who focuses her essay, 'Gender, Genius and Ireland at the Turn of the Century', on the intersection of discourses of gender and race in the debate over the incidence of 'genius'. Through the use of these mutually reinforcing elements, both Irish men and English women were, it is argued, excluded from a 'form of genius' which 'not only justifies colonialism and male dominance, but makes them inevitable'.

Gender and history are also considered in Alison Twells's account of 'Colonial Discourse and Domestic Femininity'. This essay studies the writings of Hannah Kilham, sent to Ireland by the British and Irish Ladies' Society to work among the Irish female poor. Kilham compared these Irishwomen to the African women she had also visited, and Boehmer's point about the 'difference' of the Irish case is here most clearly illustrated, as Kilham constructs from her comparisons a 'hierarchy of civilization determined by notions of domesticity'. At the same time, however, the missionaries of the society saw themselves as having a civilizing role in Ireland which is readily recognizable as an all too familiar element of the relationship between the colonizer and the colonized.

Two essays on Irish history and literature make connections between literary works of the twentieth century and the psychic and physical wounds suffered by Irish society and individuals in contemporary and recent memory. In '"Eater and eaten": The Great Hunger and De-Anglicization', Laura O'Connor examines Yeats's later poetry, and traces its themes of satire and self-contempt back not only to 'post-Parnellite rancour' but also to Irish 'painful memories' of the Famine, of 'attempted ethnocide', and of 'Irish complicity with it'. The barely-disguised images of cannibalism in Irish history are thus explored in this essay, which, considered alongside Kay Schaffer's 'Whose Cannibalism', underlines both the similarities and the differences between Ireland and other postcolonial societies. Laura Doyle's essay, 'Alter/natives for the Colonial Body: Matter and Memory in O'Faolain's *No Country for Young Men*', examines another set of narratives of the body, discussing the exhibition of women's sexual bodies as the site of memory and resistance in the work of Julia O'Faolain.

The final section comprises three essays on the role of art and artifacts, dealing with their status as objects carrying the weight of colonial history but also displaying, in their contemporary re-interpretations, both the legacy of colonialism and the new concerns of postcolonial cultures. These essays continue, as well, the analysis of the placement and representation of the human body in cultural and economic contexts. In 'From the Spectre to the Specular: Imaging the Colonial Body in Post/Modern Times', Janet Harbord discusses the body as an object susceptible to appropriation and representation in the service of many conflicting discourses. Focusing on reproductions of a single image, a photo titled 'Adrianna, Transvestite, Brazil', the essay also details the ways in which 'the circumstances of its circulation' point towards a complex of gender, political and cultural relationships between individuals and nations. Andrea Noble's 'Framing the Mexican Body' examines the circulation of the photographer Tina Modotti's images, and her signature, in a dual exploration of the operation of Marxian 'commodity fetishism' and Freudian 'psychic fetishism' in the exchange and use of these representations of the body.

Finally, Lisa Botshon's 'African Remains of the Day: Art and Object at the American Museum of Natural History' outlines her fascination with the Museum itself, its policies with regard to acquisitions and exhibitions, and the versions of history it offers its audience. She sees in some of its work an attempt to re-contextualize the material in its exhibitions, placing the objects on display in the framework of the colonial societies which produced them. In other cases, however, the displays are characterized by the discourse of 'an antiquated American anthropology', thus forming, in effect, another chapter in the colonial history. The Museum, in her analysis, becomes the location where a neo-colonial contemporary cultural landscape reveals both knowingly and unknowingly its colonial past. In this interaction of past and present histories lies the story told, in different ways, by all the contributors to this book.

Works Cited

Bhabha, Homi K. (1994) *The Location of Culture*. London and New York: Routledge.

Boehmer, Elleke. (1995) *Colonial and Postcolonial Literature: Migrant Metaphors*. Oxford & New York: Oxford UP.

Deane, Seamus, Andrew Carpenter and Jonathan Williams, eds. (1991) *The Field Day Anthology of Irish Writing*. 3 vols. Derry: Field Day Publications.

Said, Edward W. (1995) *Orientalism*. 1st pub. 1978. Harmondsworth: Penguin.

Spivak, Gayatri Chakravorty. (1986) 'Imperialism and Sexual Difference', *Oxford Literary Review* 8.i/ii: 225-240.

Young, Robert J.C. (1995) *Colonial Desire: Hybridity in Theory, Culture and Race*. London: Routledge.

GENDER AND COLONIAL SPACE

Sara Mills

My aims in this essay are to analyze the gendered nature of colonial space and to begin to sketch out a framework for a materialist-feminist postcolonial practice.[1] I will be drawing on theoretical work on gender and space which has been developed primarily by feminist geographers and anthropologists, and I will read this critical work through/against some of the theoretical material developed within postcolonial literary and cultural theory. I will attempt this fusion in order to analyze spatial relations without relying solely on the psychoanalytical models developed within postcolonial cultural theory which polarize and essentialize gender and racial divisions. I begin with an examination of the possibility of developing a more materialist postcolonial theory/practice. I then critically examine the theoretical work which has been undertaken on space and gender, which generally considers the confinement of women to be the determining factor in women's sense of their position within spatial frameworks. I argue that the complexity of gendered spatial relations, particularly within the colonial context, cannot be encompassed within the notion of confinement. I then move to an analysis of the importance of viewing position for the construction of gendered spatial relations. Finally, I consider two levels of colonial space, the idealized level of distance and separation embodied within colonial architecture and town planning, and the 'contact zone' of sexualized colonial space (Pratt 1992). In this way, by being critical of the reductiveness of much psychoanalytical postcolonial theory, I hope to produce an analytical framework within which it is possible to make general statements about the gendered nature of colonial space, at the same time as being aware of the material specificity of different colonial contexts. Throughout this discussion I will examine briefly a number of primary texts written within different colonial contexts; my main focus of attention will be on India in the late nineteenth century.

Materialist Feminism and Colonial Spatial Relations

Like many critics working in the field of colonial discourse, I have felt politically committed to work on colonial material, but have not felt comfortable working within the frameworks currently in circulation (see Young 1990 and 1995; Williams and Chrisman 1993; and Ashcroft, Griffiths and Tiffin 1995 for general surveys). So ingrained is the use of psychoanalytical concepts within this type of theoretical work that it is difficult to engage in theoretical debates without, of necessity, reinflecting the usage of certain terms to allow a more materialist analysis to develop. My principal objection to the reliance on psychoanalysis for the analysis of colonialism is that the specificity of the colonial context is lost—the materiality of invasion, discrimination, murder, rape, expropriation of land and also of resistance are erased.

I will be viewing space not as a given, but as a set of superimposed spatial frameworks, as many social spaces negotiated within one geographical place and time. Colonial space has often been described in monolithic terms, since it is the dominant spatial representations of British male colonists which have been examined. Instead of this monolithic view of space, I will attempt to examine the possibilities of developing a materialist feminist analysis of representational space which will be aware of the way that women and men, colonized and colonizer, negotiate their positions in space through their interrogations with their respective social positions. Rather than simply arguing, for example, that British women have imposed upon them a spatial confinement within the colonial context, thus assuming that British males have complete freedom of movement, I will analyze the variety of spatial frameworks which are operating both for women and men within this context. I will be concerned to examine the way that discursive constraints work to produce often conflicting and contradictory spatial frameworks, where within certain colonial contexts, confinement for some women is the dominant mode of negotiating spatiality, whereas for other women, in other colonial contexts, transgressing these boundaries will be sanctioned. In still other situations, transgression will be a strategy of resistance. Indeed, I am concerned to examine whether spatial relations do not in fact determine the differences within gender and racial relations operating within a particular colonial context (Pratt and Hanson 1994). As Massey has argued, 'it's not just that the spatial is socially constructed; the social is spatially constructed' (Massey 1984, cited in Spain 1992, 4).

Space and Gender

The relationship between gender and space has been the subject of rigorous enquiry especially by feminist theorists (Ardener 1981; Blunt and Rose 1994; Massey 1994; Moore 1986; Spain 1992). Early feminist work on women and space tended to focus on women's confinement and restriction in movement; for example, Iris Marion Young's article 'Throwing like a girl' stressed the way that women learn to situate themselves and move in space in a way which is significantly more restricted than men—even simple actions like sitting or walking are ones where the female subject is selfconsciously not allowing herself to transcend the limits of the body as an object (Young 1989). However, within the colonial sphere, this sense of restriction is not as clearly experienced as in the British context. In many of the accounts of women travelling, and in autobiographical and fictional accounts, British women stress the freedom they found within the colonial context, which seemed free of some of the constraints of British society. It should also be noted that for Indian and African women within colonial society, their freedom was often curtailed not by their families within the harem or purdah, but through fear of attack or rape by British soldiers. As I show later, colonial spatial relations were sexualized.

The public/ private sphere divide has been critically analyzed by many feminist theorists, since the domestic is positioned as primarily a woman's space, and her access to the public sphere is sometimes seen as marked or exceptional. Gillian Rose describes the work of feminist theorists who have charted the ways in which women's sense of place within the public sphere is bounded by a fear of physical attack. But Milroy and Wismer have shown that much of women's work cannot be fitted into this binary divide, and that the spheres themselves are more interconnected than has previously been recognized; they thus argue for a disengagement of the conflation of gender and the private/public spheres (Milroy and Wismer 1994). Certainly once one begins to move the analysis of the public/private sphere away from a concern with British middle-class women, the distinction becomes untenable.

This work clearly calls for a reappraisal of analysis of gender and colonialism where it is assumed that colonizing and colonized women are confined to the private domestic sphere, whilst colonizing and colonized men operate in the public sphere. As I hope to show in this essay, colonized space troubles some of the simple binary oppositions of public and private spheres, since some of the values circulating within the colonized countries are profoundly at odds with the values of the imperial culture. There seem to be extreme forms of the public/private divide at an idealized, stereotypical level: for example, the perceived restriction of some Indian women in the private sphere within the harem or zenana, and the ultra-conservative spatial arrangements within the Civil Lines in British Indian cities (see Callan and Ardener 1984). Yet at the same time, British women's travel writing in colonized countries, together with the accounts of British women in outpost situations, by their very presence alone in the public sphere destabilize notions of a clear female-private/male-public sphere divide (Mills 1991; see also Paxton 1992).

Doreen Massey's work demonstrates the necessity of discussing women and men in space in materialist terms, for she states that 'what is at issue is not social phenomena in space but both social phenomena and space as constituted out of social relations'. We therefore need to think of 'the spatial [as] social relations "stretched out"' (2). This notion of space being imbricated with social relations is important in considering women in space, because it moves discussion away from simple notions of women as a group having a consistent relation to spatial frameworks. Whilst Massey's basic premise is essential for this kind of analysis, I have found it very difficult to forge a materialist form of analysis from her work. Her lack of specificity in terms of different forms of spatial relation has led me to draw more on Henrietta Moore's anthropological work, since she has produced very detailed practical analyses (Moore 1986). Thus, through an analysis of the socially constructed differences in women and men's access to the public and private sphere, it is possible to map out the differences this may entail for women and men when they negotiate spatial boundaries for themselves and for other subjects.

Viewing positions: knowledge and colonial space

In analyzing space, it is important to consider not simply that which is represented spatially, but also the position from which that representation is produced. I would like to consider in this section the importance of viewing and knowing positions in constructing spatial relations. Rose's work on the landscape has been very important in understanding Western women's different access to that position of intelligibility which is the viewer of landscape (Rose 1993 and 1995). For her, whilst bodies are 'maps of the relation between power and identity', those maps do not simply trace subjection (Rose 1993, 32). Within the colonial context, as Mary Louise Pratt has shown, a particular type of knowledge was produced: what she terms planetary consciousness. This universal view of natural history led to Europeans travelling the globe in search of specimens and extracting those specimens from their meaning within indigenous systems of signification and functionality, in order for them to take their place within a Eurocentric and colonial system of knowledge. As John Noyes states in his analysis of German South West Africa: 'the colony is a space in which meaning is possible' (6). The position which a European traveller could adopt because of his or her role in the production of knowledge of natural history was one which was elided with the colonial state; and, as Pratt states, travellers were 'central agents in legitimising scientific authority and its global project alongside Europe's other ways of knowing the world' (29). British women travellers, in the same way as male travellers, produced scientific knowledge which was fundamentally connected to European expansion and the promotion of a view of the world that sees European activities as essentially civilizing. The naturalist figure may have had some appeal to women travellers since it seemed so innocent, in relation to an 'assumed guilt of conquest', as Pratt puts it (29). But this production of knowledge set up a network of spatial frameworks within which the colonized country is constructed as simply a repository of unusual specimens which Europeans may explore and plunder at will. The colonized country is produced as a space empty of systems of signification other than the order which European scientific knowledge imposes.

Levels of Colonial Space

In describing the gendered nature of colonial space it is important to examine a range of different spatial relations both at an ideal or stereotypical level, and at a more experiential level in what Mary Louise Pratt terms 'the contact zone' where 'disparate cultures meet, clash and grapple with each other, often in highly asymmetrical relations of domination and subordination' (38).

Although architectural space does not determine social relations, it may attempt to set out the parameters within which certain types of relation may be negotiated; as Spain states:

> architecture itself does not directly determine how people act or how they see themselves and others. Yet the associations a culture establishes at any particular time between a "model" or typical house and a notion of the model family do encourage certain roles and assumptions (Spain 108).

At an ideal level, British colonial space in India and Africa is primarily divided into clear-cut territories where distance between the colonized and the colonizers is emphasized. At an actual level, this distance is impossible to maintain and instead there develops what King has termed a third culture, that is, a very different form of cultural system to the colonial culture in Britain, modified as it is by the indigenous culture (King 1976).

As King has shown, the Civil Lines in India are generally located some way from the 'native' town; the justification for this distance is made on perceived health grounds, and colonial cities are designed to emphasize the distinction between ruler and ruled. In contrast to what are seen as the sprawling accretions of the crowded 'native' town, the civil lines are generally planned with mathematical precision on a grid-plan, including strategically placed grand public buildings which dominate the cityscape and are easily viewed from a range of vistas, and wide straight avenues which give ease of access and visibility. Colonial residences are often set in spacious landscaped grounds and built on classical lines, emphasizing the perceived imperial heritage of the inhabitants. Colonial town planning is an idealized embodiment of colonial relations. But this notion of the complete separation of the 'native' area from the British area is one which only holds at an ideal level, since the separated Civil Lines contain within them large numbers of indigenous people.

Spatial segregation seems to be 'figured' around British females. The stereotypical representation of the memsahib is invoked at moments when British colonial power is threatened, for example, in the case of the Ilbert Bill in 1883 and Gillies case of 1859 (see Chaudhuri and Strobel 1992). Whilst sexual contact often took place between white males and indigenous females/males, this sexual contact was figured at an idealized/stereotypical level as between white women and indigenous males. The confinement of British women because of the fear of sexual attack has a history which is an integral part of the justification of colonial rule. Sharpe focuses on the fictional 'origins' of the image of British women subjected to rape by 'native' insurgents in the 1857 Indian Uprising/Mutiny, and states that:

> the idea of rebellion [in the 1857 revolt] was so closely imbricated with the violation of English womanhood that the Mutiny was remembered as a barbaric attack on innocent white women. Yet Magistrates commissioned to investigate the so-called eyewitness reports could find no evidence to substantiate the rumours of rebels raping, torturing and mutilating English women (2).

By meticulously examining the fictional accounts and historical records, she is able to document the way that this figure of women serves to displace consideration of the oppressiveness of colonial rule and also to obscure its fragility in moments of conflict. She states that the 'savaged remains [of British women] display a fantasy of the native's savagery that screens the "barbarism" of colonialism' (233) and also 'displaces attention away from the image of English men dying at the hands of native insurgents' (231). She shows how focusing on representations of the rape of British women at times of conflict in colonial rule also has the effect of moving our attention away from political insurrection towards a concern with racial difference and Otherness. Thus, she stresses that it is important to see these images and the subsequent protection of British females as serving a function within the maintenance of colonial rule in a time of crisis—a crisis which was both a political crisis within India and also a wider crisis relating to the moral and ethical position of colonial rule (see also Donaldson 1992 and Sunder Rajan 1994). This concern with rape and protection also had the effect of sexualizing space for women.

It is important to recognize that the confined spaces of Indian women operate at the ideal level of stereotype rather than the actual level. Whilst the concept of the stereotype is important, as Bhabha has shown, I would like to question the monolithic quality of stereotype prevalent in psychoanalytic theorizing, since these stereotypes changed over time and were challenged by other representations (Bhabha 20). As Moore has shown, stereotypes do not determine thinking, but need to be seen as forming part of a practice which is developed in negotiation with other people and other practices. Just as colonial history is being rewritten through the matrices of race and gender, it is necessary to examine colonial spatial frameworks in order to construct subaltern spatiality (see Sangari and Vaid 1990; Bhadra 1988). Subaltern space within India and Africa can be defined as the complex where indigenous spatial frameworks and colonized evaluations of those frameworks collided, within the context of the imposition of imperial spatial frameworks. To colonized subjects, practices such as sati and the confinement of women had been viewed differently before colonial rule, and once colonial rule was instituted colonized space was inflected differently. For many subjects, these practices figured large in nationalist struggles. It is not possible to 'retrieve' this subaltern space, but it may be possible to 'figure' it out from examining a range of representational practices, much as Rajan has done with her re-examination of sati (Rajan 1992).

To sum up, I have argued that within the colonial sphere, British and indigenous women's interventions in the production and negotiation of spatial frameworks cannot simply be considered in terms of notions of confinement. The architectural constraints and ideological strictures on women's movement within the colonial zone were important in shaping a notion of a woman's place and contributed to a sexualizing of space. Nevertheless, the spatial frameworks which developed as a result of the clash between these constraints and women as agents, as producers of knowledge and viewers of landscape, meant that a variety of spatial roles existed for women. For example, British women's travel writing with its ambivalent position, wavering between openly transgressive qualities and acceptance of the domestic sphere and protection, forces us to consider the complexity of the role of gender in mapping colonial space. Similarly, when considering colonized women and their spatial frameworks it is not possible simply to consider the stereotypical representations of confinement in the harem. It is necessary to consider these representations together with critical subaltern re-evaluations of those spaces, and alongside other representations of the majority of colonized women who were not confined. Thus, I have not been arguing that women have separate spatial frameworks, but that women negotiate meanings within the context of dominant discursive fields; whilst the dominant discourses may place emphasis on confinement, passivity and protection, these discourses are themselves challenged and reaffirmed by representations produced by both women and men.

Notes

1. A version of this paper will be appearing in *Gender, Place and Culture*, forthcoming.

Works Cited

Ahmed, S. 'Identifications, gender and racial difference: moving beyond the limits of a psychoanalytical account of subjectivity', in *Representations of Gender and Identity Politics in South Asia*, ed. J. Rencka Shama. (forthcoming).

Ardener, S., ed. (1981) *Women and Space: Ground Rules and Social Maps.* London: Croom Helm.

Ballhatchet, K. (1980) *Race, Sex and Class under the Raj: Imperial Attitudes and Policies and their Critics 1793-1905.* London: Weidenfeld and Nicolson.

Barnes, T.J. and J.S. Duncan, eds. (1992) *Writing Worlds: Discourse, Text and Metaphor in the Presentation of Landscape.* London: Routledge.

Bhabha, Homi K. (1994) 'The other question: stereotype, discrimination and the discourse of colonialism', in *The Location of Culture.* London: Routledge, 66-85.

Blunt, A. and G. Rose, eds. (1994) *Writing Women and Space: Colonial and Postcolonial Geographies.* New York: Guilford.

Callan, H. and S. Ardener, eds. (1984) *The Incorporated Wife.* London: Croom Helm.

Callaway, H. (1987) *Gender, Culture and Empire: European Women in Colonial Nigeria.* Basingstoke: Macmillan.

Chaudhuri, N. and M. Strobel, eds. (1992) *Western Women and Imperialism: Complicity and Resistance.* Bloomington: Indiana UP.

Colomina, B., ed. (1992) *Sexuality and Space.* Princeton, NJ: Princeton University.

Donaldson, L. (1992) *Decolonising Feminisms: Race, Gender and Empire-Building.* London: Routledge.

Ferguson, M. (1993) *Colonialism and Gender Relations from Mary Wollstonecraft to Jamaica Kincaid: East Caribbean Connections.* New York: Columbia UP.

Guha, R. and Gayatri Chakravorty Spivak, eds. (1988) *Selected Subaltern Studies.* New York and Oxford: Oxford UP.

Haggis, J. (1990) 'Gendering colonialism or colonising gender?: Recent women's studies approaches to white women and the history of British colonialism', *Women's Studies International Forum* 13.i/ii: 105-15.

Hyam, R. (1990) *Empire and Sexuality: The British Experience.* Manchester: Manchester UP.

King, A. (1976) *Colonial Urban Development: Culture, Social Power and Environment.* London: Routledge and Kegan Paul.

Massey, D. (1994) *Space, Place and Gender.* Cambridge: Polity Press.

McClintock, A. (1995) *Imperial Leather: Race, Gender and Sexuality in the Colonial Contest.* London: Routledge.

Mills, Sara. (1991) *Discourses of Difference: Women's Travel Writing and Colonialism.* London: Routledge.

Mills, Sara. (1994) 'Knowledge, gender and empire', pp 29-50, in A. Blunt and G. Rose, eds: *Writing Women and Space: Colonial and Postcolonial Geographies.* New York: Guilford.

Minh-ha, T. (1989) *Woman, Native, Other: Writing Postcoloniality and Feminism.* Bloomington: Indiana UP.

Moore, H.L. (1986) *Space, Text and Gender: An Anthropological Study of the Marakwet of Kenya.* Cambridge: Cambridge UP.

Noyes, J. (1992) *Colonial Space: Spatiality in the discourse of German South West Africa.* Chur: Harwood.

Pratt, Mary Louise. (1992) *Imperial Eyes: Travel Writing and Transculturation.* London: Routledge.

Rose, G. (1993) *Feminism and Geography: The Limits of Geographical Knowledge.* London: Polity.

Rose, G. (1995) 'Geography and Gender, Cartographies and Corporealities'. *Progress in Human Geography* 19.4 (1995): 544-48.

Sharpe, J. (1993) *Allegories of Empire: the Figure of Woman in the Colonial Text.* Minneapolis: University of Minnesota Press.

Spain, D. (1992) *Gendered Spaces.* Chapel Hill: University of North Carolina Press.

Young, Robert J.C. (1995) *Colonial Desire: Hybridity in Theory, Culture and Race.* London: Routledge.

Young, I.M. (1989) 'Throwing like a girl: a phenomenology of feminine bodily comportment, motility and spatiality', in *The Thinking Muse: Feminism and Modern French Philosophy*, eds J. Allen and I.M. Young. Bloomington: Indiana UP: 51-70.

'LOST DAUGHTERS OF AFRIK'?

Caribbean Women, Identity and
Cultural Struggles from Slavery to Freedom

Barbara Bush

The study of slavery is an area fraught with problems, for the 'racial terror' of enslavement still has a powerful and emotive influence on the 'social memory' of black women in the Atlantic Diaspora. It is linked to politically loaded contemporary debates over black identity and the nature of gender, class and race oppression. My focus within these debates is how black women's history has been interpreted through what Catherine Hall has dubbed 'white visions' of black lives (Hall 1993). White men (and in certain ways, white women) had the cultural and economic power to define slave identities in a way that reinforced their own superiority. But an examination of white defined 'identities' also demands recognition of black cultural resistance produced in the mediation of those identities. The cultural struggles that developed over the negotiation of black identity are central to understanding the divided or 'double consciousness' of slaves in simultaneously adapting to and resisting enslavement. For black women the term 'triple consciousness' may be more appropriate: they had to negotiate not only conflicts between a racist white and a formative Afrocentric creole culture, but also gender identity in relation to white men, black men *and* white women.

My central argument is that women redefined the 'imagined identities' created for them by whites by effecting a fusion between African-derived cultural beliefs and powerful resistance strategies which undermined the slave system. I refer here primarily to women field slaves who constituted the most culturally 'independent', if the most harshly treated, slaves. Ironically, it was the powerful tensions they experienced between production in the formal economy and biological and cultural reproduction of the slave community that ensured their pivotal contribution to the general resistance against, and successful survival of, slavery. I have concentrated on the later and, arguably, most exploitative phase of slavery when a conjunction of disintegrative forces culminated in the overthrow of a system which had indelibly reshaped the world. Developments in this epoch are also seminal in the mapping of black women's experiences in freedom.

In the first section I will try to clarify my interpretation of culture, identity, power and resistance in the context of women's location in slave society and the complex web of interactions between black and white. This addresses the crucial question of what identity is. I will then examine how black women's identities were interpreted through 'the eyes of the [white] beholder'. This is followed by a closer look at the link between white oppression and resistance struggles in which women engaged to defend themselves and the slave community against psychic and cultural disintegration. Finally, I have included an analysis of the transition to freedom and the reworking of black identities that emerged with developments in colonial society in the nineteenth century. Here, I will argue that the slave experience, brutal and reifying as it was, forged a particularly dynamic cultural resistance that became subdued and more covert in freedom.

The Cultural Interface? Identity, Power and Resistance in Slave Society

Analyses of slave women's lives focalize the relationship between culture and resistance in the shaping of new identities within complex and changing patterns of gender, race and class oppression. Slaves did not simply react to material conditions; resistance also embraced a struggle against forces that undermined the slaves' Afrocentric culture. I do not use this term in the sense of a static, 'authentic' culture or 'mythologised Africanity', which Paul Gilroy has so eloquently criticized (Gilroy 1993) but as a recognition of the significance of Africa as a source of origin of black diaspora culture. The deep significance of cultural resistance is now being recognized in both conflict and compromise, reflecting the 'ingenious ways of which the weak make use of the strong' (De Certeau xvii). Slave women employed a multiplicity of resistance tactics and survival strategies that ranged from 'compromise'—in, for instance, concubinage with white men—to cultural resistance against pressures that threatened to undermine the Afrocentric family, marriage and childbearing customs. Women were also able to turn the system to their own advantage in their participation in the informal economy centred on the provision grounds and slave markets, allowed by the planters to boost food supply. All these tactics involved either tensions or 'contracts of compatibility' between white and slave cultures.

Culture is a term frequently used loosely, without any precise, shared understanding. It is interpreted here as a shared set of values coherently linking language, religion, kinship, work, family, leisure and individuals' concepts of the world around them. This conceptualization of culture aids discussion of both white and black identity and links identity to wider political struggles against the slave system. Women, globally, are arguably the principal transmitters of culture within the family and local community and it is women's work that ensures that the world—and indeed humanity—continues (Rosalda and Lamphére 1976). Links between culture and material survival are clear in the vital contribution slave women made to social and biological reproduction in the slave community as the primary 'cultural shield' that frustrated the efforts of whites to dehumanize Africans through servitude (Rodney 345). The cultural contribution of women, however, must be located within their relationship to white patriarchy and black sexism. The definition of patriarchy as the manifestation and institutionalization of male dominance over women and children in the family and wider society (Lerner 242) is arguably applicable only to white men in slave society. Sexism, as an ideology of male supremacy and of beliefs that support and sustain it, has validity for relations between slave men and women. Women were more likely to be concentrated in the less skilled jobs in the formal economy, in contrast to men who comprised the vast majority of elite, skilled slaves. Overseers were predominantly male slaves, and slave men in general benefited from women's domestic labour. Gender differences perpetuated a specific 'women's culture' that developed within, and sometimes in resistance to, the primarily male-defined elements of slave and white cultures. Such 'women-centred culture' was vital to the development of identity and encompassed friendship networks of women, their affective ties, rituals and 'folk knowledge'. In the present-day Caribbean there is an increasing recognition of the deep significance of this 'womanist culture' that has been overshadowed by the more dominant 'masculinist culture'—two 'sharply gendered cultural visions' marked by competition and struggle (Arnold 5).

The labyrinthine interpenetrations of culture, gender, class and power reverberated more dramatically on the lives of slave women than those of slave men. Slave women's material reality was that of profound economic exploitation. In establishing some autonomy of action and self identity they had to fight against deep constraints of law, punishment and complete lack of human rights. Power relations between masters and slaves have always been ambiguous and some black women may have had limited sexual power over white men, securing favours, including manumission, for themselves and their children (Bush 1990, 111). However, the very nature of chattel slavery led to a peculiarly strong concentration of power. Women as field slaves worked in the harshest conditions and had the additional burdens of childbearing. This has led to a tendency in the historiography of slavery to see women on large-scale plantations as atomized production units estranged from kin, community and culture (e.g. Morissey 1989), when it was arguably those very material pressures that inspired communal solidarity and resistance and kept the goal of liberation alive.

These relationships of power are paramount in understanding how black women made sense of their world and defined their identity. Their relationship to white women is central here. Black women became the 'other', whose debased and sexual nature reinforced white women's identity as pure and feminine, the white patriarchal ideal of womanhood. Contrasts with white women were central to white-defined identities of black women, but in the culturally fluid creole society, white women's identities were also influenced by close proximity to black women. Visitors to the Indies commented adversely on the habits of white creole women. The portrayal of Antoinette (Bertha) Cosway as Rochester's mad first wife (starkly contrasted with the devoted and sensible Jane Eyre) in Jean Rhys, *Wide Sargasso Sea* (1966) is a reflection of such negative attitudes. According to the Jamaican planter Edward Long, white women suffered from 'constant intercourse with negroe domestics' whose 'drawling dissonant gibberish', modes of dress and manners they 'insensibly adopted'. Women on remote plantations were particularly vulnerable:

> We may see in some of these places, a very fine young woman awkwardly dangling her arms, with the air of a negroe servant lolling almost the whole day upon beds or settees, her head muffled up with two or three handkerchiefs, her dress loose, and without stays. At noon, we find her employed in gobbling pepper pot, seated on the floor, with her sable handmaids around her (2: 412-13).

Poorer and urban white market women and female slave-owners were also culturally influenced by spacial proximity to black women (Beckles 1993). If creole women were not 'untainted' by contact with black culture, likewise, female slaves in habitual contact with whites, especially the 'light skinned obedient' housekeepers and long-term mistresses of white men, emulated white women (Wright 112; Stewart 330).

There is an ambiguity of culture in the Atlantic diaspora, and in the Caribbean both black and white permeated cultural barriers (Gilroy 31). The term Afrocentric is useful, however, in defining the primary cultural ambience of slaves. There were common threads of Afrocentric culture throughout the English, French and Spanish Caribbean that had important implications for cultural struggles and identities. In the cultural cauldron of slave society, cultural negotiation had to take place not only between black and white, creole and African-born women, but also amongst slaves taken from different parts of Africa. However, a link was forged through resistance to slavery and the overarching economic and ideological power of whites. White men defined the limits and discourses of this power but white women were integral to the racist culture of slavery and male cultural honour. In contrast, black women's identities were uniquely influenced by resistance to enslavement and to the identities constructed for them by contemporary racial ideologies.

At this point it is essential to explore the idea of 'identity'. There are two main ways of looking at identity. Both are intrinsically related and applicable in this analysis. The simplest concept of identity is as a tag or label, that is, how you are seen by others. This applies to some extent to white constructs of black identity, explored below. But identity is also how you see yourself, your consciousness of being and where you fit into the world. This more complex definition raises the question as to what the distinction is between identity and consciousness, and how do both concepts relate to cultural struggles? Kum Kum Bhavnani defines identity as a concept that has provided motivation for many struggles that challenge social, economic, political and ideological injustices, including those against enslavement. It is, however, a 'slippery concept' as it is not fixed and is never closed. Hence identities are always being reworked and individuals can have different 'identities' in different contexts (Bhavnani 1993). Similarly, images and stereotypes, the white-constructed identities of blacks, shift and change with time (Pieterse 1992). Arguably, this has relevance to African Caribbean women both in terms of historical time-scales (periodization of the changing character of slavery and processes of personal transformation through capture, creolization and emancipation) and the way in which women had to negotiate a multiplicity of overlapping and frequently conflicting identities, as in the tensions between the white-defined public and the more Afro-defined private spheres of their lives. Identity negotiation is integral to securing a coherent individual and group self-consciousness of the material and ideological forces that shape human beings' diverse 'realities': it informs political action and/or resistance against oppression. The deep problems inherent in this process in slave societies are revealed through an analysis of African women's identities and white constructs of slave womanhood.

Daughters of Injur'd Afrik?: White Constructs of Slave Women

Gender, race and class inequality are equally fundamental to understanding slave women's identities. Why and how did such inequalities originate? Women have always been vulnerable to enslavement because of their status in patriarchal societies, and women slaves predominated in the internal African slave trade. Indeed, on the earliest pre-literate tablets from the Middle East, the term for slave girl appeared before the more general term 'slave' (Davis 35). In Africa, as in the Caribbean, women were highly valued for their labour, not simply as child bearers. Moreover, it may be argued that women experienced slavery of a sort within the family through the practice of 'bride price', and were accustomed to being bartered and having little control over their own destinies (Robertson and Klein 4-9). So for some women, their identity was already defined, pre-capture, as domestic slaves. For those who were not enslaved, identity came primarily through motherhood and in relationship to the deeper structures of family and kin that cohered African societies. It can be argued that in such societies collective as opposed to individual identity prevailed and women were supported by a 'remarkable degree of female solidarity' (Cutrufelli 146). Unfortunately, the lack of contemporary evidence relating to the lives of eighteenth-century African women is even more acute than for Caribbean slave women. Rare accounts, however, provide a slim testimony to how they were taken into captivity. Women were taken in dawn raids as the first up and out of their houses, sometimes being surprised drawing water at wells outside the village. Deception and bribery were used, not simply violence, and women could also be sold into slavery to settle debts or as punishment for adultery or crime. Richer women could substitute slaves (Boulègue 243). Once in captivity, women had to struggle against cultural and psychic annihilation. The sense of fear and loss must have been profound, and they resisted from the moment of capture. Women, separated from the men, were reputedly 'sulky' and sang 'sad laments'. They were forced by 'threats and blows' to make them eat and if they were still recalcitrant they were flogged (Falconbridge 32). The ultimate denial of their new 'reality' was suicide, evidence for whites that they were 'raving mad': failed suicide was punished by floggings. But evidence suggests women also registered their collective protest at the ways in which they were treated. The Reverend John Riland, a planter turned abolitionist, who sailed in 1801 from Liverpool to Jamaica in a slave ship, recorded that, when forced to dance on the deck, women maintained their dignity and 'kept themselves aloof', manifesting 'an indignation that long continued habit could not suppress when forced to behave childishly' (Riland 51, 59-61).

These destructive transformations, paradoxically, sharpened women's resistance to the plantation work regime. This actively disrupted and negated African cultural patterns, particularly gender relations, upon which women's identities were premised, producing new cultural struggles and consciousness. In defining slaves as commodities and denying their human reality and bonds, whites sought to create identities for slave women and men that would disempower them through cultural 'stripping' to ensure an atomized work force that was as controllable and productive as the animal 'stock' on their plantations. Slavery was arguably a form of 'social death' where slaves became 'dishonoured persons', outside the society in which they lived. This was achieved through 'natal alienation', the denial of the slave's history, kinship bonds and right to a past or future (Patterson 56-8) and reinforced through branding and renaming, often with ridiculous, inappropriate names such as Clarissa or Lavinia or distorted versions of African names.

Names are the very essence of an individual's identity. In rural African societies, naming had deep social significance associated with ritual and symbolism and linked to transmission of ancestral spirits. Denial of this process in matriarchal cultures broke the female line, leading to 'loss and confusion in identity' (Simmonds 110). 'Secret' names are common in many societies and frequently received on initiation into adulthood and cults. Such names can be used harmfully in sorcery (Patterson 55). It is possible that slaves concealed their own names to deflect the wickedness of whites and protect themselves against strange fellow slaves. We can never know if African-born slave mothers, for instance, gave their children 'secret' African names, although there is evidence that African-derived rites associated with newborn infants persisted into late slavery and even into the twentieth century in rural areas in the Caribbean (Smith 133-4). The existence of these 'secret identities' is an exciting speculation but impossible to verify. What is clear is that slaves, male and female, often had several names or aliases that confused masters and public authorities (Viotta da Costa 11). Such ambiguity over names suggests complexities of responses to enslavement that white observers were either unable or unwilling to comprehend.

Yet African names persisted: evidence of women's attempts to cling on to the vestiges of identity, but simultaneously employed by whites in a bastardized form to confirm their 'otherness'. In Jamaica these were frequently based on Asante (Akan) day names: Quasheba, Cuba and Yabba, from the Asante words Akosuwa, Akuwa and Yaa or Yawa (Sunday, Wednesday, Thursday). Such names were still given to newborns by 'an old woman' in August Town in British Guiana in the 1950s, a testimony to the enduring social significance of naming in African Caribbean communities and of women to cultural continuity (Smith 131). Sale advertisements, however, simply described both male and female as 'young, healthy negroes of the Ibo country' (or Popo, Ashanti etc.) whilst advertisements for slave runaways often identified African slaves by owners' brands or markings associated with their ethnic origins such as tattoos, ritual scars and filed teeth. The complexity of this naming and identification is clearly shown in one such advertisement for a Kingston-born woman named Flora who had run away with her daughter, Phiba (*sic*) 'who calls herself often Cuba and Abba'. Here we have evidence of names in existence other than those given by masters. Cuba was also 'marked on both shoulders A.W.' but the brand was 'raised in lumps from endeavouring to take them out', a testimony to how one woman rejected her slave identity.[1] Some African names persisted, but with creolization, English names, such as Mary or Lucy, became more common, added to surnames identifying women with their owners. It was mainly these names that carried through into freedom and which inspired, for instance, Malcolm X's own self-renaming, the X symbolizing the lost identity of blacks in the diaspora.

The traumatic fragmentation of women's identity through slavery still reverberates on black women's consciousness. 'Modern life begins with slavery' writes Toni Morrison; '[slave] women had to deal with…certain kinds of dissolution, the loss of and the need to reconstruct certain kinds of stability' (Morrison 221). By creating 'imagined identities' for slave women, whites defined their 'otherness', in qualities that were simultaneously denigrated and desired. I am wary of using this concept too loosely here, as psychoanalysis is rooted in twentieth-century Western culture that centralizes the individual as opposed to the collective consciousness. However, it does have validity in understanding cultural struggles and the need for whites to deny and actively repress slave culture, demonizing slave women as 'she devils' and 'harlots' whilst being seduced by their exoticism. It also has relevance to black women's transformations through migration. Women in other migrant diasporas have, where possible, retreated into their own families and communities as a means of defence against a hostile society; this was not possible for slave women and they were brutally forced to confront their 'otherness'.

Women's lives, writes Maya Angelou, were dissolved through slavery into a 'fabulous fiction of multiple personalities' (Angelou 209). Women were 'concrete in their labour and surreal in their humanness'. This is reflected in the images of black women that have been projected through white history and visual representation. Symbolic but powerful metaphors created by the white imagination were profoundly distorting. Such images of black women did change over time, but a core of negative stereotyping has remained, especially around black female sexuality. Such images predated women's capture in Africa and have helped obscure the concrete exploitation of black women, sexual and economic, and precluded a more positive appraisal of black women's identities.

When the Moroccan traveller Ibn Battatu visited Mali in 1352, he was shocked by the sexual freedom and nakedness of women but did not express any objection to the sight of both males and females working in copper mines (Davis 46). Travellers' tales from Africa enlarged upon this dual persona, commenting on women's strength and muscularity and the way they competed with men in 'enduring toil, hardship and privations'. Women's drudge status was confirmed by 'polygamy' which whites believed simultaneously promoted promiscuity and reduced women to 'the domestic slaves of men' (Sells 33). They were depicted as submissive workhorses, emasculating matriarchs or 'hot consitution'd' scarlet women, lewd and promiscuous in their relations with black *and* white men. Physically, they were adversely contrasted with the white bourgeois ideal of female beauty, emphasizing their animality and inferiority. Interestingly, there is no 'good' Caribbean stereotype equivalent to the 'loyal Mammy' of the American South (White 1985).

White male obsession with the sexual otherness and exoticism of black women is clear in this extract from 'The Sable Venus: An Ode' (1765) by Isaac Teale, which Robert Young describes as '[an] ... extraordinary ... articulation of the sexual economy of desire in the fantasies of race' (Young 1995, 153):

O Sable Queen! Thy mild Domain
I seek and court thy gentle reign
So soothing, soft and sweet.
Where meeting love, sincere delight
Fond pleasures, ready joys invite,
And unbrought raptures meet.

Do thou in gentle Phibia smile,
In artful Benneba beguile,
In wanton Mimba pout
In sprightly Cuba's eyes look gay
Or grave in sober Quasheba
I still shall find thee out

(Cited in Edwards 2: 33).

Tempting, scheming, wanton—all is here except the concrete reality of labour. In late slavery, British abolitionists created other 'personas', from 'sable beauties' and 'dusky Venus's' to the innocents betrayed in need of pity

25

and protection. Abolitionist poetry created biographies of African women's lives graphically charting the horrors they suffered from capture to sale in Jamaica. In two very similar abolitionist poems published in the 1790s, 'Cruelty Extraordinary Committed On a Female Slave of the Name of Yamba in the Island of Jamaica' and 'The Sorrows of Yamba; or, a Negro Woman's Lament', Christian abolitionists advocated redemption through Christian conversion and 'moralization'. The Ladies Society For the Relief of Negro Slaves was particularly concerned that slave women lacked male protection and were prevented from leading the lives of 'normal good wives'. In female abolitionist propaganda, they were identified as the 'weakest...of the human race' and worthy of white women's special 'maternalistic' attention (Midgely 28). Slave women were now expected to embrace Christianity, assume the 'respectability' of the bourgeois ideal of womanhood and deny their 'bad' African side. This identity transformation is chronicled in *The History of Mary Prince* (1831), a unique autobiography of a Caribbean slave woman that also provides insight into her ambiguous relationship to white culture.

Abolitionist constructions of such 'redeemed' black women strongly contrast with the cruder stereotypes of slave women that were in widespread circulation in England as the debate over slavery intensified. These were evident in the caricatures of influential cartoonists, the popularity of exhibits such as the South African Saartjie Baartman, the 'Hottentot Venus', commercially exploited for her large buttocks; and the many written accounts that stressed the physical unattractiveness and animality of black women. Plantocratic writers berated the licentiousness of slave women, their insubordination, sharp tongues and unruliness that justified the use of the whip. They were neglectful mothers, careless midwives, idle and malingering domestics and scheming Jezebels out to get what they could from white men (Bush 1990). More generous descriptions still tended to project white concepts of beauty and female behaviour onto black identity, as in John Stedman's account of his beloved mulatto mistress, Joanna, whose face was 'full of native modesty' with 'a perfectly formed, rather small nose' and only slightly prominent lips (Stedman 1: 52-3) A beautiful mulatto slave on Matthew Lewis's Jamaican estate, was described as having an 'air and countenance' comparable to the Virgin Mary as depicted in Renaissance art, the 'most picturesque object' Lewis had seen for twenty years (Lewis 69-70). Mulatto women were thus generally viewed in a more favourable light than African women, although it can be argued that in many ways their identities were more problematic.

Little attention has been given in mainstream histories to these thorny questions relating to images and identities of slave women. Yet it may be argued that images of women signify the extent of respect accorded to them in any society. There were glaring 'silences' in black women's history up to the late 1970s. Recently, black women have begun to explore their own history through literature, drawing on the 'long memory' forged through slavery that is central to the search for meaning and identity in the contemporary African diaspora (Fabre and O'Meally 1994). New challenges to orthodox history have centred on the relationship between history and 'fiction', and the argument that all historians are imaginatively interpreting 'histories' through their own constructed narrative (Young 1990) has validated this approach. How then can we deconstruct the identities of slave women and tease out the oppositional identities that they struggled to forge for themselves? This is where women's involvement in the cultural struggles in slavery and freedom is centralized.

Searching for the Invisible Woman: Cultural Struggles in the transition from Slavery to Freedom

Cultural struggles involved powerful resistance to white-constructed identities of slave women. They facilitated the negotiation of new identities rooted in women's 'African' memory which enabled them to reclaim their own destinies. In the intimidating new environment of the Caribbean, both men and women found 'fictive kin' among established slaves to replace their lost families, arrangements that also reinforced the identities of established slaves. In conversation with newcomers they were able to 'revive and retrace the remembrance of ideas and past pleasures and scenes of their youth', reinforcing bonds with Africa and assuring cultural continuity of the African extended kinship group, the basis of social organisation and cultural interaction. The building of slave villages 'beyond the ken' of masters, the 'yard', deriving from the communal African compound, and the family provision grounds were also vital to the rebuilding of a viable cultural matrix of which whites had little understanding (Bush 1987). Away from the 'inner life' of the slave community, the reality of slave women's life was a daily round of hard labour, punishment and the negotiation of white-defined 'slave identities'. Yet from white descriptions, slave women come over as strong, defiant individuals who are neither dependent on nor repressed by slave men.

In contemporary art, women were frequently shown working in the field and mill wearing European dress. But often they are also wearing the head tie, perhaps more typically African than the nakedness focused on by whites in depictions of African women. The head tie can be interpreted as one of the clearest assertions of an 'African' identity and a reflection of the fact that proportionately more women than men were field hands on emancipation and the African element in field slave culture remained strong (Goveia 244-5). As the pioneering anthropologists of 'Black Atlantic' culture, Melville and Francis Herskovits, concluded:

> The custom of wearing…headkerchiefs originated in Africa and appeared most strongly in those areas of the New World in which African values retained their greatest strength, in some areas, in some cases, in which revolutionary resistance to slavery had been most pronounced and successful (4-5).

The head-tie is symbolic of women's centrality to an oppositional slave culture. This is reflected in their participation in the cultural life of the slave village. Song, music and dance accompanied all the important events in a slave's life. Entertainment in the slave village was provided by the voices of female slaves, sometimes accompanying themselves with 'home-made' instruments. Women were often the leading singers and William Beckford noted that in Jamaica, singing was 'confined' to the women, the men 'but seldomly … excepting on extraordinary occasions' joining in the chorus (Beckford 2: 120, 211). In the field women sang songs 'of their own composing' which were answered in the same manner by men. At crop-over they sang 'wild choruses of joy' but also expressed the sorrow of enslavement through 'plaintive' songs (Stewart 271-3). Through such singing (which was typically African in structure, based on a pattern of statement and response), work could be rendered less burdensome, slave morale could be raised and white masters mimicked, satirised or even subtly threatened (Brathwaite 225). 'Plays' were also highly popular, combining verbal dexterity, music and dance. Both sexes participated, forming a ring around a male and female dancer who performed to the music of the drum. Entrepreneurial women in Trinidad organised Saturday night dances (attended by slaves from neighbouring plantations) providing the 'supper, liquor and music' and sometimes charging a small entrance fee (Carmichael 2: 26-9).

In African-Caribbean creole, with its rich nuances, double entendres became the language of resistance. Verbal abuse was frequently used by female field hands and it was alleged that female slaves talked 'worse' than males and their language was described in derogatory terms (Long 2: 211). The slaves' everyday language preserved and dynamically adapted the rich linguistic structures of Africa and associated oral cultural forms. Caribbean oral traditions still retain strong links with West Africa, where they embrace poetry, music, dance, religion and collective histories which together

28

comprise a powerful holistic belief system, a moral universe that Christianity has failed to counteract (Collins 1995). Even though slaves came from different ethnic groups and some may even have been converted to Islam, this cultural framework cohered life in the slave community. The power of this cultural base is evident in the continuing importance of religion, music and oral expression, from calypso to rap, in the modern African diaspora. As a focus of cultural definition and creative defence against a dominant white culture it remains central to black identity. Contemporary black Caribbean women writers now draw on oral traditions preserved and passed on through women in exploring facets of their own history, culture and identity.

Cultural struggles intensified with economic development and white identities of slave women became more racist and derogatory (but also more fragmented and conflictual). It was arguably in the 'high' and most oppressive period of slavery (c.1780–1838) that the most significant and sophisticated cultural negotiations occurred, linked to important changes in individual and group consciousness. These coincided with more intense exploitation of female labour combined with fuller creolization. Concepts of freedom stimulated by abolitionism, the French revolution, the Haitian liberation struggle and a more literal reading of the essence of Christianity were also influential. Slaves seemed even more ungovernable and women, as the 'backbone' of the labour force and internal marketing system through their informal economic activity, became the epitome of this 'ungovernability', as contemporary records show (Bush 1982; Da Costa 1994).

The area which engendered the most fierce cultural struggles between master and slave was religion and associated 'bad African practices' such as medicine and witchcraft (obeah, vodun). In animist sub-Saharan African societies religion coheres an individual's understanding of her or his world, determining both individual identity and sense of place and collective consciousness. In the eighteenth century, African religion was connected to slave uprisings in Dutch, French and English colonies in which powerful women slaves or 'prophetesses' enjoined slaves to rebel or run away in an 'an aura of spirit possession' (Gautier 1983; Bush 1990). Fear of African culture and its potential to 'excite rebellion' is evident in the laws, linked to severe punishments, that were passed to suppress it (Senior 1835, 149-52). Such fears were enhanced by white experiences of European witchcraft. 'Witchcraft', however, may also be interpreted as a response to the cultural dislocations that affected African women's position in the family and wider society (Cutrufelli 162-3). Older slave women had extensive knowledge of herbs and plants that could be used for healing as well as more sinister purposes such as poisoning. In Jamaica, for instance, an old woman of the

'Popo country' (Dahomey), described as the 'terror of the neighbourhood', had brought her 'evil' arts with her from Africa and practised them with allegedly devastating consequences for both black and white.

During late slavery there was thus more planter tolerance of missionary projects to 'moralize', and hence subdue slaves, particularly women, through Christianity. But female slaves often resisted Christian marriage and baptism, confirming their primacy as cultural guardians. 'Well acquainted with all the customs and mythology of their native country' (Riland 104), they arguably rejected Christianity to a greater extent than men, having little to gain from its deep seated misogyny and patriarchal doctrine emphasizing female subordination. Cutrufelli has noted a similar rejection of Christianity by African women under colonial rule (52). Outwardly, some slaves may have accepted Chistianity (particularly elite male slaves who increasingly became designated by whites as 'leaders' in the slave community), but value and belief structures remained African, shaping an important counter identity that gave meaning and validity to their lives. On the eve of emancipation, slaves were still allegedly 'addicted to witchcraft' and obeah men and women 'had a great ascendancy over other negroes' (Atwood 269). This is reflected in the continued legal suppression of the cornerstones of Afro-Caribbean religions: 'obeah', drumming and 'negro burials' (Madden 160-1). Slave funerals were rumbustious, life-affirming collective celebrations, and evidence suggests that women resisted Christian baptism to ensure an African burial that reunited them with the ancestors (Bush 1990, 103). They may also have performed ceremonial functions. In modern-day Ghana, for instance, older women, who are important traditional poets, characteristically deliver funeral dirges (Collins 1995).

Invasive and disorientating cultural change stimulates religious cults as individuals seek solidity and meaning to their lives (Cutrufelli 65). In the cultural dislocation generated by slavery, participation in 'subversive' religions had a direct bearing on the redefinition of slave women's identities and the development of a group consciousness which challenged slavery and the transmission of a specific 'women's culture'. It was in the area of childbirth and childrearing that the transmission of this 'woman's culture' was particularly important, affording women both psychic and practical support. Older women were the slave midwives and were able to pass on to younger women their skills and knowledge. These arguably included abortifacients and contraception, an area always confined to the 'shadow' world of women because of male hostility or strong social taboos on such practices.

Childbirth, healing and medicine, informed by African religious beliefs, constituted key areas of female cultural struggles during late slavery when abolitionists pressed for improved slave conditions and planters grew concerned over low female fertility after the ending of the slave trade (Bush 1993). The ways in which birth, sickness and death are conceptualized are integral to cultural identities. Similar conflicts to those which emerged in slave societies still exist in parts of Africa where western medicine has a problematic relationship to traditional healers and magic, with important social consequences (Allen 1992). Folk medicine developed in the Caribbean with essentially the same features and, in Sheridan's estimation, women's contribution as healers and nurses outside the plantation hot-house may have exceeded all the health services provided by the white establishment (Sheridan 1985, 137).

In women's contribution to slave culture we have an important example of the reworking of identities through struggle and negotiation which presented a positive counterbalance to the predominantly negative 'white visions' of slave lives. These struggles continued after emancipation, and women retained a powerful profile in African-based religious and magical practices. Women still outnumber men in syncretic Caribbean religious sects and black Christian churches in Britain that continue to provide psychic support and a language of resistance in a hostile environment; they are frequently the evangelists, choir singers and worship leaders (Alexander 93-4). To gain insight into this ongoing process of cultural identification and conflict it is useful to explore briefly the mechanisms of change during the transition to freedom and the post-slavery colonial society.

Out of Bondage?: Women, Culture and Colonialism

Afrocentred creole culture arguably developed through an interchange of cultural traits between black and white in an atmosphere of creativity but also tension (Brathwaite 41). During late slavery this generated powerful cultural struggles. Did this dynamism ironically become subdued in freedom when the absolute power of planters was replaced by a more diffuse but no less significant colonial power? The power wielded by whites in slave society was enormous, but it arguably was not as destructive of Afrocentric culture as the more subtle forms of cultural imperialism which emerged in the nineteenth century. Slaves, simply by virtue of the fact that they were not recognized as having a viable society and culture, were able to retain a degree of cultural autonomy where no direct conflict with planters' economic interests emerged. Pro-slavery whites were not interested in 'culturally civilizing' Africans. They were also wary of missionary activity as, in their view, it led to slave insubordination and serious uprisings such as the 1823 Demerara rebellion (Viotta da Costa 1994). After abolition, however, there was a strong movement, promoted initially by abolitionists, to create a vigorous and free but also 'respectable' (Europeanized) peasantry. Whereas the slave system was characterized for the most part by coercion, punishment and, in the formal economy, cultural annihilation through 'social death', whites now had increasingly to resort to more subtle mechanisms in their suppression of what they perceived as inferior cultural forms. How did these developments affect black women's identities?

There has, to date, been little research into the specific responses of women to nineteenth-century colonialism in the Caribbean. Historians of this period tend to emphasize the improvements in the living conditions and situation of black women which, by the mid 1840s, had restored the population to normal levels from the negative population increase that existed throughout slavery. With abolition, it is argued, women abandoned field labour on the estates, 'devoting their time to housekeeping and raising their families' (Sheridan 1993, 36-7). This cosy scene of bourgeois domesticity provides sharply contrasting images to those evoked for the times of slavery, more aptly fitting the white abolitionist and missionary ideal of free black peasant society. What happened in freedom to all those defiant, insubordinate and actively resistant women? More pertinently, how were identities of women changed and re-negotiated? My argument is that the more subtle mechanisms of colonial legitimization, particularly missionary activity and the 'education' of blacks in 'Victorian values', subdued (but did not destroy) the cultural dynamism of the slave period. As standards of 'civilization' and 'progress' were frequently assessed in terms of the 'behaviour' of women and the nature of gender relations, in freedom women were once more central to cultural struggles but this time as the key to the moralizing projects of whites.

Catherine Hall has argued that '[t]hreaded through missionary discourse...was the vision of a new gender order', centred on Christian marriage and a good family life where men were urged to become 'men of property' and women were withdrawn from labour outside the home. The urgent need was stressed for the training of 'pious and intelligent' female teachers to instruct the 'rising female race' and counteract the 'degrading influence of slavery' (Hall 110). For some women, adoption of white norms led to a complete break with Afro-Caribbean culture. This resulted in greater social acceptance but also in 'self-hatred', intensifying role conflicts. It undermined women's autonomous economic activities—holding dances in their houses, Sunday marketing and lucrative pottery making—which missionaries viewed with contempt. 'Respectable women' were thus forced to retreat into 'domestic invisibility' to ensure recognition (Fog Olwig 114).

But the economic reality of women's lives was such that it was impossible for most to live up to white bourgeois standards of femininity. In freedom the black woman remained 'de mules uh de world' (Zora Neale Hurston, cited in Jarrett Macauley 43). Such women were excluded from Western respectablity and remained closer to their African cultural roots.

In the way whites saw women as the key to their moralizing campaigns among the free blacks there are clear parallels with other colonial societies. In her study of the Jesuits' project to subdue Huron women in seventeenth century New France, Karen Anderson suggests that the Jesuits also saw women as the key to moralization of a 'barbaric' society. But the reputed 'unruliness' and sexual promiscuity of Huron women created serious barriers, and they were obliged to work through male converts who would then 'police' their own women. The Jesuits thus skilfully tapped a patriarchal misogyny deep-rooted in the creation myths of many cultures, and in so doing curbed female power and undermined the more egalitarian relationships which had existed between men and women before colonial intervention (Anderson 179). Similar processes of change can be charted in other societies oppressed by European colonization and cultural and racial arrogance (Vaughan 1991; Bell 1983). In all cases women were seen as the key to the 'civilizing' mission and this resulted in conflicts with indigenous women over childbirth, marriage, and religion—the primary definers of gendered identities. Men were thus coopted through Christian conversion to control their 'unruly' women, and the importance of women's culture and political participation to collective identities was increasingly ignored. Similarly, in the 'free' Caribbean, such undermining of 'women's culture' has arguably had serious implications for identity, gender relations and ongoing cultural resistance (Senior 1992).

Can we, therefore, suggest ways in which women's identities may have changed in freedom? Certainly 'identities' constructed by whites shifted with the moralization project, and with the increasing need to contrast the 'civilized', respectable Caribbean woman with the 'primitive', naked and sexual African woman, as imperialist energies were targeted on Africa, nourished by a new and virulent scientific racism. Moreover, women lost their source of cultural renewal from Africa as creolization was completed. New identity conflicts also emerged with the renegotiation of gender relationships, as a patriarchal colonialism emphasised male 'progress' and engagement in the public sphere, further marginalizing women in history. Colonial structures assumed gender power relationships along the public/private divide similar to that which existed in Europe and prioritized black male headship of families and community leadership.

33

Paradoxically, these developments ensured that it was primarily women who kept alive a vernacular Afrocentric culture surviving through slavery into the colonial period. Martha Beckwith's patronizing study of Jamaican folk culture in the 1920s provides insight into the degree to which an Afrocentric culture was retained as a foundation of black identity and defence against the psychic oppression and inferiorization of white racism. She observed that women 'perhaps more than men' hesitated to be 'bound irrevocably' by legal marriage and were prominent in the 'heathen practices' which could only be eradicated if folk culture could be tamed into a 'more robust and healthy way of thinking and living' (Beckwith 102). Such rejection of Christianity and embracing of 'African' religions like Pocomania was more sympathetically commented on by Una Marsen, the Jamaican playwright, who also testified to the 'solace and security' women found in each other's company (Marsen 1937, cited in Jarrett Macauley 43-4). By this time the gulf between black men and women had widened through the tendency of men to 'marry upwards on the colour scale' into respectablity. Transmission of 'creoleness'—including Obeah—thus became (and remains today) primarily a female activity passed on from older to younger women (Arnold 17), confirming women as the main 'guardians' of African memory.

Cultural imperialism was perhaps most 'successful' in the way that upwardly mobile black men absorbed western male 'Victorian values' of the bourgeois family and female 'respectability'. For them, black renewal and progress hinged on a reconstituted patriarchal black family and the honour of the race was increasingly invested in the 'good behaviour' of women. The black search for new identities post-slavery was thus intimately linked to redefinitions of gender and sexuality characterized by the emergence of an idealized black patriarchy (Gilroy 85-6) that increasingly confined women to the private sphere. As new black political movements emerged, women once again became central to cultural struggles, as icons of cultural purity essential to the reconstruction of a black masculinity that had been distorted and undermined by slavery. In the extreme, these developments have led to a powerful black misogyny (reflected in, for instance, calypso, reggae and rap) which, combined with persistent negative white images of black womanhood, still creates problems for contemporary black women (Senior 1992). The reassertion of 'traditional' gender relations in black consciousness movements is evident, for instance, in Rastafarian beliefs. In Jamaica, Rasta women are economically subordinated to men and 'acceptable female behaviour' for 'ladies' (that is wives) is established by male-defined boundaries emphasizing subservience to their 'kingmen' (Lake 1994).

Summary

In this paper I have tried to chart the fluidity and dynamism of black cultural resistance, and argued that both material conditions and white constructs of black women's identity intermeshed with elements of African culture to reshape black women's cultural landscape and gender identity. Placing culture centre-stage has thrown into relief subtle gender differences and a diversity of individual experiences absent from more orthodox economic and demographic studies of slavery. Culture and identity have been shown as significant in two main ways: firstly, in interpreting the resistance struggles that intersected the formal and informal spheres of slave women's lives; and, secondly, in understanding the ways in which women continuously challenged their white-defined identities. In freedom, black women were 'reinvented' by both white and black men, and shifting identities led to new cultural struggles intertwined with gender conflicts that have ongoing significance in the African diaspora. Through imaginative media such as film, literature, poetry and oral history, black women are now articulating their own histories as part of a concrete struggle to recover the 'princess in darkness' and a more equal place in contemporary diaspora societies.

Both academic research and the 'imaginative recovery' of black history in the creative writings of African diaspora women increasingly centralize women's seminal contribution to the development of a vibrant and challenging 'counterculture'. In combating the demeaning and confusing identities created for them by whites during slavery, women asserted powerful elements of 'women's culture'. After emancipation new tensions developed between the dominant white culture, imposed from above through increasingly sophisticated media, and the vernacular black culture, with clear implications for contemporary cultural struggles and black female identity. Yet women continued to be the principal exponents and bearers of Afrocentric culture and the anchors of Afrocentric family and local networks. This was crucial to black survival when poverty and migratory patterns of employment ensured that the 'respectable' stable family promoted by concerned whites became an ideal impossible to live up to except for a better off minority. Poorer women's marginality to white society also preserved a woman's culture to counterbalance the 'hypermasculinity' of post-emancipation creole culture. Afro-centered rituals preserved and played out by women were and are a 'metaphor' of togetherness in adversity, as the Jamaican theatre collective Sistren has demonstrated. They have helped to solidify black women's reality in a world where the negative white images of black womanhood stretching back to slavery and before still persist.

Notes

1. Slave advertisement placed by Alexander Walker, Luana, St. Elizabeth, August 30 1779. *The Jamaica Mercury*, June 26, 1779.
2. *Report of the Lords of Trade into t he Slave Trade, British Parliamentary Papers (Commons)*, 1789, vol. XXXVI, 646a, appx D.3.

Works Cited

Alexander, Valentina. (1996) '"A mouse in a jungle": The Black Christian woman's experience in the church and society in Britain', in D. Jarrett Macauley, ed. *Reconstructing Womanhood, Reconstructing Feminism*. London: Routledge.

Allen, Tim. (1992) 'Upheaval, Affliction and Health: A Ugandan Case Study', in H. Bernstein, B. Crow and H. Johnson, eds. *Rural Livelihoods: Crises and Responses*. London and Milton Keynes: Oxford UP.

Anderson, Karen. (1991) *Chain Her By One Foot; The Subjugation of Women in 17th Century New France*. London: Routledge.

Angelou, Maya. (1989) 'I Dream a World: America's Black Women', *National Geographic* 176.ii (August).

Arnold, James A. (1994) 'The Erotics of Colonialism in Contemporary French West Indian Literary Culture', *New West Indian Guide* (NWIG) 68.i&ii.

Atwood, Thomas. (1835) *History of Domenica*. London.

Beckford, William. (1790) *A Descriptive Account of The Island of Jamaica*. 2 vols. London.

Beckles, Hilary. (1993) 'White Women and Slavery in the Caribbean', *History Workshop* 36 (August): 72-5.

Beckwith, Martha. (1969) *Black Roadways: A Study of Jamaican Folk Life*. New York: Negro Universities Press. 1st pub. 1929.

Bell, Diane. (1983) *Daughters of the Dreaming*. Melbourne: Allen and Unwin.

Bell, Hesketh J. (1893) *Obeah: Witchcraft in the West Indies*. 2nd ed. London.

Bhavnani, Kum Kum. (1993) 'Towards a Multi-Cultural Europe', *Feminist Review* 45, Special Edition, 'Thinking Through Ethnicities'.

Brathwaite, Edward Kamau. (1978) *The Development of Creole Society in Jamaica*. Oxford: Oxford UP.

Boulègue, Jean. (1987) 'l'éxpression de refus de la traite nègriere dans les sociéties Sénégambiennes, XVIIème-XVIIIème siècles', in Serge Daget, ed. *Les Actes du Colloque international sur la traite des Noirs*. Nantes, 1985. 2 vols. Paris: Editions Garrard. 1: 102-26.

Bush, Barbara. (1993) 'Hard Labour: Women, Childbirth and Resistance in the British Caribbean', *History Workshop* 36: 83-100.

Bush, Barbara. (1990) *Slave Women in Caribbean Society, 1650–1838*. London: James Currey.

Bush, Barbara. (1987) 'The Family Tree is not Cut: Women and Cultural Resistance in Slave Family Life in the British Caribbean', in Gary Y. Okihiro, ed. *Resistance*

Studies in African, Caribbean, Latin American and Afro-American History. Stanford: Stanford UP.

Bush, Barbara. (1982) 'Defiance or Submission?: The Role of Slave Women in Slave Resistance in the British Caribbean', *Immigrants and Minorities*, 1.i.

Bush, Barbara. (1981) 'White Ladies, Coloured Favourites and Black Wenches: Some Consideration on Sex, Race and Class in White Creole Society in the British Caribbean', *Slavery and Abolition* 2.iii.

Carmichael, A.C. (1833) *Domestic Manners and Social Condition of the White, Coloured, and Negro Population of the West Indies.* 2 vols. London: Whittaker, Treacher & Co.

Collins, Merle. (1995) 'Africa to the Caribbean: A Journey of the Oral Tradition', *Out Of Africa Series.* BBC Radio 4, December 13.

Cutrufelli, Maria Rosa. (1983) *Women of Africa: Roots of Oppression*, trans. from Italian. London: Pluto.

Davis, David Brion. (1984) *Slavery and Human Progress.* New York: Oxford UP.

De Certeau, Michael. (1988) *The Practice of Everyday Life.* Berkeley and London: University of California Press.

Edwards, Bryan. (1801) *The History, Civil and Commercial of the British Colonies in the West Indies.* 5 vols. London.

Fabre, Genevieve and Robert O'Meally, eds. (1995) *History, Myth and Memory in African American Culture.* London: Blackwell.

Falconbridge, Alexander. (1788) *An Account of the Slave Trade on the Coast of Africa.* London.

Fanon, Frantz. (1986) *Black Skin, White Masks.* 1st pub. 1968. London: Pluto.

Fergusson, Moira. ed. and intro. (1987) *The History of Mary Prince: A West Indian Slave Narrated by Herself, 1831.* London: Pandora.

Fog Olwig, Karen. (1993): *Global Culture, Island Identity: Continuity and Change in the Afro-Caribbean Community of Nevis.* Chur, Switzerland: Harwood Academic Publishers.

Gautier, Arlette. (1983) 'Les Ésclaves, femmes aux Antilles françaises, 1635–1848', *Reflexions Historique* 10.iii.

Gilroy, Paul. (1993): *The Black Atlantic: Modernity and Double Consciousness.* London: Verso.

Goveia, Elsa. (1965) *Slave Society in the British Leeward Islands at the End of the Eighteenth Century.* New Haven: Yale UP.

Hall, Catherine. (1993) 'White Visions, Black Lives: The Free Villages of Jamaica', *History Workshop* 36: 100-33.

Herskovits, M.J. and F. (1936) *Surinam Folk Lore.* New York: Knopf.

Herskovits, M.J. and F. (1947) *Trinidad Village.* New York: Knopf.

Jarrett Macaulay, Delia. (1996) 'Exemplary Women', in D. Jarrett Macauley, ed. *Reconstructing Womanhood, Reconstructing Feminism.* London: Routledge.

Lake, Obiagele. (1994) 'The Many Voices of Rastafarian Women: Sexual Subordination in the Midst of Liberation', *New West Indian Guide (NWIG)* 68.iii&iv.

Lerner, Gerder. (1986) *The Creation Of Patriarchy*. New York and Oxford: Oxford UP.

Lewis, Matthew Gregory. (1845) *Journal of a Residence among the Negroes of the West Indies*. London.

Long, Edward. (1774) *The History Of Jamaica*. 5 vols. London.

Madden, Richard. (1835) *A Twelve Month Residence in the West Indies*. 2 vols. London.

Midgley, Clare. (1992) *Women against Slavery: The British Campaigns, 1780–1870*. London: Routledge.

Morrison, Toni. (1988) *Beloved*. London: Cape.

Morissey, Marietta. (1989) *Slave Women in the New World: Gender Stratification in the Caribbean*. Kansas: Kansas UP.

Patterson, Orlando. (1982) *Slavery and Social Death: A Comparative Study*. Cambridge, Mass.: Harvard UP.

Pieterse, Jan Nederveen. (1992) *White on Black: Images of Africans and Blacks in Western Popular Culture*. New Haven and London: Yale UP.

Riland, John. (1837) *Memoirs of a West Indian Planter*. London.

Robertson, Claire and Herbert Klein, eds. (1983) *Women and Slavery in Africa*. London: Frank Cass.

Rodney, Walter. (1969) 'Upper Guinea and the Origins of Africans Enslaved in the New World', *Journal of Negro History* 54.iv.

Rosalda, Michelle and Louise Lamphere, eds. (1976) *Women, Culture and Society*. Stanford: Stanford UP.

Sells, William. (1823) *Remarks on the Condition of the Slaves in the Islands of Jamaica*. Shannon: Irish UP, 1972.

Senior, Bernard Martin. (1835) *Jamaica as it was, as it is, and as it may be. By a Retired Military Officer*. London.

Senior, Olive. (1992) *Working Miracles: Women's Lives in the Caribbean*. London: James Currey.

Sheridan, Richard. (1985) *Doctors and Slaves: A Medical and Demographic History of Slaves in the Caribbean, 1680–1834*. Cambridge: Cambridge UP.

Sheridan, Richard. (1993) 'From Chattel Slavery to Wage Slavery in Jamaica', *Slavery and Abolition*. 14.i.

Simmonds, Felly Nkweto. (1996) 'Naming and Identity', in D. Jarrett Macauley, ed. *Reconstructing Womanhood, Reconstructing Feminism*. London: Routledge.

Smith, Raymond T. (1956) *The Negro Family in British Guiana: Family Structure and Social Status in the Villages*. London: Routledge and Kegan Paul.

Stedman, John. (1798) *Narrative of a Five Years Expedition Against the Revolted Negroes of Surinam, 1772–1777*. 2 vols. London.

Stewart, John. (1823) *A View of Jamaica*. London.

Vaughan, Megan. (1991) *Curing their Ills: Colonial Power and African Illness*. Cambridge: Polity Press.

Viotta Da Costa, Emilia. (1994) *Crowns of Glory, Tears of Blood: The Demerara Slave Rebellion of 1823*. London and New York: Yale UP.

White, Deborah Gray. (1985) *Ar'n't I A Woman?: Female Slaves in the Plantation South*. New York: Norton.

Wright, P., ed. (1976) *Lady Nugent's Jamaica Journal*. Kingston: Institute of Jamaica.

Young, Robert J.C. (1990) *White Mythologies: Writing History and the West*. London: Routledge.

Young, Robert J.C. (1995) Colonial Desire: Hybridity in Theory, Culture and Race. London: Routledge.

'PSYCHIC REGENERATION THROUGH CATASTROPHE':

The Recovery of History through Magic Realism in the Fiction of Toni Morrison

Deirdre Reddington

The operation of magic realist devices in the work of Toni Morrison is indicative of changing perspectives in late twentieth-century fiction. Salman Rushdie writes that 'the mingling of fantasy and naturalism is one way of dealing with the problems of the incompatibility of opposing descriptions of society' (Rushdie 1991, 56), and Carlos Fuentes attributes the formal diversity of the twentieth-century novel to the proliferation of realities in the modern world (xlii). In a world where the uniformity of standards, tastes and rational process has dissolved in the face of historical variety and cultural pluralism, new novel forms are emerging in which the power of the imagination to refigure perceptions of the real contests the strict delineations of rationalist discourse. Combinations of naturalistic detail and magical epiphany in Toni Morrison's novels constitute an alternative, postcolonial discourse which interrogates hegemonic structures of meaning. Juxtaposing the known contours of reality with the heightened vision of a folk imagination, she forges a distinctly magic realist language with which to reappropriate a buried Afro-American past.

Magic Realist fiction is essentially characterized by the amalgamation of fantasy or magic and realism in a narrative which sustains opposing views of the world on equal terms. In contrast to the fantastic, the occurrence of the supernatural in magic realism does not disconcert the reader, nor do characters express surprise or dismay when confronted with the unreal. The juxtaposition of contradictory perspectives does not represent a flight into the purely fabulous but serves to expand the dimensions of the real, 'combining myth, magic and other extraordinary phenomena in Nature and experience which European realism has tended to exclude' (Williamson 132).

Magic Realism has found fertile ground in Third World contexts where historical and political conditions have consistently blurred the boundaries of the real and where fact and meaning have myriad, unlimited dimensions. In Latin America the use of magic realist devices in fiction reflects dislocations in the understanding of the real caused by a continuing cycle of dominations, both colonial and neo-colonial. The tendency to marry antinomies and elaborate the real, typical of magic realism, has characterized the descriptive and historical records of Latin America's colonization and development. In the chronicles of discovery and conquest which were written by men who could not find words for the phenomena they encountered in the New World, dream and reality became, as Mario Vargas Llosa describes it, 'incestuously confused' (17). The confusion persists in modern Latin America where the diversity of ethnic groups, each with its own repertoire of forms, myths, superstitions and religions, has an established cultural heterogeneity, and where an uneven material development enables the coexistence of primitive agriculture with advanced technology. This proliferation of different ways of seeing forbids the application to Latin American history of a linear or totalizing perspective.

Timothy Brennan calls magic realism 'the style popularly associated with Gabriel Garcia Marquez and Alejo Carpentier but actually a more general and inevitable outcome of mature postcolonial fiction' (xii). In areas of conflict where issues of historical and political truth are subject to distortion, meaning and reality are necessarily shifting and provisional categories. The degree to which a magic realist text appears strange, incongruous, magical or improvisational can be related to the condition of its historical referents. The defamiliarizing of concepts which are absolute and immovable in naturalist narratives is part of the attempt to understand a place where knowledge is not representative but arbitrary and dialectical.

J. Michael Dash attributes the dialectic at work in magic realist texts to a particular historical consciousness. He focuses specifically on African cultures in the Americas for whom magic realism has provided a more constructive historical paradigm than Negritude. The Negritude movement of the 1950s responded to the violence and cultural loss incurred by the enslavement and colonization of African peoples by advocating the annihilation of the past through decolonization and the promotion of a unique African identity based on racial essence. Dash argues that Negritude failed because it was based on a conception of a historical past so destructive that its 'inheritors were frozen in a prison of protest' (64). The Guyanese writer Wilson Harris and the Haitian artist Stephen Alexis have challenged the refusal of both Western commentators and Negritude theorists to envisage a continuum of Third World history evolving beyond the ruptures of slavery and colonization. They claim that, far from being silent and irrevocable, the historical past was a 'creative process in which the continuous process of survival had given birth to a distinct national culture'. Their work, with its range of cross-cultural references, recognized that the oppressed people of the Caribbean did not relinquish their spiritual and creative originality to the imperial hegemony but developed a 'counterculture of the imagination' (Dash 64, 65). The dispossessed African and indigenous peoples preserved and syncretized myths, legends and rituals in what was 'a complex culture of survival'. Contemporary Third World writers reject the negativity of the protest cry which rails against the void of an 'uncreative past', and have discovered in magic realism a mode which identifies positive 'patterns of reemergence from the continuum of history' (Dash 64, 66). In *The Womb of Space*, Wilson Harris suggests that a culture capable of projecting figurative meaning beyond an apparently real world or 'prison of history' will produce a more complete and ultimately revolutionary picture of reality.

Magic realist devices in Toni Morrison's fiction derive from the same anti-rationalist, historically-charged energies that characterize Africanist art of the Caribbean. Her work demonstrates what Harris identifies as 'psychic regeneration through catastrophe' (quoted in Dash 67). He argues that the 'transforming power of the imagination' can retrieve from the violence of race hatred and racial oppression positive creative forces capable of countering fixed attitudes or beliefs. The 'imaginative transformation' of Afro-American history from a condition of unspeakable loss to one of creative process involves the reordering of realist perspectives. In Morrison's novels structures of meaning imposed by the dominant culture are disturbed by alternative discourses which often have their roots in Afro-American folk culture. Defining magic realism, Gerald Martin writes that 'it requires...the treatment of folk beliefs, superstitions and myths with absolute literalness' (149). Many Latin American practitioners of the style include in their narratives marvellous manifestations of folk belief in order to suggest the extraordinary reality of their surroundings. Gabriel Garcia Marquez traces his capacity to cast aside the restrictions of a purely rationalist or empirical outlook to the rich cultural history of the Colombian region where he grew up. Most significantly he attributes the 'taste for the supernatural' (35) which came naturally to his grandmother and her contemporaries, and which he inherited, to the region's African heritage. Integral to the epistemological structures of Caribbean culture, he maintains, is a certain multi-dimensional perception of reality which derives from the imaginations of African slaves. This African heritage, a pivotal feature of Marquez's aesthetic vision, is also part of Toni Morrison's genealogy. Common mythic lines spanning large geographic spaces connect the fabulous reality of her Afro-American literature with the magical epiphanies which surface in many Latin American narratives. The elements of magic and the supernatural which occur in Morrison's novels as unavoidable aspects of everyday life have their source in the folk history of slavery and, beyond that again, in the religious and cultural rituals of Africa. Researchers have agreed that these beliefs and practices enabled slaves to construct 'a psychological defense against total dependence on and submission to their masters' (Levine 163). In contemporary Afro-American fiction references to magic passed down along ancestral lines are in the same way a challenge to cultural and political domination, an expression of autonomy and difference.

Forms of magic known as 'tricking', 'conjuring', 'obeah', and 'voodoo' were integral to the sacred world of the slaves. Many slave communities deferred to the wisdom of a 'conjurer', a man or woman who was deemed to have supernatural powers and insights. The conjurer was called upon to cast spells, chase away evil spirits, prevent whippings or simply cure illnesses. Folk beliefs were most important for the sense of worth and assurance they gave to slaves, offering them 'sources of power and knowledge alternative to those existing within the world of the master class' (Baker 79). Even when converted to Christianity slaves enjoyed an intimate communion with the spirit world, summoning dead ancestors in clandestine religious gatherings, and translating signs occurring in the surrounding world. In a tradition directly inherited from African beliefs, slaves saw themselves as not alien to but part of a Natural Order comprising all things animate or inanimate, all spirits, visible or not. Slave folk beliefs can be seen as a cognitive system developed in response to the precarious nature of slave existence. Bronsilaw Malinowski argues that magic is found 'wherever the elements of chance and accident and the emotional play between hope and fear have a wide and extensive range...' (Levine 61). In the slave communities of the American South, magic served as a language which eliminated the fear of chance by redefining the unpredictable world as an intricate system of interpretable signs. A new level of factuality emerged in which the notion of knowledge, truth and reality as historically-determined replaced teleological prescriptions of meaning.

Magic Realism in Morrison's novels asserts the co-existence of several layers of reality in the same way that slaves combined the master's discourse of fact with alternative 'facts' of their own. In *Sula* the heroine's return to the black community is heralded by a plague of robins, a peculiarity calmly received as a sign from nature in the tradition of slave cosmology. The narrative treats this phenomenon not as an aberration of reality's known principles but as something central to the engagement with Afro-American cultural experience. The presence of the conjurer figure in Morrison's novels is another reflection of continuity between slave history and black American culture. Pilate, the powerful ancestral figure in *Song of Solomon*, is a conjurer who derives much of her mythic status from a peculiar physiological defect—the lack of a navel. The marvellous reality of her physique is corroborated by her talent for voodoo which she practices to influence the fortunes of her family. The fantastic possibilities of Afro-American magic exert an incontestable influence over the reality of the narrative, providing a space where African ancestors, slave history and contemporary black American culture converge. Characters like Pilate serve to demonstrate that what is rational is a matter of perspective, culturally determined: that, as Morrison points out, 'what distinguishes the colonizers from the colonized is viewing what is rational and what is not' (Jones 1985).

Images of flight in *Song of Solomon* also draw attention to the ambivalence surrounding representations of the real in Afro-American culture. Central to the magic realist aesthetic of the novel is the way Morrison incorporates details of an important Afro-American folktale about flying Africans into the narrative. This myth, which has been described as a 'touchstone of New World black folklore' (Wilentz 1984), tells the story of Africans who flew home across the sea as soon as they realized what slavery entailed. Recorded historical data suggest that the legend grew out of genuine acts of resistance by slaves attempting to exert some control over their lives and bodies. One historian records that 'in several cases slaves who had recently arrived from Africa sang songs in the evening and then some walked in a trance to the ocean and drowned while trying to swim home' (Owens 52). Folkloric stories of slavery in the Caribbean and Latin America attest that the story was common throughout the diaspora. Research on slavery in Jamaica and other Caribbean islands shows that slaves genuinely believed that Africans had the power of flight and that many of their fellows had taken this route of escape. Gay Wilentz argues that the Afro-American flight myth demonstrates 'how the collective unconscious (memory) functions for a particular group of people with a unique historicity' (120). It has become embedded in what Salman Rushdie calls 'race memory: that is the sediment of highly concentrated knowledge that passed down the ages, constantly being added to and subtracted from...' (Brennan 52). Latin American literature reveals both explicit and hidden manifestations of the tale. A short story by Gabriel Garcia Marquez called 'A Very Old Man with Enormous Wings' demonstrates the connection between New World Africanist mythology and the desire to subvert hegemonic or other controlling codes of expression. Vera Kutzinski sees parallels between the treatment of the winged old man—who is captured, branded and entreated to perform acts of conjury—and the fate of African slaves, and suggests that his wings are a 'synecdochial representation of...the magic power of transformation' or the power of flight known as 'volateria' on which the legend is based (138). The flight myth in United States as well as Latin American contexts provides a lexicon for addressing unresolved legacies of the past. The idea of human beings who can fly, one which defies 'the conceptual categories officially employed to define truth and reality', becomes a motif capable of both expanding and disrupting accepted ideas of historical reality and historical process.

In *Song of Solomon* the key to Milkman's quest for origins rests in the flight myth. The song which accompanies Milkman's birth contains the story of his family's history: as the narrative unravels he will discover that his great-grandfather was one of the legendary flying Africans who escaped slavery by flying back to the homeland. Fable turns to fact in Milkman's attempt to map his genealogy. The possibility of human flight becomes as real as Pilate's smooth, navel-less belly and conjuring powers. The unresolved ending of the novel in which Milkman is shown to leap into the air sustains both the verity of the Flying African tale as legend and the real possibility of flight. The question of whether the slaves drowned in the sea or mastered the air to fly home is suspended at the end, as Milkman is suspended between death at the hands of his misguided revolutionary friend, Guitar, or escape through flight. What is achieved in Milkman's final realization that 'if you surrendered to the air, you could ride it' is an understanding of the compact of triumphal resistance and community solidarity which defines freedom (Morrison 1979, 337). Ultimately the struggle between Western and African cultural perceptions is represented by the expanding dimensions of a reality in which the magical vision of the folk imagination defies rationalist demands for closure.

It is in *Beloved* that Morrison most dramatically illustrates her engagement with the marvellous aesthetic of her Afro-American heritage. In *The Literary Fantastic* Neil Cornwell locates *Beloved* within the genre of the fantastic, arguing that the doubt surrounding *Beloved's* origins, and the 'virtual absence of any independent and confirmatory narratorial voice', disqualifies its inclusion in the category of magic realism (203). However the easy acceptance of the supernatural throughout the narrative, coupled with the fact that the possibility of *Beloved's* being a ghost does not engender undue fear or disbelief, aligns the novel very closely, I believe, with magic realism; and I would contest Cornwell's contention that a 'confirmatory narratorial voice' is absent. The voice which links together the 'internally focalised' narratives of various characters communicates a belief in the existence of ghosts and a generally unsurprised response to manifestations of the unreal. This voice opens the novel in matter-of-fact tones with the information:

124 was spiteful. Full of baby's venom. The women in the house knew it and so did the children. For years each put up with the spite in his own way, but by 1873 Sethe and her daughter Denver were its only victims. The grandmother Baby Suggs was dead, and the sons, Howard and Buglar had run away by the time they were thirteen years old—as soon as merely looking in a mirror shattered it (that was the signal for Buglar); as soon as two tiny hand prints appeared in the cake (that was it for Howard)...

The voices whose interior consciousness transmits most of the novel's action and information also portray an unastonished acceptance of a reality which accommodates hauntings and other intrusions from the spirit world. Baby Suggs tells her daughter-in-law that moving away from the ghost-ridden house will not extirpate the anxiety of restless spirits since 'there's not a house in this country's ain't packed to its rafters with some dead Negro's grief'. As a young girl, Denver looks through the window of Baby Suggs's room at Sethe who is kneeling in prayer and sees that 'a white dress knelt down next to her mother and had its sleeve around her mother's waist' (Morrison 1987, 3, 5, 29). Sethe does not question the validity of her daughter's vision, but merely grills her for some detail that might indicate its significance. It is Denver also who perceives Beloved's true identity as the ghost of the baby girl come back to haunt the living, and who asks her: 'What's it like over there, where you were before? Can you tell me?' Even the men who do not share the women's easy communion with the supernatural world are slow to dispute its interference in their own. When Paul D arrives at Sethe's house he steps 'through the door straight into a pool of red and undulating light that locked him where he stood'. Sethe assures him that the company is 'not evil, just sad' and he has the courage to keep going: 'Walking through it a wave of grief soaked him so thoroughly he wanted to cry. It seemed a long way to the normal light surrounding the table, but he made it dry-eyed and lucky' (Morrison 1987, 75, 78, 79).

The narratorial point of view, whether represented by the internal voices of the characters or the linking commentary of the omniscient narrator, conveys an awareness and a tolerance of the supernatural which reflects the magic realist consciousness of Afro-American cosmology. Barbara Christian recognizes correspondences between *Beloved* and her own Caribbean culture. 'In the Caribbean', she writes, 'spirits are everywhere, are naturally in the world, and are not ghosts in the horror-genre sense of that term. For African Americans, at least until the recent past, the experience of spirits communicating with the living was a natural one rather than some kind of weird, unnatural event' (9). She also finds significant the fact that although Beloved appears to have reached the age she would have been had she lived, she acts like the 'crawling already? baby' she was when her mother killed her. There are many references to the newness of her skin and eyes, the unsteadiness of her feet, her huge capacity for sleep and greedy appetite for sweet things. The manner of Beloved's return, Christian points out, is in keeping with the beliefs of African-derived cultures in the New World:

> If ancestors are consistently not fed, or have not resolved some major conflict, especially the manner of their death, they are tormented and may come back to the realm we characterize as that of the living, sometimes in the form of an apparently newborn baby. So often I have heard someone in the Caribbean say, 'This one is an old one and has come back because she needs to clear up something big' (Christian 10).

This conception of a world whose boundaries with death are fluid and shifting informs the tone of *Beloved*. The marvellous reality of a spirit world emerges out of the slave's deeply rooted cultural psychology and is harnessed to the evocation of a traumatic history. It provides an alternative logic with which to read the past. In South Africa white psychiatrists have noted that in diagnosing black patients they must first decide whether something is a symptom or a cultural belief. In the Xhosa world-view, illness is often attributed to 'manfunfunyana', that is 'sorcery in which the use of dirty medicine is involved'. One doctor cites an example: 'A patient says he was pursued by a snake, the same snake which he saw visit his mother's grave at the funeral. At first glance this is a delusion, yet there is a Xhosa sect which believes snakes protect them. So the patient could be mad, he could not' (Carlin 28). The reader of a magic realist text such as *Beloved* is also required to judge culturally and not clinically. In *Beloved* the presence of ghosts is shown to be no more incredible or delusory than the unspeakable horrors of slavery. Morrison applies at textual level the tenets of a world view in which reality can dilate to admit more than is immediately discernible on the surface. The possibilities of an anti-rationalist cultural code and an infinitely malleable narrative perspective are employed to link Beloved's mysterious identity to the 'disremembered' millions, the black and angry dead whose names were never recorded. Beloved's interior monologue—'I am Beloved and she is mine. Sethe is the one that picked the yellow flowers in the place before the crouching'—suggests a collective history emerging out of a personal story. Salman Rushdie's novel *Shame* enacts a similar expansion of fictionalized personal history into mass, national history. The retarded young girl, Sufiya Zinobia, who blushes so intensely that the kissing lips of her grandmother burn on contact with her cheek, and who metamorphoses into a man-devouring 'Beast', replete with the shame of the world, is conceived within the tradition of grotesque, magical reality. Here as in Beloved the unreal provides a structure on which to assemble a critique of history. The ghostly Beloved speaks for all the forgotten and tormented victims of slavery, while in Sufiya Zinobia the shame of an evil and unregenerate world is horrifically personified.

Using the returned spirit of Beloved as a medium through which to refract the forgotten histories of enslaved Africans, Morrison illustrates magic realism's function as a 'cognitive mode'. Where fact, in this case the experience of African slaves from the Middle Passage through to their lives in the Americas, is obscured and distorted by historical or political mediation, magic realism emerges as a code which can 'assert another level of factuality' and which enables an emergent society like Black America to formulate a 'renewed self-description' based on an engagement with 'local' sources of knowledge. Describing Garcia Marquez's use of magic realism in a way which could equally apply to Morrison's style in Beloved, Kumkum Sangri argues that 'he realigns the notion of history as a set of discoverable facts with the notion of history as a field of diverse human and cultural possibility' (220-2).

To conclude, I will return to the Caribbean and Wilson Harris, whose claim that 'a philosophy of history may well lie buried in the acts of imagination' approximates something of magic realism's potential as a literary mode for the postcolonial world. That this philosophy of history is one which reaches beyond the limited zone of Western European realism is evident in magic realist literature which suggests that, across the Americas, African-derived cultures provide access to alternative cognitive systems in which meanings are not singular or fixed by subject to the transformative influence of a non-rationalist perspective. In Toni Morrison's fiction, the charged language of the marvellous real forges a space where the historical and spiritual imagination of the first slaves merges with the real landscapes of the New World, shattering the sacred concept of 'America' with vivid glimpses of an alternative black reality.

Works Cited

Baker, Howard, Jr. (1991) *Workings of the Spirit: The Poetics of Afro-American Women's Writing*. Chicago: Chicago UP.

Brennan, Timothy. (1989) *Salman Rushdie and the Third World*. London: Macmillan.

Carlin, John. (1994) 'Empire of Delusions'. *The Independent on Sunday*, 27 Nov.

Christian, Barbara. (1993) 'Fixing Methodologies: *Beloved*'. *Cultural Critique* (Spring).

Cornwell, Neil. (1990) *The Literary Fantastic: From Gothic to Postmodernism*. London: Harvester Wheatsheaf.

Dash, J. Michael. (1973) 'Marvellous Realism: The Way out of Negritude'. *Caribbean Studies* 13.iv.

Fuentes, Carlos. (1984) 'New Novel, New World.' *Modern Language Review* 84.iv.

Garcia Marquez, Gabriel. (1982) *The Fragrance of Guava*, trans. Ann Wright. London: Verso.

Jones, Bessie and Audrey Vinson. (1985) *The World of Toni Morrison: Explorations in Literary Criticism*. Dubuque, Iowa: Kendall/Hart.

Kutzinski, Vera. (1985) 'The Logic of Wings: Gabriel Garcia Marquez and Afro-American Culture'. *Latin American Review* xxiii.25.

Levine, Lawrence. (1978) *Black Culture and Black Consciousness: Afro-American Folk Thought from Slavery to Freedom*. Oxford: Oxford UP.

Martin, Gerald. (1989) *Journey through the Labyrinth: Latin American Fiction in the 20th Century*. London: Verso.

Morrison, Toni. (1979) *Song of Solomon*. London: Picador.

Morrison, Toni. (1987) *Beloved*. London: Picador.

Owens, Leslie Howard. (1977) *This Species of Property: Slave Life and Culture in the Old South*. Oxford: Oxford UP.

Rushdie, Salman. (1991) *Imaginary Homelands*. London: Granta.

Rushdie, Salman. (1983) *Shame*. London: Jonathan Cape.

Sangri, Kumkum. (1990) 'The Politics of the Possible', in *The Nature and Context of Minority Difference*, eds. Abdul Jan Mohammed and David Lloyd. Oxford: Oxford UP.

Vargas Llosa, Mario. (1987) 'Latin America: Fiction and Reality'. *Modern Latin American Fiction: A Survey*. London: Faber & Faber.

Williamson, Edwin. (1987) 'Magical Realism and the Theme of Incest in Gabriel Garcia Marquez's *One Hundred Years of Solitude*', in *Gabriel Garcia Marquez: New Readings*, eds. B. McGuirk et al. Cambridge: Cambridge UP.

Wiltenz, Gay. (1984) 'If you surrender to the air: Folk legends of Flight and Resistance in Afro-American Literature'. *Melus* 16.i.

JAMAICA KINCAID'S *LUCY*:

A Sexual and Literary Subversion
of (Post) Colonial Subjectivity

Lee A. Talley

Jamaica Kincaid's *Lucy*, the 1990 novel to follow her critically acclaimed and popularly praised *Annie John*, was, upon publication, criticized for its bitterness. Kincaid's defiant construction of postcolonial subjectivity in her protagonist Lucy prompted reviewers to focus on its anger and sometimes to praise it solely for its formal brilliance or for its rendering of love, glossing over the novel's political import.[1] While Kincaid is deliberately invoking the voice of Charlotte Brontë's cold Lucy Snowe from *Villette*, she is also subversively revising Wordsworth's Lucy poems.[2] Her challenge to cultural authority is rendered through her transformation of his poetry into a vehicle for rebellion and articulation of (post) colonial subjectivity.[3]

Kincaid disrupts accepted (and expected) literary and social roles for women—and their bodies—through her subversion of Wordsworth's poetic construction of the protagonist, Lucy. This is much more than merely an ingenious and important structuring device for this novel, as Kincaid's living character, Lucy, a young Antiguan woman, breathes new life into Wordsworth's Lucy poems, the series of five poems that glorify a dead (white) Lucy—one whose body no longer exists. Each of the five chapters in *Lucy* corresponds directly and meticulously to one of the five Lucy poems, and the novel even works with Wordsworth's own revision of their order.[4] His ordering of these poems creates a woman who begins in his 1799 manuscript as a dead woman who did have a voice in 'Strange fits of Passion I have known', one who is ultimately not just rendered mute and dead, but nameless as well ('A slumber did my spirit seal').[5] Kincaid's novelistic Lucy proudly speaks, claiming her life, body and voice. Through her reconstruction of the poetic Lucy, Kincaid renders the long-lasting effects of colonialism visible and challenges canonical literature, making what one learns in the classroom explicitly political.[6]

Kincaid's revisions are powerfully linked to a complex understanding and depiction of postcolonial subjectivity that are very much embodied. *Lucy's* protagonist begins as a young woman rebelling against her mother and her country's colonization. Lucy works at creating her self despite her repressive British education and her mother's 'proper' desires for a daughter who is well mannered and chaste. Lucy rebels bodily, delighting in her sexuality, using

51

it for pleasure and for power, embracing and subverting the status of the 'fallen', and writing home to tell her mother proudly she has become her mother's worst fear—a 'slut' (128). The theme of the fallen state as defined by the metropolis is fully explored in the novel, providing a sharp contradiction to the virtuous, English Lucy Wordsworth's narrator extols. Here, 'the fallen'—women, people and countries—are all offspring that are orphaned because of their perceived imperfection.

Kincaid's fascinating reworking of a series of Wordsworth's poems produces a powerful dialogue about colonialism as Lucy's very human body responds to and refracts the poetic body Wordsworth created.[7] My paper explores the intersection of 'bodies' of knowledge, land and literature with the female human body. The power dynamics of motherland, literature and culture flesh themselves out and struggle for supremacy through the body, and in the production of subjectivity. Lucy's profound embodiedness—her fascination with her body and the ways in which she uses and perceives her body in many different relationships where a struggle for power occurs—tells the stories of colonial oppression and the difficulty of forging an identity despite systems that work to disrupt the ties that bind humans together. These include language, family and ownership of property (including the property of your own person), ultimately creating orphans for the economic good of the 'motherland'.

Colonial systems traffic in bodies, destroy families, but also police language—as Kincaid's narrator points out in *A Small Place* when s/he comments on unreflective American fascination with English royalty and the pain of having no tongue.

> All they see is some frumpy, wrinkled-up person passing by in a carriage waving at a crowd. But what I see is the millions of people, of whom I am just one, made orphans: no motherland, no fatherland, no gods, no mounds of earth for holy ground, no excess of love which might lead to the things that an excess of love sometimes brings, and worst and most painful of all, no tongue. (For isn't it odd that the only language I have in which to speak of this crime is the language of the criminal who committed the crime?) And what can that really mean?…The language of the criminal can explain and express the deed only from the criminal's point of view. It cannot contain the horror of the deed, the injustice of the deed, the agony, the humiliation inflicted on me (31-2).

Kincaid explores these concepts as Lucy, in her own way, speaks angrily of these crimes and the material reality of their consequences. I believe Kincaid deliberately uses Wordsworth as a way to structure her Lucy's story and words because Wordsworth, one of the first nineteenth century poets to become a mainstay of the (inter)national British curriculum, was an influential man in the debates about the national educational system that worked to teach its students what Kincaid's narrator in *A Small Place* would describe as decidedly criminal language. Wordsworth believed, for example, that 'a hand full of employment, and a head not above it...are the best security for the chastity of wives of the lower rank', overtly acknowledging education's restrictive functions in terms of class mobility, sexuality and acquisition of knowledge.[8]

The first chapter, 'Poor Visitor', revises 'Strange fits of Passion I have known' as Kincaid reclaims the female object of the narrator's gaze, transforming Lucy into a subject and giving her an unmistakable voice.[9] 'Poor Visitor' documents Lucy's journey into an unnamed American city to become an au pair. While we learn that the protagonist is very well read indeed, we learn even more about her body and her relationship to that body. It is invoked early on when she notes that her room's ceiling 'was very high and the walls went all the way up to...[it], enclosing the room like a box—a box in which cargo traveling a long way should be shipped. But I was not cargo. I was only an unhappy young woman living in the maid's room' (7). Despite her assertion that she is not cargo, one cannot ignore the obvious reference to slavery and to the Middle Passage. Antigua became a 'successful' colony through the 'pertinacity' of the English, especially Colonel Codrington, a man infamous for the forced breeding of slaves.[10]

Kincaid expands the colonial reference to incorporate the 'fallen' state of sexuality, having Lucy dream that 'the scenes printed on [her] nightgown' come to life, compelling her to learn her pajamas's origins: 'Made in Australia' (9). She remembers 'that Australia was settled as a prison for bad people, people so bad that they couldn't be put in a prison in their own country' (9). Lucy learned her lessons 'properly', recalling Australia's origin as Britain's penal colony—the continent used to 'house' its criminals and fallen women, getting rid of the problem at home. The fact that the first colony Lucy mentions is one famous for its forced adoption of fallen women in the nineteenth century is vital, since so much of Lucy's upbringing involves her mother teaching her not to become 'a slut'.[11]

In the second chapter, 'Mariah', Kincaid revisits the haunting process of bodily erasure found in 'She dwelt among the untrodden ways'. There, Wordsworth's Lucy *becomes* a violet, and in this chapter's central episode, Lucy's body becomes literally obscured by another type of infamous Wordsworthian flower: the daffodil.[12] At ten, Lucy Potter masters 'I

53

wandered lonely as a cloud'—the so-called daffodil poem—'nicely pronouncing each word and placing just the right amount of special emphasis in places where that was needed' (18). Lucy Potter's audience lets her know 'how proud the poet, now long dead, would have been to hear his words ringing out of [her] mouth' (18). The image of Wordsworth's proud ghost is disturbing, for he would be pleased indeed with this particular performance. The vision of a well-schooled 'native' speaking the queen's English is proof of his belief in education's duty to construct good, loyal Christians, but ones who require strict schoolmasters, ministers and 'the never ceasing vigilance of their parents'.[13] Lucy was chafing under the yoke of oppression, but at ten was already conscious in a Fanonian way of her 'two facedness…outside false, inside true' (18). And while she does politely respond to the praise, she simultaneously vows 'to erase from my mind, every line, every word of that poem' (18).[14]

Given the subject's ideological interpellation at both conscious and unconscious levels, it is no surprise that the following night Lucy is powerfully hailed by colonialism, punished for her transgression by dreaming that she is smothered by daffodils, 'buried deep underneath them [never to be] seen again' (18). As Wordsworth's Lucy is figuratively erased through her comparison to various natural objects, now Kincaid's Lucy is literally erased by those same seemingly innocuous natural metaphors.[15] Lucy Potter's dream speaks to the powers of destruction found in poetry ostensibly about creation and imaginative possibilities for any (white) man:

> I gazed—and gazed—but little thought
> What wealth the show to me had brought:
> For oft, when on my couch I lie
> In vacant or in pensive mood
> They flash upon that inward eye
> Which is the bliss of solitude;
> And then my heart with pleasure fills,
> And dances with the daffodils' (l. 17-24).

The images (and words) which are so generative for Wordsworth's narrator are positively menacing for the postcolonial subject. Wordsworth himself writes, however, of how 'words are too awful an instrument for good and evil to be trifled with: they hold above all other external powers a dominion over thoughts'.[16] Kincaid's project affirms language's potential for domination as we see the effects of colonial erasure upon Lucy's person. Both the sign and signifier of daffodil acquire infinitely more sinister meanings.[17]

54

Although Lucy tells her employer, Mariah, about her daffodil experience, Mariah does not tell her that the yellow flowers she later shows Lucy are daffodils. To Lucy they look 'like something to eat and something to wear at the same time; they looked beautiful; they looked simple as if made to erase a complicated and unnecessary idea. I did not know what these flowers were so it was a mystery to me why I wanted to kill them' (29). Lucy is unable to express her rage effectively to Mariah once she learns belatedly what they are. Although Lucy explains the connections between the flower and the domination of educational practices and colonialism, Mariah fails to understand how Lucy could 'cast her beloved daffodils in a scene of conquered and conquests' (30).

When the family vacations at Mariah's childhood summer home, Kincaid's Lucy continues to reflect Wordsworth's comments on how words have such potential for good or evil because they hold dominion over thought. Mariah makes an unfortunate joke about feeding the minions, thereby allowing Lucy to contemplate the relationship between minion and dominion. Lucy describes herself as haunted by 'minions' because 'the place where I came from was a dominion of someplace else' (37). Here, we see just how powerful words are. When Wordsworth discusses their potency he links words to thoughts through 'dominion'. For him, thoughts can be the property of words, just as countries or people could be the property of another nation or person. But, as *Lucy* shows us, having a history of being property—of not having property in the person—can literally change an individual's personal properties or personality.

The following chapter, 'The Tongue', blends in seamlessly with this one, continuing Lucy's lessons in and on the white American upper-middle class. In this central chapter, one that connects simultaneously to 'A slumber did my spirit seal' and 'I traveled among unknown men', language and power are tied together in a gordian knot. Here one sees the detail of Kincaid's revisions as 'The Tongue', the very center of the novel, explores life at the margin. Kincaid appears knowledgeable not just of the conventional ordering of Wordsworth's poems, but also of his own final ordering of the poems in which 'I traveled' is the middle, not final, poem. The reference to 'I traveled' is particularly poignant as Lucy travels to America's 'heartland', a type of figurative—and certainly a powerful imaginative site for mainstream America's ideal of 'American-ness'—metropolis of American power. Wordsworth's narrator moves away from the mother land while Kincaid's narrator moves to one of its centres. Yet while his narrator becomes increasingly patriotic, vowing never to 'quit thy shore / a second time', (l. 6-7) pining for his Lucy 'turn[ing] her wheel / beside an English fire' (l. 11-12),

Kincaid's narrator, Lucy, has an opposite experience. Her country of origin is repeatedly referred to solely as a lovely vacation spot, making Lucy long to come from a 'place filled with slag and unexpectedly erupting volcanoes' (65). Kincaid's indictment of colonialism is extraordinary, making the patriotic narrator and the very English Lucy in 'I traveled' foolish indeed. This knowledge becomes incorporated with many other concepts and relationships connected to the chapter's apt title, 'The Tongue': themes of motherhood, mother tongues, mother land, story telling, feeding and sex .

In 'The Tongue', not only is Lucy sexually involved with Hugh, a family friend of her employers, reveling in her body, their bodies, and their tongues, but she also meets people whose names 'were easy on the tongue, names that made the world spin' (64). Her memories of her earlier sexual encounters are connected through her memories of various boys' tongues; but Lucy is playing with English too, a system of signification ineluctably linked with colonialism. Lucy's earlier sexual encounters take place in libraries—for her, a place where literal and figurative tongues meet. This helps demonstrate how deeply colonial educational practices penetrate its subjects, for as Ashcroft, Griffiths and Tiffin note, 'the English 'tongue' (and thus English literary culture and its values) was learned 'by heart': a phrase that captures the technology [of education's] particular significance' (426). This chapter, literally the heart of the novel, embodies and subverts both of Wordsworth's poems through Lucy's control of her sexuality—her person.

'The Tongue' is interestingly followed by 'Cold Heart', a comment, perhaps, on what happens when one is estranged from her tongue or heart—an integral part of colonial subjugation and postcolonial identity. 'Cold Heart' explores the links between girls' bodies, coming of age, dominion and domination. It parallels 'Three years she grew in sun and shower', the poem in which Lucy is a child, and the one in which the narrator is vying with an ominous suitor (nature) for Lucy's hand in marriage.[18] Again, Lucy is compared to a flower, but now she is, according to nature, the loveliest flower on earth, prompting nature to want her for himself. Wordsworth's Lucy has become a valuable and contested piece of property. Kincaid's Lucy moves from describing her current lover Paul's hands, to describing a girl she once knew, Myrna, who, as did the Lucy of 'Three years she grew', never finished growing. Lucy reflects on girls' sexuality, vulnerability and power when she remembers discovering that Myrna was sexually abused by a man at home. Lucy, at the time, was envious of her friend for getting attention, and for learning more about sexuality than she. Lucy was not ignorant, however, because when her friend recounted the meetings with Mr. Thomas in the alley and the exchange of a sexual favour for money, Lucy admits 'I was afraid that if I asked one thing I would reveal my feelings and show how familiar I was with what she had just described' (107-8). We never learn how this is familiar to Lucy, but she shifts from this scene, in which she cruelly asked the young girl 'if it hurt' (108), to her adult relationship with Paul, explaining how 'familiar' she would become with his hands. Given that this is the part of his person that captures Lucy on film and on canvas, the part of the body that violated Myrna, and the figurative hand nature wants in the Wordsworthian antecedent to this chapter, one could infer that perhaps her relationship with Paul is unequal. Here, one sees how domination, property and exchange are fraught *and* linked with representation.[19]

Lucy, however, learns another medium of (self) representation in this chapter. When she decides to buy a camera, this twentieth century Lucy refuses to be the passive Lucy that Wordsworth's nature decides to construct: 'This Child I to myself will take; / She shall be mine, and I will make / A Lady of my own' (l. 4-6). Lucy Potter uses her camera to speak and to contest the historical ways in which photography was used—most often in the social sciences—to truthfully represent 'deviant' members of society like the insane, the criminal and the exotic Other. Nineteenth-century photography upheld white, bourgeois values, but Lucy's photographs do not. She photographs the ordinary: everything from sanitary napkins to domestic disputes that topple the family for whom she works. Like Kincaid's inversion of the Lucy poems, Lucy Potter's use of photography continues to articulate not just the representation of self, but its inherent difficulty, potential duplicity and its multiplicity. Yet while her interest in photography is liberating, the sexual transactions that surround the purchase of her camera signal the recurring themes of power imbalance and the commodification of bodies and bodies of knowledge.

Sexuality becomes more fraught and bound up with colonialism once Lucy's father dies. After his death, she coldly writes to her mother reminding her:

> my whole upbringing had been devoted to preventing me from becoming a slut[.] I then gave a brief description of my personal life, offering each detail as evidence that my upbringing had been a failure and that, in fact, life as a slut was quite enjoyable, thank you very much. I would not come home now, I said. I would not come home ever (128).

Her departure from home and the death of her father allow her to define herself sexually against her mother, the person whom Lucy believes occupies an extraordinary position of power. In writing her mother in this way, she is defining herself against the other chaste, literary Lucys, and against her mother's injunctions to be a 'good girl'. She takes her body spitefully away from the maternal body that birthed her, that 'carried [Lucy] for nine months inside [her]', a fact that threatens Lucy's tenuously individuated identity (90).

The final chapter, 'Lucy', returns to origins and to Lucy's quest to know herself and her history. Unlike Wordsworth's Lucy who is 'rolled round in earth's diurnal course, with rocks and stones and trees' ('Slumber'), this Lucy moves away from the bourgeois white family and deeper into the metropolis on her own. She comes alive. 'Lucy' parallels 'A slumber did my spirit seal' and 'I traveled among unknown men' where Wordsworth moves from bemoaning the loss of Lucy to discovering a deeper patriotism because of her death. Interestingly, in 'Slumber' Lucy is never named, and yet in this revision of it she names herself, becoming the author of her being. In this final chapter Kincaid has her Lucy see colonial oppression, her self, her life and the place from which she has come; she is anything but dead, patriotic, or the vehicle for someone else's patriotism.

Lucy re-authors herself through anger—a vital and life-giving muse—in both naming herself and embracing the 'fallen state', a state aligned most often with constructions of social Others and one explicitly aligned with her name—a point to which I will return shortly. These acts enable her to write and see lucidly what much of the world would like to forget: the visible and invisible scars of colonial oppression that can never be forgotten or erased. She comes to terms with her name and embraces two very different canonical writers to do this, writers who I believe sum up Kincaid's project of recasting not just Wordsworth, but the many other authors that accompany a good British colonial education: writers whose Others need to be reclaimed.

Lucy writes of how, in her youth, she 'disliked the name Lucy, because it seemed slight, without substance, not at all the person I thought I would like to be even then', thus distancing herself from the small, cold, Lucy Snowe of *Villette* and the dead Lucy of the poetry (149). She called herself other names 'Charlotte, Emily, Jane…the names of the authoresses whose books I loved. I eventually settled on the name Enid, after the authoress Enid Blyton' (149). Lucy admires the Brontës and Austen, but it is Blyton's name she claims as her own, the author almost every colonial or postcolonial child reads despite knowledge or rules forbidding the simplistic but engrossing fiction she creates. Blyton's work is disturbingly full of problematic representations of racial Others, but is nevertheless devoured by children around the world. Thus, Lucy's choice simultaneously rejects 'good' literature, and also whispers of the insidious ways in which colonial ideology is globally consumed.

The other name she embraces is from Milton: 'Lucy, a girl's name for Lucifer' (153). And, while in her youth she memorized Milton's *Paradise Lost*, and knew well 'the stories of the fallen…[she] had not known then that [her] own situation could even be distantly related to them' (152). As an adult she learns this, and while her embrace of the fallen state speaks of colonial systems' power, and narratively reflects the Romantic writers' reclamation of Milton's Satan as (fallen) hero, it is also a step in reclaiming and recreating her self on her own terms.

When Wordsworth told Coleridge about the Lucy poems, he said, 'as I have had no books I have been obliged to write in self defense' (Moorman 415). He was trying to fight depression. Kincaid's Lucy also writes in self defense, only her writing is more *offensive* (by which I mean both attacking *and* provocative)—it is a type of 'back talk'. Lucy writes to stave off attacks from books that inadequately and incorrectly describe her and her history. Kincaid's revision of Wordsworth's series of five poems that represent the same subject also speaks to the discursive fragmentation of postcolonial subjectivity, neatly problematizing simplistic, essentialist representations of the Other.

At the very end of the text Lucy writes out her full name, Lucy Josephine Potter, in what will become her journal, and then writes 'I wish I could love someone so much that I would die from it' (164). Full of shame, she weeps, leaving only a trace of the words that articulate her desire as one watery blur. The anger that offended the critics, that power that made them comment repeatedly on the novel's formal brilliance and silenced them about colonialism, is connected to the pain of longing for home most often discursively figured in the maternal. The properties colonial societies attempt to wrest away from their subjects (a mother land [home], mother tongue [language], and comforting mother's body [family]) are the properties of Lucy's person that she is reclaiming through her non-canonical appropriation and revision of a very oppressive and often unwelcoming body of literature. Unlike Wordsworth's Lucy, Lucy Potter is anything but 'a thing that could not feel the touch of earthly years' ('Slumber'). Kincaid creates a Lucy who has motion, force, aurality, sight, but most importantly, voice. The 'laughter light' that Wordsworth took away from his poetic Lucy in his revision of 'She dwelt' becomes a voice that expresses the pain, knowledge and cynicism borne out of colonialism. This Lucy does not laugh at England's educational or literary attempts to erase her. She refuses to be rendered mute.

Notes

1. See for example, the *Washington Post*, October 7, 1990; *Newsweek*, October 1, 1990; and *USA Today*, November 8, 1990. The following presents a more complex picture of the novel, but still complains about, for example, finding 'it difficult to recognize the lively, curious and engaged child Annie in the angry but disengaged Lucy': *The New York Times Book Review*, October 28, 1990. The *New York Times* article of October 12 praises the anger, but notes that readers will have difficulty with it. The *Los Angeles Times* (October 21, 1990) and especially the *Nation* (February 18, 1991) perform much more politically insightful analyses of the novel.

2. Moira Ferguson (1993) notes the significance of the Lucy poems in the novel, but subsumes them in importance to the Miltonic Lucy, Lucifer, after whom Lucy is named. I argue that all three Lucys (Milton's, Wordsworth's and Brontë's) are of importance, and that the multiple origins of Lucy's name signal the multiplicity of the postcolonial subject, and also the colonial and postcolonial inheritance of an oppressive literary tradition.

3. I use the term '(post) colonial' to invoke the history of colonialism surrounding the literature that Kincaid is revisiting. While *Lucy* is clearly a postcolonial novel, its revision of a group of poems used in colonial *and* postcolonial educational systems cannot be ignored. (Post) colonial signals that dual history.

4. The order in which these poems are traditionally taught follows the order of their composition ('Strange fits of Passion I have known', 'She dwelt among the untrodden ways', 'A Slumber did my spirit seal', 'Three years she grew in sun and shower', and 'I traveled among unknown men'). Wordsworth did, however, change the placement of 'Slumber' to be the final poem rather than 'I traveled'. See Frances Ferguson (1973) for a detailed reading of how the poems' revisions affect one another and for an analysis of temporality, the act of writing and the power of language.

5. While this plotting of Wordsworth's poems is clearly central to my analysis of voice in *Lucy*, I also explore the connections between the more traditional arrangement of the poems.

6. Bill Ashcroft, Gareth Griffiths and Helen Tiffin (1995) note that 'education is perhaps the most insidious and in some ways perhaps the most cryptic of colonialist survivals, [with] older systems now passing, sometimes imperceptibly, into neo-colonialist configurations' (425). They argue that in *Lucy* Jamaica Kincaid 'examine[s] and challenge[s] that persisting gap between the so called 'first world' production of knowledge (the 'authoritative' text) and its consumption at colonial and post-colonial sites' (426). They have also compiled an excellent group of texts exploring colonial educational practices.

   Two autobiographical accounts of the formative experiences of education in the Caribbean and the act of writing are Merle Hodge, 'Challenges of the Struggle for Sovereignty: Changing the World versus Writing Stories' (in Cudjoe 1990, 202-8) and Lorna Goodison, 'How I Became a Writer' (in Cudjoe 1990, 290-

4). For Jamaica Kincaid's comments on her own literary education referring specifically to Milton, see Leslie Garris (1990).

7. This undoes at a literary level what Gauri Viswanathan (1988) writes of when she explains how the exportation of literature reversed the Cartesian notion of self, presenting a 'de-actualized' and disembodied yet materially powerful English presence (103). At a literary level Kincaid has recreated Wordsworth's Lucy into a profoundly embodied young woman. At another level, however, Lucy's subjectivity actively resists the colonial attempts at bodily erasure, not only of the colonizers' bodies as Viswanathan points out, but also of the (sometimes) more threatening colonized body. For a more expansive study of colonial educational practices see Viswanathan (1989).

8. Letter to the Reverend Hugh James Rose, quoted in *Prose Works* (299).

9. Moira Ferguson does not make comparisons between particular poems and chapters of Kincaid's novel, but her analysis of Wordsworth's poems in '*Lucy* and the Mark of the Colonizer' is useful. She explores the ambiguities of the narrator's gaze in 'Strange fits' as representing Lucy Potter's later desire in the novel for her mother's death. Although the importance of the mother-daughter relationship cannot be downplayed, and nor should be Ferguson's analysis of its importance, I believe this poem's significance is more specific than that. I see the significance lying in Kincaid's defiant reconstruction of Lucy's voice.

This was the one poem in which Wordsworth gave Lucy a voice, but he edited out that stanza in his final version, leaving her utterly mute. The 1799 MS. ends with an extra stanza in which after the narrator cries, 'O mercy...[if] Lucy should be dead', he follows with: 'I told her this; her laughter light / Is ringing in my ears; / And when I think upon that night / My eyes are dim with tears' (Matlack 52).

10. A fascinating and disturbing representation of the 'uplifting' presence of the British is provided by Frederick A. Ober (1916, 306-16; 1920, 346-8).

11. For other scenes of instruction on girlhood and sexuality read Jamaica Kincaid's earlier short story 'Girl' in *At the Bottom of the River* and also *Annie John*. For criticism on these other works and their connection to the anxieties regarding female 'promiscuity', see Helen Pyne Timothy, 'Adolescent Rebellion and Gender Relations in *At the Bottom of the River* and *Annie John*' (in Cudjoe 233-44), Laura Niesen de Abruna's 'Twentieth-Century Women Writers from the English-Speaking Caribbean' (in Cudjoe 86-97), and Moira Ferguson (248).

12. Moira Ferguson reads 'She dwelt among the untrodden ways' as being about the silenced female figures of empire against which Kincaid's Lucy struggles. I agree, but also believe that both Wordsworth's and Kincaid's fascination with language's ability to erase subjects needs to be considered as well.

13. William Wordsworth, 'Speech at the Laying of the Foundation Stone of the New School in the Village of Bowness, Windermere, 1836' in *Prose Works* (295).

14. In their introduction to their section on education Ashcroft, Griffiths, and Tiffin note how the 'recitation of literary texts...becomes a ritual act of obedience often

performed by a child...as if s/he were the imperial speaker/master' (426), and note the insidiousness of memorizing things by heart. While this is alarmingly true, one sees how this Lucy fights against and is conscious of the potential damage of this type of memorization and performance.

15. Frances Ferguson notes 'when Lucy is given corporeal form it is a flower form and not a human form', arguing that 'these flower similes become impediments rather than an aid to any imaginative visualization of a woman' (534). Lucy is thus quite literally 'colonized' by language. Ferguson argues that this process is most obvious in 'Strange fits' and 'She dwelt'. In Kincaid's work it is most prominent in 'Mariah', the chapter that corresponds to 'She dwelt'. Note, too, that this chapter is the one chapter title that cannot be tied to Lucy's body or self. Not only is this chapter the one in which the scene of colonial oppression is dramatized with the daffodils, but it is the one chapter title that directly applies to Lucy's white, politically naive employer.

16. William Wordsworth, 'Essay on Epitaphs', in *Selected Prose* (361).

17. Moira Ferguson argues that the daffodils are a trope of colonialism and analyzes the importance, repetition and growing meaning of the colour yellow during this and other incidents in the novel (240).

18. Frances Ferguson analyzes nature in this poem as a 'child molester' (544). The configuration of the colonial relationship—often represented as a parent- or adult-child dyad—resonates well with the exploitative relationship Wordsworth describes.

19. Moira Ferguson notes the connection between Paul and Mr. Thomas and links them to Lucy's desire to subvert the 'maternal injunctions' about sexual behaviour found both in 'Girl' and *Annie John* (249). While I agree that Lucy is rebelling against a colonial (and maternal) system that works to control the bodies of 'natives', I view the relationship as more sinister. I too see the similarities between Paul and Mr. Thomas, but I read Paul as being possibly similar in his position of power to Mr. Thomas. The more sinister connection between Paul and Mr. Thomas lies in the power imbalance implied in colonial systems of oppression and in incestuous or sexually abusive relationships, where the (most often) younger, or more powerless, participant views him/herself as making choices when, in fact, those choices do not represent true agency, but rather, subtle and insidious manipulations of power by the person in the dominant position. I believe it is this similarity between colonialism and sexually abusive relationships that makes Myrna's relationship with Mr. Thomas 'familiar' to Lucy in some way, whether or not she is sexually knowledgable about the specifics of their transactions.

20. Moira Ferguson mentions photography's ability to distort and rearrange reality, and also 'level the playing field' of power (248-9). For a detailed pictorial and theoretical account of how native Others were depicted and commodified, especially in the nineteenth century, a vital period in photography's artistic and colonial history, see Alloula (1986).

21. Lucy, I believe, is meant to be 'offensive' in both senses of the word. Kincaid states, 'I think after writing *A Small Place* and seeing the reaction to it, I realized that people couldn't stand a certain sort of frankness.... But yet I wanted to be very frank and to be unlikable within the story. To be even unpopular. In the last two stories [*A Small Place* and *Lucy*] I wanted to risk more' (Perry 506).

Works Cited

Alloula, Malek. (1986) *The Colonial Harem*, trans. Myrna Godzich and Wlad Godzich. Minneapolis: University of Minnesota Press.

Ashcroft, Bill, Gareth Griffiths and Helen Tiffin. (1995) *The Post-Colonial Studies Reader*. New York: Routledge.

Cudjoe, Selwyn R., ed. (1990) *Caribbean Women Writers: Essays from the first International Conference*. Wellesley: Massachusetts: Calaloux Publications.

Ferguson, Frances. (1973) 'The Lucy Poems: Wordsworth's Quest for a Poetic Object', *ELH* 40.iv: 532-48.

Ferguson, Moira. (1993) 'Lucy and the Mark of the Colonizer', *Modern Fiction Studies* 39.ii: 237-59.

Kincaid, Jamaica. (1986) *Annie John*. New York: Plume/New American Library.

Kincaid, Jamaica. (1989) *A Small Place*. New York: Plume/Penguin.

Kincaid, Jamaica. (1983) *At the Bottom of the River*. New York: Farrar, Strauss, Giroux.

Kincaid, Jamaica. (1991) *Lucy*. New York: Plume/Penguin.

Matlack, Richard E. (1978) 'Wordsworth's Lucy Poems in Psychobiographical Context', *PMLA* 93.i.

Moorman, Mary. (1957) *William Wordsworth A Biography: The Early Years 1770-1803*. Oxford: Clarendon Press.

Ober, Fredrick A. (1916) *Our West Indian Neighbors: The Islands of the Caribbean Sea, 'America's Mediterranean': Their Picturesque Features, Fascinating History, and Attractions for the Traveler, Nature-Lover, Settler and Pleasure Seeker*. New York: James Pott & Company.

Ober, Fredrick A. (1920) *A Guide to the West Indies, Bermuda and Panama*. New York: Dodd, Mead & Company.

Perry, Donna. (1990) 'An Interview with Jamaica Kincaid', in *Reading Black, Reading Feminist: A Critical Anthology*, ed. Henry Louis Gates, Jr. New York: Meridian/Penguin.

Viswanathan, Gauri. (1988) 'Currying Favor: The Beginnings of English Literary Study in British India', *Social Text* 19/20 (Fall).

Viswanathan, Gauri. (1989) *Masks of Conquest: Literary Study and British Rule in India*. New York: Columbia UP.

Wordsworth, William. (1974) *Prose Works of William Wordsworth*, eds. W. J. B. Owen and Jane Worthington Smyser. Vol. 3. Oxford: Clarendon Press.

Wordsworth, William. (1988) *Selected Prose of William Wordsworth*. London: Penguin Classics.

WRITING HOME:

Constructing the Caribbean Subject
in the Poetry of Derek Walcott

Paula Burnett

'*poets, as is well known, don't know what they're saying, yet they still manage to say things before anyone else*' (7)

Jacques Lacan

An observation from Stephen Slemon elaborates some implications of the Lacanian epigraph: 'It has become commonplace in poststructuralist criticism to regard the critical text as essentially fictional, but the possibility that the fictional text might equally function as a work of literary criticism or as a genuinely theoretical document seems to be the occulted "other" in the deconstruction of this particular binary' (in Brydon & Tiffin 145). To look to fiction for kinds of knowledge deemed non-fictional is unfamiliar, perhaps unheimlich, the Freudian 'uncanny' (literally 'un-homely'), which disturbs as it disrupts a familiar order; to read off from fiction a theory of psychology may seem perverse. Derek Walcott's work can be seen to encode profoundly innovative ideas, yet because the signs it uses embrace the givens of the canon it tends to be interpreted as evidence of assimilation to the Western bourgeois tradition. Just to draw on a tradition, however, is not necessarily to reinscribe its values. As Wilson Harris, the Guyanese novelist, poet and philosopher, puts it, 'Homer, Dante, Shakespeare, Goethe are as much the heritage of black men and women as of white men and women because the triggers of conflicting tradition...lie in...the cross-cultural psyche of humanity' (in Maes-Jelinek 137).[1] Writing such as that of Walcott and Harris may be the place to look for new models of possibility, for new understandings of our complex and hybrid individualities which are the building blocks of society. Lacan's arrogant presupposition that the wisdom of poets is not deployed consciously may be, rather, about defending the status of nonfictional inquiry. His acknowledgement of their lead (whether knowingly or not) is made in a context which historicizes Rimbaud's *I is an other* as precursor of the Freudian thesis—an innovation which had 'exactly the same implication of decentring as that brought about by the Copernican discovery' (Lacan 7). It is used here to introduce an interpretation of Walcott because it obliquely confirms a rather unconventional approach. Kristeva lists the three innovations in textual critique as the materiality of writing, its immersion in history, and its sexual overdetermination which 'orients it toward psychoanalysis, and through it toward the set of a corporeal, physical, and substantial "order"' (100). The topic here is the way fiction can be read as theorizing new insight into the psychological order, although it should be noted that Walcott himself professes little interest in the 'dead fish' of criticism.[2] He is convinced of art's lead in identifying and developing the 'cross-cultural psyche of humanity'.

Home is a term which is immediately problematized in relation to the postcolonial predicament. 'Writing home', underneath its apparent symmetry with the idea of the empire writing back (to write home implying a subject position of not being at home, as the empire writing back implies a counter-discursive position) raises a contrary notion. 'Home', as well as being the indirect object of the participle 'writing', is perhaps also its direct object—a matter not so much of address as of production. The ambiguity of the phrase 'writing home' thus draws attention to the gap between the intentionality of writing as social practice, and its product, the text, and raises the possibility of the text in some sense being able to make home happen, to call it into existence. Inevitably it also raises the question of a dialectical relationship with the meaning of the phrase in colonial discourse. Under empire, 'home' was constructed in relation to the imperial heartland (in the British case the 'home counties' remains a current usage), functioning as a centrist myth to alienate those who inhabit the colonial space from their own in-placeness. Counter-discourses have identified the need to reclaim the notion of home, positing its pluralism, its openness to multiple determinations. These may involve differences not just of location but of kind. Home may be a matter of psychology and of culture—to do with the construction of the subject—as much as a spatial concept. In essence, home may be the opposite of alienation.

Walcott 'writes home' in a number of ways. Most obviously, he inscribes the particularity of his Caribbeanness into literary discourse to such a degree that his whole oeuvre can be read as an elaboration of the lines, 'moi c'est gens Ste. Lucie. / C'est la moi sorti; / is there that I born' ('Sainte Lucie', *CP* 314), lines which he chose to quote to the welcoming party on his first visit back home to St. Lucia after winning the 1992 Nobel Prize for literature.[3] As well as celebrating his own geographical in-placeness, however, he has eloquently addressed its antithesis, the migrant's displacement and hence ambivalence about place, shared with the Caribbean diaspora worldwide and with other emigrés. From vigorous protestations of his commitment to the archipelago as home, in the sense of the location for utterance—'may I speak here'—he moved in mid-life to Boston and to explorations of the condition of the 'single, circling, homeless satellite', the emblem of mobile communication, remote, but articulating each to each ('As John To Patmos' and 'North and South', *CP* 5, 405).

Concerns that the 'metaphorization of postcolonial migrancy is becoming so overblown, overdetermined, and amorphous as to repudiate any meaningful specificity of historical location or interpretation' (Krishnaswamy 128) may be quietened by the interactive specificities of Walcott's epic poem *Omeros*, which brings these oppositional identities into relationship, reconciling them in a 'homing' action on which the poem's intertextual relationship with Homer provides a kind of pun. The poem maps in-placeness as well as journeys, trauma as well as healing, and Seven Seas utters the wisdom that:

> there are two journeys
> in every odyssey, one on worried water,
>
> the other crouched and motionless, without noise.
> For both, the 'I' is a mast; a desk is a raft
> for one, foaming with paper, and dipping the beak
>
> of a pen in its foam, while an actual craft
> carries the other to cities where people speak
> a different language, or look at him differently
>
> (*Omeros* 291).

Seven Seas finally privileges stasis as 'the right journey', because from travel 'you have learnt no more than if you stood on that beach...except your skill with one oar'. The text, stitching together the two shores of the Atlantic with its journey images, presents a double sign of the oar, with which Homer's Odysseus was to travel on until he reached a land where the people did not recognize it. It is a tragic cleaver in the African episode when it becomes a weapon wielded against the slavers, but it is transformed in the new world to the mast/pen emblem, repairing schism through the harmony of the text: not a utopian dream of oneness, but a seamed conjunction. The poem repeatedly models binary pairings between its personae, both within and across gender and racial groups, but these are never romantic. The toughness of the poem lies in its refusal of utopianism; its strength lies in its mapping of loving interpersonal relationships both despite and because of history. In this and other works Walcott effectively remodels identity politics, placing alongside Western psychology's understanding of the individualist subject, constructed against alien others, a self which exhibits and seeks hybridity and pluralism as positive signs.

It thus calls into question the Freudian and post-Freudian interpretations of the psyche which have dominated twentieth-century thought, focusing on relations between the self and its others. Freud has enabled an exegesis of the modern condition as characterised by alienation, both individually and socially. In the phrase of Trinidadian poet Wayne Brown it has been a 'century of exile'. It would be an error, however, according to Jameson, to attribute 'postmodern schizo-fragmentation', psychology's new 'speculative mapping of fractured and multiple subject positions', to 'some unimaginably complex new internal human nature rather than to the social templates that project them' (372). In the work of Julia Kristeva, a post-Freudian who studied with Lacan, the dynamic is inverted, with the difficulty of social relations derived from the difficulty of integrating the individual personality:

> Living with the other, with the foreigner, confronts us with the possibility or not of *being an other*. It is not simply—humanistically —a matter of our being able to accept the other, but of *being in his place*, and this means to imagine and make oneself other for oneself. Rimbaud's *Je est un autre* ["I is an other"] was not only the acknowledgment of the psychotic ghost that haunts poetry. The word foreshadowed the exile, the possibility or necessity to be foreign and to live in a foreign country, thus heralding the art of living of a modern era... Split identity, kaleidoscope of identities: can we be a saga for ourselves without being considered mad or fake? Without dying of the foreigner's hatred or of hatred for the foreigner? (Kristeva 1991, 13-14).

The logic of Kristevan inquiry is to argue from recognition of the presence of the stranger within the self to acceptance of the stranger without: from the psychological to the social. For her, the route out of xenophobia (otherwise inescapable, omnipresent, even genetic) is acknowledgement of the alienation within the individual. This is close to a tragic philosophy, however, in which the individual consciousness collapses back on itself in despair of ever knowing itself or sharing with others. The best Kristeva can offer is the fatalism that 'we are all "others", that hell is within us, that the foreigner is within us, that we must accept it' (1993; cf. Burnett 1996), which is predicated on a xenophobic construction of the idea of the 'étranger', translated here as 'foreigner'. Perhaps at the point when the North's Freudianism has backed itself into a corner, the South, as Walcott presents it, can offer a way out, a fresh perspective on the problematic arising from the Freudian preoccupation with boundaries, and principally with the delineation of the limit between selfhood and alterity—in other words, with difference.

Western thought traditionally proceeds by difference—it classifies by division, defining homogeneity by its antithetical relationships to otherness. Such systems of knowledge, however, tend to essentialize, suppressing difference within the groups being demarcated, in order to conceptualize the boundary with greater firmness and clarity. Scientific and social taxonomies appear to be conceptually accurate, recording real divisions between distinct classes, when in fact they often suppress other potential groupings and obliterate median positions. Notions of nation are conspicuously problematic in this way, as are those of race, the privileging of simplistic essentialisms functioning to obliterate, disparage or suppress the hybrid and the plural. The conceptual basis of Western rationalism, now understood as a patriarchal hegemony, has real political consequences. Our understandings of the pernicious psychological effects of European imperialism, initiated by Fanon, Mannoni and Memmi, are still developing. As Fanon anatomizes, it is at the most fundamental level that the colonial subject is traumatized: the imperial discourse (particularly in its racial dimension) prevented (prevents?) the healthily integrated construction of the ego, producing self-alienation: 'It was no longer a question', he writes, 'of being aware of my body in the third person but in a triple person... I was not given one, but two, three places' (Fanon 1967, 112). The colonial schizophrenia affects the colonized, the colonizer and those in between. As Hawthorn puts it, in a discussion of Jean Rhys's *Wide Sargasso Sea*, 'in an exploitative society all involved are, in different ways, denied the possession of their full humanity' (100). It is this full humanity which Walcott attempts to retrieve.

While the terminology of difference is the language through which we speak our perceptions of the world, we risk repeating the old myths. The dialectical embrace of the opposite pole to the dominant, while understandable, and perhaps a necessary phase, in the end is limited by its inscription within the old binary system, just as negritude is limited by its reciprocity: negritude 'writes back' to hegemonic constructions of race as polarity by privileging the formerly negative pole, instead of rejecting polarization altogether. The need is rather to break out of the restrictive binaries. The particular usefulness of Walcott's aesthetic project is that it offers ways of reconceiving difference without either suppressing it in assimilationist taxonomies or allowing it to proliferate as absolutist fragmentation, the first tending conceptually towards fascism and the second towards balkanization (a term which has acquired an urgent new political contemporaneity).

To unite or to divide are not, after all, the only options; the continuum between them offers many median positions partaking in part of both one and the other. A region such as the Caribbean, fragmented as its communities are—geographically on small islands, historically by dislocation from ancestral communities, and culturally in terms of language, race, class and background—nonetheless also exhibits shared sensibilities, its hugely various people having more in common than they have dividing them. It is therefore a case of both difference and sameness, simultaneously. It involves the recognition of otherness specifically as the point of sameness, of identification—of what I choose to call the sharedness of difference.[4] Walcott, I believe, reconstitutes the schizophrenic subject position as a plus— the West Indian position is one of 'creative schizophrenia' (cf. 'What the Twilight Says')—as the means to a richer selfhood than that postulated under the western epistemology derived from Freudian and post-Freudian thought. The Oedipus complex, as Deleuze and Guattari point out, is not the only means of addressing the formation of the psychological subject.

They define the task of what they term 'schizoanalysis' in terms both of deconstruction—'tirelessly taking apart egos and their presuppositions' in order to liberate 'the singularities they enclose and repress'—and of construction—'assembling the desiring-machines that countersect everyone and group everyone with others' (362). Having exposed Oedipal psychology as a despotic monoculture internalized throughout society from microcosm to macrocosm, the argument of *Anti-Oedipus* revises the 'breakdown' of the schizophrenic as a 'breakthrough', an essentially creative and revolutionary process, a rejection of an intolerable order: 'society is schizophrenizing at the level of its infrastructure, its mode of production, its most precise capitalist economic circuits' (359, 362, 361). The great artist (and in 1972 it seems the idea of greatness was not deemed problematic) is necessarily, in their view, of the schizophrenic party. Great writers, those 'capable of performing a breakthrough in grammar and syntax, and of making all language a desire', speak 'from the depths of psychosis' and demonstrate 'for our benefit an eminently psychotic and revolutionary means of escape' (134). As opposed to the 'oedipalization' of literature which reduces it to 'an object of consumption conforming to the established order, and incapable of causing anyone harm', the great author is the one who 'cannot prevent himself from tracing flows...that necessarily nourish a revolutionary machine on the horizon... For literature is like schizophrenia: a process and not a goal, a production and not an expression' (133). By privileging schizophrenia as revolutionary sign, Deleuze and Guattari postulate the disruption of the Western-defined 'norm' in terms which resonate profoundly with the Caribbean experience and its aesthetic, as expressed by artists such as Walcott, and with current theorization.

Bhabha applies the idea of the split to postcoloniality: 'power must be thought in the hybridity of race and sexuality…nation must be reconceived liminally as the dynastic-in-the-democratic, race-difference doubling and splitting the teleology of class-consciousness' (251). Said identifies the new ex-centric dynamic:

> In a totally new way in Western culture, the interventions of non-European artists and scholars cannot be dismissed or silenced, and these interventions are not only an integral part of a political movement but, in many ways, the movement's *successfully* guiding imagination, intellectual and figurative energy reseeing and rethinking the terrain common to whites and non-whites (256).

Walcott, in inscribing his people's subject-position (writing home), addresses the world. His focal image is the tiny island of St. Lucia, from which he disrupts Northern centrism with his etiolating discourse.

Centrism attempts to preserve its dominance by privileging its own. Walcott challenges the constructions of race which serve that project. The one who is most on the margins of cultural constructions of identity, the person of mixed race, is psychologically most at risk since, in Hawthorn's phrase, s/he 'symbolizes the human internalization of external divisions in a racially divided society' (106). The imperialist construction of race exhibits the manichean pattern very clearly: the privileged pole of so-called whiteness is defined by its antithesis, so-called blackness. The person of mixed race, like Walcott, therefore has a special authority to speak of race. Empire had a horror of the hybrid, because in the mixed-race person it recognized the destruction of its system of racial classification, the trampling of the boundaries, as its ever more hysterical devising of new terms of classification exhibits. As Young notes, in the nineteenth century, 'racial difference became identified with other forms of sexual and social perversity as degeneracy, deformation or arrested embryological development. But none was so demonized as those of mixed race' (180). The theorization of the 'between' as unheimlich, the Freudian term usually translated as 'uncanny' but literally meaning 'unhomely', is developed by Allon White into the theory of 'abjection':

the abject feels split between a self and internalized otherness which s/he attempts to expel. This split or *Ich-spaltung* (Freud) destroys the fundamental subject-object boundary which both preserves subjective identity as such and keeps the world at bay. The abject is split between subject and object, neither fully an independent self nor completely determined by the objective realm, falling uncontrollably between both (166).

Such theorization, however, proceeds from a number of totalizing assumptions, such as the 'fundamental' nature of the subject-object 'boundary', and the presumed projection of hostility implicit in the need to 'keep the world at bay'. While these may be apt accounts of certain aspects of the construction of the psychological subject position, they are neither complete nor exclusive. The implicit politics of the denial of the validity or manageability of that which falls 'between' is not addressed, yet it is acutely present, and requires a response such as Walcott gives. Representations of both miscegenation and creolization (the bodily and linguistic hybridizations) are central to Walcott's creative project. The Caribbean personae he models are essentially plural, and are shown engaging creatively with colonial trauma. The locus of 'between' is, for him (in cultural just as in bodily terms) the site of fertility, product of interactive desire, where the generation of the new holds out the endless possibility of hope. Patriarchal Western preoccupations with origin, with retrospective lineage, are, in Walcott's aesthetic, countered with the privileging of originality, here and now. Dennis Plunkett in *Omeros* is engaged in the sterile search for an ancestor as putative son, but the poem ends with the image of the heterosexual couple, and the implied promise of Helen's foetal child, the identity of whose biological father is unimportant.

In suggesting that pluralism might be regarded as an empowering heritage, however, Walcott does not underplay the difficult reality, the product of socialized constructions of alterity as negative, and of the 'between' as 'abject'. His Shabine persona in 'The Schooner *Flight*', an implicit self-image in which a recurrent theme of his work culminates, is a tragic figure of alienation, suffering a specifically mixed-race angst as his name suggests:

After the white man, the niggers didn't want me
when the power swing to their side.
The first chain my hands and apologize, "History";
the next said I wasn't black enough for their pride (CP 350).

Shabine is homeless, but it is an historically specific alienation, the legacy of a colonial displacement, which informs his question:

Where is my rest place, Jesus? Where is my harbour?
Where is the pillow I will not have to pay for,
and the window I can look from that frames my life? (*CP* 350).

The colonial specificities simultaneously, however, open out to engage with the existential questions of our time. When Walcott names the origin as 'that cry, / that terrible vowel, / that I!' ('Names', *CP* 306), he addresses a crux of the human condition which goes beyond spatial and temporal categories, and groupings of culture, race or gender. Literacy, literature, culture, the poem indicates, are ultimately unimportant, compared with the daring of the primal utterance of self-consciousness, an elemental 'wild' voicing. The loneliness of that self-perception is real, but so also is the possibility of sharing, of the social: the poem's 'I' migrates to 'we', and from the oral to the scribal in the tracing of 'our names'. Walcott postulates that the continuum between individual and community requires *both* polarities to be given forceful representation, so that the multiplicity of intermediate possibilities can emerge.

The creole principle is evident not just in representations of the body (miscegenation) and in the language (creolization), but in Walcott's construction of the Caribbean subject position. His project of 'writing home' is not like the empire writing back to the centre, but an inscription of 'home' in the sense of a defining of the in-placeness of the Caribbean person, the wholeness of the Caribbean subject in all her or his pluralism—which he calls 'assimilating the features of every ancestor' (1974, 1)—thus revisioning the centrist construction of Caribbeanness as alienation, locked in to trauma and tragedy. He does not deny the trauma—that would be romance—but reconceptualizes it in such a way that it opens out into both negative and positive, producing the balance of epic: at the end of *Omeros* the sea is 'still going on'.

Clearly, the idea of alterity has been appropriated with enthusiasm by cultural producers of all kinds in the project to counter totalizing discourses with inscriptions of heterogeneity, such that to give a sceptical critique of difference is to risk accusations of revisionist universalism. The task may be, however, to cherish heterogeneity while mapping congruence: the two are not necessarily incompatible. The binarism of self and other can be reconceived without implacable oppositionality. The Freudian concept of splitting can be positive as well as traumatic, as Deleuze and Guattari postulate. Walcott, as a twin, begins his approach to the world perhaps with a different relationship to alterity; and as a Caribbean person, inheriting both a hard history and a heartfelt humanity, he is able both to give expression to the loneliness of the 'I', and to model the fundamental community I suggest is symbolised in 'I-an-I', the Rastafarian pronoun which serves as both 'I/me' and 'we/us'. This coinage offers an apt symbol of Walcott's practice, in its refusal to recognize a fixed boundary between self and other, and in its creative inclusiveness: it not only marks the dyad (and other multiples) without suppressing the individual, but also preserves the subject position in all grammatical formations by its rejection of any differentiated object case. Historically, it was the repudiation of the commodification of the psychological subject implicit in the grammatical object case, understood as a semiotics of slavery, that led to the origination of the 'I-an-I' formation in Rastafarian speech, which is a highly politicized discursive practice. Walcott (who has lived in Jamaica, and took his degree at the Jamaican campus of the University of the West Indies) mines its significance in his Jamaican play *O Babylon!*; he has Rude Bwoy explain that 'in Rasta language / there is no accusative case. Dem feel not guilty', and has a final chorus which elaborates the dyad to a symbolically plural form, 'I-and-I-and-I-and-I' (1978, 216, 275).[5]

Walcott thus sets alongside his explorations of the lonely individualist self a different concept of the subject, constructed by means of positive reciprocities in which the self-other formulation is less a problematic than an enrichment. Walcott's epic poems are constructed out of emblematic dyads. In *Another Life*, the narrator makes 'I-an-I' pairings both with Gregorias and with Anna; in *Omeros*, Achille makes similar pairings with Hector, with Philoctete and with Helen, while Helen is seen paired with Hector, with Achille and with Dennis, who is himself paired with Maud. Understood as the singular pronoun, 'I-an-I' marks a complex sense of the plural individual which contests the Freudian notion of schizophrenia as pathology. The narrator of *Another Life*, and Achille, the protagonist of *Omeros*, are complex individuals whose creative response to the socially induced trauma of alienation enables them to outwit the conspiracy of history, Anansi-like, to assert their full humanity, if anything enhanced by the depth of their suffering and the difficulty of working through the potentially crippling negatives. Healing is not easy, but it is possible, and in *Omeros* it is enacted, through the Philoctete story, in the faith that the language rite may have the magic power to deliver that which it narrates. The particular difficulty of constructing the masculine subject in colonial and neocolonial societies is addressed in *Omeros*, culminating in the symbolic androgyny of Achille and

Philoctete's masquerade. Instead of being *unheimlich*, the median of gender, the Tiresias figure which is both genders rather than neither—a Jungian positive rather than tragic—is modelled as heroic, the energy of the cross-gender creative act showing an alternative to either phallic violence or emasculation.

The revolutionary nature of this aesthetic can be seen not only against the discourse of Western psychology, but against traditional constructions of Caribbeanness. The Caribbean experience has a particular place in postcolonial discourse, and Walcott's work has an interrogative place in both. Within the global postcolonial story, the region is often cast in a Cinderella role, foregrounding the painful dislocations and alienations suffered historically by the Caribbean people. Philip Sherlock, the Jamaican poet and intellectual who did so much to nurture the Caribbean cultural flowering of the second half of the twentieth century, put it forcefully: 'Colonialism, however important, was an incident in the history of Nigeria and Ghana, Kenya or Uganda; but it is the whole history of the West Indies' (Sherlock 13-14, quoted in Brydon and Tiffin 37). The authors of the critical handbook *The Empire Writes Back* use the region as negative pole in the scale of colonial experience:

> The West Indian situation combines all the most violent and destructive effects of the colonizing process… In the West Indies [in comparison with settler colonies] the processes of maintaining continuity or of "decolonizing" the culture are much more obviously problematic…[in] part…because the process of disruption brought about by imperialism was not only more violent but also more selfconsciously disruptive and divisive (Ashcroft *et al* 26).

The extremity of the West Indian condition within the British empire extends in this formulation even to language: 'English', say these Australians, 'had a much more tainted historical role in the Caribbean' (26-7). That it should be the terminology of impurity, of 'taint', which comes to mind to express the particularity of the West Indian language story is indicative of the tenacity of old ideologies, even among the most aware thinkers. For while the West Indians lived the extreme of language-as-power, they also generated the opposite pole of language-as-creative-survival, and of language-as-subversion (as Ashcroft, Griffiths and Tiffin go on to acknowledge). It was in the fire of language in the West Indies that the creative response to tyranny was tempered, and that a uniquely hybrid culture was forged.

Walcott is not alone in placing a high value on that uniqueness. John Hearne, the Jamaican novelist, made the large claim that the people of the Caribbean are 'the last hope of a nearly beaten human race, because we, the hybrids, were beaten into the ground and have risen, furnished with an obstinate belief in the *person*—in the man, woman and child—that astonishes the institutionalised world' (xi). Walcott shares with Hearne, who was a close friend, the conviction that to read Caribbeanness as locked into a psychology of alienation and an aesthetic of loss and suffering is not the only way to formulate its particularity in the global cultural story. As Walcott puts it in a miniature epic poem, 'that was just Lamentations, / it was not History' ('The Sea is History', *CP* 366).

The boldness of claims such as Hearne's implicitly casts any artist who expresses that culture in a potentially over-reaching role. Walcott, aware of the risks, has repeatedly ironized his role as priest-like artist serving his community, through the figure of the 'light of the world'. *Another Life* presents the near-blasphemous daring and faith of the young artists' commitment as like a drunken passion. When the poet-narrator shows himself, in the more recent poem 'The Light of the World',[6] as left behind in the dark by the transport which takes his fellow St. Lucians onward in a capsule of light, and records his humble recognition that in the cultural economy of human exchange they lacked nothing which he had to offer, a genuinely revolutionary moment is expressed. The supposed superiority of the poet—literate, educated, the world traveller, revisiting a home projected by centrism as marginal—is deconstructed as in relative lack, while the ordinary citizens of the island are given superior status in both wisdom and spirituality. The ambivalence is crucial. The poem's narrator, apparently Walcott himself, is both at home and away—a sharer but also different, othered by his intellectual role. The originality of his perception is the realization that, to the extent that the individual shares, s/he does so as the gift of the group; it is not something s/he can claim, or to which s/he has a right. It is only through the generosity of the group that the loneliness of the 'I' can be assuaged, as its metropolitan presumption of superior knowledge is othered by the egalitarian spirituality of the so-called powerless community.

A poem which marked the move into the alienation of geographical exile, 'The Schooner *Flight*', explores the pluralism within, containing the twin statements, 'I have Dutch, nigger, and English in me, / and either I'm nobody, or I'm a nation', as well as 'I had no nation now but the imagination' (*CP* 346, 350). The idea of the miscegenated individual as in his or her own person 'a nation', and its doubling with the idea of the life of the imagination as being in some sense a country or an identity, offers an important counter to reductive ideas both of the individual and the social. As Walcott has said:

> I'm constantly running into this idea…that I'm not sure which world I'm in, that I don't know who I am. I know very precisely. You can only dissect and understand the spiritual instability of the West Indian if your hands are calm… But perhaps to an American living in such an atmosphere as black-is-black and white-is-white and never-the-twain-shall-meet, a mixed person like myself has to be seen as a mixed-up person (Rodman 255).

And this is not to claim unusual self-knowledge. He asserts it as a distinctive condition of Caribbean people, however humble—'Fisherman and peasant know who they are and what they are' (in Hearne 127)—and calls himself 'this neither proud nor ashamed bastard, this hybrid, this West Indian' ('Twilight' 10).

The reading of the Caribbean experience as tragic, with schizoid distress the product of past exploitation, is thus revealed as conspiring with the neocolonial project, which it is the artist and intellectual's task to counter. Fanon, also a Caribbean, argues that the 'colonized man who writes for his people ought to use the past with the intention of opening the future, as an invitation to action and a basis for hope', in a revolutionary practice which 'aims at a fundamentally different set of relations between men' (1961; 187, 198). Walcott endorses Hearne's claim that the 'fundamentally different' human relations are not just a matter of aspiration but of reality. Rex Nettleford, the Jamaican social theorist, relates it to a global position:

> The Caribbean…has no reason to indulge the now endemic doubts about its self-worth since it demonstrates its capacity for having all modes of artistic cultural expression, classical, popular and ancestral, which co-exist in cyclical dynamic inter-relationship. This is a good enough basis for the region's call for a new international cultural order… (x).

In his formulation it is the writers, 'literate, healthily schizophrenic, insightful', who have been 'truly among the first to explain formally the Caribbean to itself' (52), and he mentions Walcott as among those who have:

> something unique to say about the human condition, and where they come from and how they were socialized and bred just happens to

give that something a special pitch and tone of importance and relevance to a North Atlantic world, itself in search of new patterns and new designs for its continuing existence (53).

Walcott writes for the Caribbean first, but he offers the good news of Caribbean 'I-an-I' humanity to the wider world, inverting, with a fine irony, the old missionary project. This is not a manichean counter-discourse but something of much more intricate pluralism, accepting and counter-balancing in one deft movement.

Bhabha, in an evaluation of Walcott's poem 'Sainte Lucie', quotes Richard Rorty's phrase that 'solidarity has to be constructed out of little pieces, rather than found already waiting', and concludes, 'from the little pieces of the poem, its going and coming, there rises the great history of the languages and landscapes of migration and diaspora' (235). This recalls Walter Benjamin's figure for translation:

Fragments of a vessel which are to be glued together must match one another in the smallest details, although they need not be like one another. In the same way a translation, instead of resembling the meaning of the original, must lovingly and in detail incorporate the original's mode of signification, thus making both the original and the translation recognizable as fragments of a greater language, just as fragments are part of a vessel (79).

The image—of a whole composed of different but congruent parts—shadows Deleuze and Guattari. After defining the task of 'schizoanalysis' as 'assembling the desiring-machines that countersect everyone and group everyone with others', they go on:

For everyone is a little group (un *groupuscule*) and must live as such— or rather, like the Zen tea box broken in a hundred places, whose every crack is repaired with cement made of gold (362).

Walcott uses a memorably developed variant of the metaphor in his Nobel speech, to explain the distinctively Caribbean cultural synthesis:

Break a vase, and the love that reassembles the fragments is stronger than that love which took its symmetry for granted when it was whole... It is such a love that reassembles our African and Asiatic fragments, the cracked heirlooms whose restoration shows its white scars. This gathering of broken pieces is the care and pain of the Antilles, and if the pieces are disparate, ill-fitting, they contain more pain than their original sculpture, those icons and sacred vessels taken for granted in their ancestral places. Antillean art is this restoration of our shattered histories, our shards of vocabulary, our archipelago becoming a synonym for pieces broken off from the original continent (*Antilles* 9).

The Ramleela drama, a folk ritual, which he describes being enacted in rural Trinidad, is such a fragment, reassembled differently in a new time and place, as part of a different, plural culture. As he has said:

> Fragments survive. Most languages survive in fragments anyway, they don't survive entire, and so that access, that tonal access, makes the Caribbean, just because of history, logically a place that is going to create an immensely fertile, varied and different kind of literature (Scott 16).

The task of writing, the task of 'creative schizophrenia', is 'the god assembled cane by cane, reed by weaving reed, line by plaited line' (*Antilles* 9). The artist is the community's shaman, its servant not its master. S/he articulates the community to itself. The Caribbean artist articulates a plural identity, of fragments tightly knit into a new whole, each individual bearing the pluralism of the ancestral presences at the heart of her or his uniqueness. And the proffered wisdom is that this is not a condition unique to the Caribbean; that we are all plural in this way, bearing many selves within us, functioning within hybrid cultures, using languages which continually creolize.

As well as writing home in *Omeros* by articulating his vision of St. Lucianness as plural identity both to his own people and to the world, Walcott gives expression to his faith in the individual's power of creation, the power to defeat alienation by creating a symbolic 'home', in whatever external conditions life may be lived. Instead of modelling Caribbeanness on nostalgia for a lost Africa, he shows the African ancestors, drawn by the creativity of their descendents across the Atlantic, as a silent, ghostly audience to the dance of Achille and Philoctete. The whole poem may be seen as centred on a passage of metamorphic magic, creating home. It boldly disrupts the epic metre—the Dantean *terza rima* with its resonating hexameters—by shifting gear into the incantatory binary rhythms of the traditional English spell, with its insistent rhymes. Significantly, it comes at the heart of the poem, in the third section of Chapter 33, suggesting a numerological magic which medieval and renaissance writers would have recognized, and is an incantation to turn a seemingly hostile house into a home. Walcott empowers the unhappy, alienated consciousness to transform its exile to in-placeness, teaching that it is available to each individual to use his or her creativity to bring into being the world of aspiration. The rite begins by naming the House of Horror which we all recognize, the house of fear, memories and broken relationships, a manmade environment which isolates the senses from the natural—the 'Unlucky house that I uncurse / by rites of genuflecting verse'. The relationship between place and consciousness is then inverted in a carnivalesque transformation: 'I do not live in you, I bear / my house inside me, everywhere'. In the concluding lines of the spell, which deliver the magic, there is a potent echo of George Herbert's dramatisation of his faith in a hospitable God, rejoined in the ultimate homecoming:

House that lets in, at last, those fears
that are its guests, to sit on chairs

feasts on their human faces, and
takes pity simply by the hand

shows her her room, and feels the hum
of wood and brick becoming home (*Omeros* 173-4).

The rite of transformation is enacted not as by a *deus ex machina*, with all its politics of hierarchy, but as a popular appropriation, a magic which is demonstrated as available to anyone, specifically through the creative practice of language. The unhoused soul—always, in Walcott's metaphysics, in a kind of exile when embodied away from its creator in the world—can, by an act of mind, create its home. For the migrant the moment of beginning to feel at home in a new location is symbolic; the spell at the heart of Omeros functions in the historical as well as the metaphysical plane. As well as particular social application, however, it has an etiolating mythic significance. Likewise the Jon Konnu dance for Christmas of Achille and Philoctete stands like the Gemini constellation over the whole poem, providing a figure for what this study suggests as the 'I-an-I' model of human consciousness.

The insight as to psychological alienation, which Lacan traces back beyond Freud to Rimbaud's *Je est un autre*, the tragic insight of the late nineteenth century which transformed thought in the twentieth, is balanced by Walcott with a parallel insight, comedic, to use his term. In the late twentieth century he has shown how 'that terrible vowel, / that I!', real to all of us in its loneliness and paranoia, is only one aspect of our psychological self-perception. Not only can the individual be creatively schizophrenic, but variants of community can be both real and ubiquitous. The permutations on the sharedness of difference are endless. To rephrase Kristeva: we all share each other, heaven is within us, we must celebrate it. As Rastafarian wisdom—another original Caribbean cultural synthesis—demonstrates through its creative transformation of language, 'I-an-I' is a speech practice of openly political symbolism, and the meaning of 'dread' can be remade.

Notes

1. Fred D'Aguiar distinguishes Walcott from Harris, arguing that only Harris goes beyond binarism to the pluralism of a 'kaleidoscopic whole' (167).
2. '...since boyhood I have delighted in criticism. I cherished the essays of Eliot not because of his perceptions but because of their quotations. They induced in me the truest humility: that is, the desire to imitate, to imprison myself within those margins. Since then a lot of dead fish have beached on the sand. Mostly the fish are French fish, and off their pages there is the reek of the fishmonger's hands. I have a horror, not of the stink, but of the intellectual veneration of rot...' *et seq.* Derek Walcott, 'Caligula's Horse', in Stephen Slemon and Helen Tiffin (141).
3. *Arena*, BBC2, London, 26 February 1993.
4. Bhabha begins to address the ambiguity housed right at the centre of the construction of the subject position, responding to Fanon in terms of the 'crucial splitting of the ego', in which the colonized subject is 'primordially fixed and yet triply split between the congruent knowledges of body, race, ancestors' (80), but he stops short of investigating the potential of the split to signify as positive marker.
5. The final chorus relates faith that the individual consciousness will be reunited with God ('the great I / Am shall be one with I') and progresses from Aaron's repeated cry of 'I-and-I-and-I-and-I' to the concluding statement of faith in the coming of the New Jerusalem, 'Zion a' come, / Zion a' come someday'.
6. *The Arkansas Testament* (48). Terada adduces Rilke's version of the Orpheus and Euridice myth in her analysis of this poem, with which her postmodern reading of Walcott's poetry concludes (216-26)
7. George Herbert, 'Love', from *The Temple*, 1633, rpr. in Helen Gardner (1957, 142). An earlier poem of Walcott's may be regarded as a response to the same poem of Herbert's: 'Love After Love' (CP 328).

Works Cited

Arena. BBC2. London, 26 February 1993.

Ashcroft, Bill, Gareth Griffiths and Helen Tiffin, eds. (1989) *The Empire Writes Back: Theory and Practice in Post-colonial Literatures*. London and New York: Routledge.

Benjamin, Walter. (1955) 'The Task of the Translator', *Illuminations*, trans. Harry Zohn. London: Fontana, 1992.

Bhabha, Homi K. (1994) *The Location of Culture*. London and New York: Routledge.

Brown, Wayne. (1973) 'The Century of Exile', *Jamaica Journal* 14.iii.

Brydon, Diana and Helen Tiffin. (1993) *Decolonising Fictions*. Australia, Denmark and UK: Dangaroo.

Burnett, Paula. (1996) 'The Ulyssean Crusoe and the Quest for Redemption in J.M. Coetzee's *Foe* and Derek Walcott's *Omeros*', in *Robinson Crusoe: Myths and Metamorphoses*, eds. Lieve Spaas and Brian Stimpson. Basingstoke: Macmillan: 239-55.

D'Aguiar, Fred. (1991) 'Ambiguity without a Crisis? Twin Traditions, the Individual and Community in Derek Walcott's Essays', in *The Art of Derek Walcott*, ed. Stewart Brown. Bridgend, Wales: Seren Books.

Deleuze, Gilles and Felix Guattari. (1972) *Anti-Oedipus: Capitalism and Schizophrenia*, trans. Robert Hurley, Mark Seem and Helen R. Lane. London: Athlone Press, 1984.

Fanon, Frantz. (1967) *Black Skin, White Masks*, trans. Charles Lam Markmann. New York: Grove.

Fanon, Frantz. (1961) *The Wretched of the Earth*, trans. Constance Farrington. London: Penguin, 1967.

Gardner, Helen, ed. (1957) *Metaphysical Poets*. London: Penguin.

Hawthorn, Jeremy. (1983) *Multiple Personality and the Disintegration of Literary Character*. London: Edward Arnold.

Hearne, John, ed. (1976) *Carifesta Forum*. Jamaica.

Jameson, Fredric. (1991) *Postmodernism, or, The Cultural Logic of Late Capitalism*. London and New York: Verso.

Krishnaswamy, Revathi. (1995) 'Mythologies of Migrancy: Postcolonialism, Postmodernism and the Politics of (Dis)Locations', *Ariel* 26.i.

Kristeva, Julia. (1980) *Desire in Language: a Semiotic Approach to Literature and Art*, trans. Thomas Gora, Alice Jardine and Leon S. Roudiez. Oxford: Blackwell.

Kristeva, Julia. (1991) *Strangers to Ourselves*, trans. Leon S. Roudiez. New York: Columbia UP.

Kristeva, Julia. (1993) 'Foreign Body', *Transition* 59.

Lacan, Jacques. (1988) *The Seminar of Jacques Lacan: Book II; the Ego in Freud's Theory and in the Technique of Psychoanalysis 1954–1955*, ed. Miller, Jacques-Alain, trans. Sylvana Tomaselli. Cambridge: Cambridge UP.

Maes-Jelinek, Hena, ed. (1991) *Wilson Harris: the Uncompromising Imagination*. Denmark, Australia, UK: Dangaroo.

Nettleford, Rex. (1993) *Inward Stretch, Outward Reach: A Voice From the Caribbean*. London and Basingstoke: Macmillan.

Rodman, Selden. (1974) *Tongues of Fallen Angels*. New York: New Directions.

Said, Edward. (1993) *Culture and Imperialism*. London: Chatto and Windus.

Scott, Lawrence. (1993) 'Derek Walcott: An Interview', *The English and Media Magazine*. Autumn.

Sherlock, Philip. (1966) *West Indies*. London: Thames and Hudson.

Terada, Rei. (1992) *Derek Walcott's Poetry: American Mimicry*. Boston: Northeastern University Press.

Walcott, Derek. (1970) 'What the Twilight Says', in *Dream on Monkey Mountain and Other Plays*. New York: Farrar Straus and Giroux.

Walcott, Derek. (1974) 'The Muse of History', in *Is Massa Day Dead?*, ed. Orde Coombs. NY: Anchor Doubleday; rpr. in *Carifesta Forum*. ed. John Hearne. Jamaica, 1976.

Walcott, Derek. (1976) 'The Muse of History', in *Carifesta Forum*, ed. John Hearne. Jamaica.

Walcott, Derek. (1978) 'O Babylon!' in *The Joker of Seville and O Babylon!* New York: Farrar Straus and Giroux.

Walcott, Derek. (1986) *Collected Poems 1948–1984*. New York: Farrar Straus and Giroux; London: Faber.

Walcott, Derek. (1987) *The Arkansas Testament*. [New York: Farrar Straus and Giroux] London: Faber, 1988.

Walcott, Derek. (1989) 'Caligula's Horse', in *After Europe*, eds. Stephen Slemon and Helen Tiffin. Australia, Denmark and UK: Dangaroo.

Walcott, Derek. (1990) *Omeros*. New York: Farrar Straus and Giroux; London: Faber.

Walcott, Derek. (1993) *The Antilles: Fragments of Epic Memory*. New York: Farrar Straus and Giroux; London: Faber.

White, Allon. (1993) *Carnival, Hysteria and Writing*. Oxford: Clarendon Press.

Young, Robert J.C. (1995) *Colonial Desire: Hybridity in Theory, Culture and Race*. London and New York: Routledge.

WHOSE CANNIBALISM?:

Consumption, Incorporation and the Colonial Body

Kay Schaffer

Cannibalism was one of the more prurient fascinations of the nineteenth-century British reading public. If one examines the colonial literature in the popular press in, say, the decade of the 1830s, one finds scores of adventure stories, often purporting to be first hand 'authentic' accounts, of castaways and shipwreck victims confronting the savage other on the frontiers of the colonial world. The tales typically tell of captivity and cannibalism at the hands of 'barbarous savages'. If a white woman was involved, then so much the better: hints of miscegenation could be employed for extra titillation. The twin themes of sex and savagery were bound to attract readers and to guarantee increased circulation for a nascent colonial publishing industry. Indeed, a ship's captain with South Seas experience, an ample imagination and a good turn of phrase could earn enough as an adventure writer for the colonial press to make a new start at the end of his seafaring days.

However fabulous the stories were, their impact was by no means slight. As Benedict Anderson (1991), Mary Louise Pratt (1992) and others have shown, the rise of the print media at the beginning of the nineteenth century was integral to the formation of national consciousness and to the evolving bourgeois subjectivity of the emerging middle class. The identity of the nation, and in this case the British Empire, depended on processes of othering. To demonize the stranger, the barbarian, at the far reaches of Empire was essential to the colonial enterprise. Newspapers, broadsheets and other popular fictional forms became key sites in the formation of new knowledges about the self and its others, and by extension, about Britain and her colonies.

For the past six years I have been examining one of these 'classic' tales—one full of sex and savagery and barbarous natives who freely, indeed gleefully, were said to practice that most depraved of human sins: cannibalism. It is the tale of Mrs Eliza Fraser, who in May 1836 was shipwrecked off the coast of what is now Queensland, Australia. Her story, of an 'innocent white woman' amongst 'savages and cannibals', met with immediate appeal. The tale, wildly embellished to be sure, circulated widely, appearing within six weeks of her arrival back in Liverpool in July 1837 in the British, North American and West Indian colonial press. Full of the horrors of cannibalism (where none was known to have occurred), it fuelled the popular imagination (Schaffer 1996). After her arrival home, when a Mayoral Inquiry was established to test the truth of the tale, her story held interest for a more professional audience as well, one which included politicians, philosophers, journalists, natural scientists, missionaries and would-be ethno-graphers, all of whom pondered the evidence of cannibalism and devised various responses—none of which would bode well for the future of the indigenous peoples of the antipodean world.

Modern research indicates that these popular colonial narratives tell us more about the fears and fantasies of the British than about the actual happenings overseas (Hulme 1986; Kilgour 1993; Obeysekere 1992a; Stratton 1990). The colonial British fear and fascination with the idea of cannibalism, in particular, has sparked the interest of a number of researchers in the past few decades. From an historical perspective, scholars report that virtually no evidence can be found to support the widespread popular Western belief that the peoples of the unknown, non-Western world were cannibals (at least not in the sense that term came to be understood by Western readers). Further, anthropologists suggest that even in societies where the practice of anthropophagy was known (or the eating of human flesh, infrequently as the brutal outcome of hostilities between warring tribes, more often for survival during times of scarcity, but primarily for sacred, ritual purposes at the time of burial), indigenous peoples were not in the habit of taking Western people captive for the purposes of torture, murder and devourment (Arens 1979; Sanday 1986; Taussig 1986). Still, that belief was so widespread in the nineteenth century to instil terror in the hearts of explorers, settlers and hapless shipwreck victims, and fuel the resolve of the mission movement.

What interests me here is not the shipwreck of the 'Stirling Castle' itself, nor the unfortunate fate of Mrs Fraser, but the way in which the event and others like it entered popular discourse. It is a specific example of a more general pattern of popular literature which contributed to the promotion of inscriptions of racial superiority and inferiority in the nineteenth century. The widespread belief that so-called primitive people practised cannibalism, that ultimate mark of savage Otherness, and the reiteration of fantastic accounts of cannibalism in the colonial tales, not only influenced the ideologies of British racial superiority at the time but sustained racial prejudices and practices long after the memory of the stories had faded. Indeed, these traces continue to have political impact today. Consider the bitterly contested election campaign in Queensland in 1995 which saw the demise of the Goss Labour government. In her campaign for a national legislative seat which helped to tipped the balance in favour of the coalition Liberal/National Party in Queensland, Independent candidate for Parliament Pauline Hanson announced in a speech, widely reported in the national press, that Aborigines had much to feel guilty about in their past, including their cannibalistic practices in regard to the Chinese in the nineteenth century. It mattered little to the press or Pauline Hanson's supporters that this malicious fiction was without foundation. The same story had been circulated in the national press in 1989. Despite vigorous protests by Aboriginal and non-Aboriginal Australians to the newspapers concerned and to the Australian Journalists' Association the story was never retracted (Schaffer 1996). In 1995, Pauline Hanson won her seat in the National Parliament, despite (or because of) the fact of her unprecedented vow that she would not represent the Aboriginal people of her electorate. Since her election she has been an outspoken proponent for a new conservative force in Australia's racial politics.

White fantasies of savage otherness assuage cultural anxieties about difference. In the nineteenth century those anxieties arose out of insecurities, both personal and political, about the success of the colonial endeavour on the edges of Empire. The continued transmission of tales of cannibalism can be aligned with the new Conservatism in Australia as it, like Britain and the United States before it, turns its back on social democracy and announces the end of the welfare state. In times of complex social change, when racial issues become matters of public contestation and government measures adversely affecting indigenous peoples seeking redress from past abuses win widespread support, how we study these phenomena matters. Our approaches have political consequences.

There is a substantial contemporary critical literature on cannibalism. The commentators come from diverse backgrounds in anthropology, literary studies, history, politics, postcolonial and cultural studies; and their treatments and intentions of the topic vary considerably. Nonetheless, one can detect two general tendencies in the research. One approach is to treat the phenomenon as a fiction, that is, chiefly as a product of imagined fantasies of Western travellers in liminal zones of early contact, and then proceed to trace the power of these imaginary constructions as a force in Western history (Hulme 1986; Kilgour 1993; Stratton 1990; Taussig 1986). Another, perhaps more overtly politicized, approach is to attempt to uncover what was actually happening between indigenous and non-indigenous peoples at the time of 'first contact' by reading against the grain of colonial discourse in an attempt to revisit the originary scene and restore a sense of inter-subjectivity to all actors present.[1]

Obviously, these different approaches have bearing on the theoretical and methodological debates currently being waged within the humanities in general, as well as the antagonism between adherents of the traditional disciplines and those advocating study in the new interdisciplinary fields of cultural studies and postcolonial studies. They also affect present political relations between indigenous peoples and new settlers in nations emerging out of their colonial pasts. The first, discursive approach, is often labelled 'post-modern', and frequently accused of reducing the world to text—of having no ethics, no moral ground, no politics. The second, more materialist anti-colonial approach claims an overt political engagement, particularly in its attempt to grant agency and restore subjectivity to indigenous peoples. I shall argue, however, that the charge that discursive, postmodern approaches cannot accommodate a politics is limited and not necessarily the case, and that the latter claim of political grounding for materialist, revisionary readings may actually have contradictory effects. I take a classic Australian colonial narrative as my point of departure in order to examine these larger, more contemporary themes.

Background: the cannibal theme in the originary event

In 1836 Mrs Eliza Fraser left her three school-aged children to the care of the Minister of Stromness in the Orkney Islands in order to accompany her ailing husband, Captain James Fraser, on a journey from London to Van Dieman's Land (now Tasmania). His brig, the 'Stirling Castle', which had made at least two prior sailings to these distant waters, delivered goods and emigrant families to the new colony. En route home, between Sydney and Singapore, the ship was wrecked off what is now called Fraser Island (in honour of the Captain, who lost his life there). Of the twenty-two persons on board, including the Captain and Mrs Fraser, their steward and nineteen crewmen, only Mrs Fraser and seven crew would be saved. After the wreck the survivors set off in two leaky lifeboats. Subsequent accounts report that on about the third day at sea Mrs Fraser gave birth to a premature baby which drowned at birth and was committed to the deep.[2] When the Captain refused to put ashore, for fear of native cannibalism, the crew of the pinnace mutinied. After nearly six weeks in treacherous waters the crew of his own rescue boat, in desperation, resorted to threats of 'drawing lots' if he would not head for land. The Captain, filled with an instinctive dread, reportedly bit his tongue in a mad frenzy, fearing capture by the barbarous natives. According to surviving crew members, interviewed after the event, the Captain was convinced that the sailors in the pinnace (the group which had deserted the Captain's party on the longboat) had already been taken prisoner and 'in all probability eaten' (Curtis 33). His advice to the remaining crew was to prepare for escape during a 'corrobery' when the natives would be 'dancing in a circle around a favourite friend...[or] a miserable captive, whose flesh they would presently greedily devour' (Curtis 41).

The Captain's party in the longboat landed on the island, where they were taken in by members of the Ngulungbara, Badtjala and Dulingbara clans for about six weeks before seven men and Mrs Fraser were rescued by an official party and returned to the penal settlement at Moreton Bay. Soon after the rescue, Mrs Fraser gave an official account to the Commandant. Her report is brief: a mere 1500 words of which only 50 tell of her sufferings on the island. In the main, the report is a justification for her husband's poor performance in the light of the wreck and the recalcitrance of the crew. Of her time on the island she has this to say:

> During the whole of my detention amongst the natives I was treated with the greatest cruelty, being obliged to fetch wood and water for them constantly and beaten when incapable of carrying the heavy loads they put upon me; exposed during the night to the inclemency of the weather, being hardly ever allowed to enter their huts even during the heaviest rain ('Mrs Fraser's Narrative', rpr Buchanan and Dwyer 35).

This is the extent of her report of her treatment amongst the Aborigines on Fraser Island. Although the shipwreck and Mrs Fraser's subsequent experiences on the island would have been an ordeal *in extremis* for a colonial lady, there is no evidence in this first account of barbarism, savagery or cannibalism on the part of the Aborigines. Despite the Captain's fears, no natives were to be found circling friend or foe in a feeding frenzy with murderous intent. Nor were any such acts reported by the other survivors upon their return to Moreton Bay. In fact, several crewmen reported that they were treated with kindness and generosity by the Fraser Islanders. All the shipwreck victims were adopted, one by one, by small bands of Aborigines and taught survival skills, despite their arrival during a particularly harsh winter season. Our limited knowledge of Aboriginal beliefs at the time suggests that the frail white stragglers were apprehended as the ghosts of their dead ancestors. The survivors were not taken captive; rather they were incorporated into the society according to Aboriginal custom. In regard to the death of the Captain, upon her return to Moreton Bay Mrs Fraser informed the authorities that she believed it was never the natives' intention to kill him. He succumbed to spearing wounds inflicted by the Fraser Islanders in punishment for not carrying out the tasks that were assigned to him and for seeking the assistance of his wife. Already in a debilitated condition, he died in her presence about three days after the spearing and was carried away to an unknown fate. Yet, despite this historical evidence, the embellished tales of the captivity and sufferings which appeared in the wake of this event, read as 'authentic' first-hand accounts, focused on depraved human behaviour on the part of the indigenous people, including the murder of the Captain, beheading of the First Mate, burning at the stake of another crew member, sexual violation of Mrs Fraser and, of course, native cannibalism.

Accretions of the tale

Within six weeks of her arrival back in Liverpool the story attracted widespread attention in the popular press. A broadsheet appeared on the streets of London which announced 'The Wreck of the Stirling Castle: Horrid Treatment of the Crew by Savages'. The broadsheet was bound to entice the local audiences with its graphic woodcut which depicted savage blacks wielding axes, knives and other weapons of torture in a palm-fringed Polynesian bay. The illustration caught 'the savages' in the act of decapitating innocent women and children, whose heads, entrails and other body parts lay strewn along the sand or proudly upheld on the tip of a victor's bloody blade.

The ballad follows, a part of which reads:

And when they reached THE FATAL SHORE,
It's [*sic*] name is call'd Wide Bay,
The savages soon them espied,
Rush'd down and seiz'd their prey,
And bore the victims in the boat,
Into their savage den,
To describe the feeling of these poor souls
Is past the art of man.

The female still was doom'd to see,
A deed more dark and drear,
Her husband pierc'd was to the heart,
By a savage with his spear.
She flew unto his dying frame,
And the spear she did pull out,
And like a frantic maniac,
Distracted, flew about.

The chief mate too they did despatch,
By cutting off his head,
And plac'd on one of their canoes
All for a figure head.
Also, a fine young man they bound,
And burnt without dread,
With a slow fire at his feet at first
So up and to his head

('Wreck of the Stirling Castle', 1837).

These gruesome details, including the 'murder' of the Captain, would quickly find their way into popular narratives of the story, similar versions of which were published in North American, British and West Indian colonial magazines. The first to appear was published in New York and advertised as a classic American captivity narrative—replete with Indians, tepees, papooses and squaws. It was entitled 'The narrative of the capture, sufferings and the miraculous escape of Mrs Eliza Fraser, wife of Captain Samuel [*sic*] Fraser commander of the ship the Stirling Castle'. The frontispiece provides the reader with the following synopsis of the story:

A part of the crew, having been taken in the long boat, were driven to and thrown onto an unknown island inhabited by savages, by whom Captain Fraser and the first mate were barbarously murdered, and Mrs Fraser with 21 crew and a steward were for several weeks held in bondage. After having been compelled to take up her abode in the wigwam to become the adopted wife of one of the Chiefs, Mrs F. was providentially rescued from her perilous situation ('Narrative of the Capture...', 1837).

One notes a number of new elements here, common to the American captivity genre, of bondage, murder and miscegenation— or the 'marriage' of the innocent white victim to the 'chief'. Two sketches accompany the narrative. The first, a full-page engraving, shows Mrs Fraser attired in full Georgian costume, grieving over the death of her handsome, young Captain whose body is watched over by caricatures of three North American Indians, standing in stoical postures, dressed in togas, moccasins and feather head-dresses. To the right of this scene, a pair of Indians engage in a bloody duel with knives and axes raised, while another two in the distance grip the imploring arms of a crew member who is being burned alive at the stake. The second illustration, appearing just below the synopsis cited above, needs no explanation. It depicts what its title describes: 'An Indian Chief in the act of forcibly conveying Mrs Fraser to his hut or wigwam'. Obviously, there is a chilling inevitability in the relationship between the two events: the death of the Captain and 'marriage' of his wife to the Chief. These illustrations, like so many discussed by Robert Berkhofer in his study *The White Man's Indian*, portray the worst (stereotypic) traits of the 'bad' Indian of the American West—including human sacrifice, cruelty to captives, brutal warfare, indolence and lechery (Berkhofer 28-30).[3] Two further versions of this same story, differing only in regard to the replacement of the North American terminology, appear in the British journal *Tales of Travellers* and the *Alexander East India Magazine* at about the same time. Each carries its own tantalizing headline; each features graphic illustrations of the deliberate murder of the Captain.

With the advent of these narratives, we have left the realm of 'what really happened' (at least as events might have been understood through the limited colonial perspectives of the British survivors), and entered the world of pure fantasy. In separating the information gleaned from testimonies given by survivors to the Commandant at Moreton Bay from the popular ballads and tales prepared for the colonial press, I am not relying on the traditional division between truth and fiction. The early testimonies and official reports, too, are discursive representations, structured within regimes of colonial power, infused with Western ideological beliefs, and motivated by the subjective intentions of the actors. They, too, need not only to be assessed in traditional historical terms for their reliability but also to be contested through social and cultural theory and read as discursive formations. Nonetheless, within these limitations, the early accounts provide the modern reader with a touchstone, however tenuous, on which to ground a comparative critique of the transformation of the event from official testimony, to story, to pure fantasy. No doubt these melodramatic tales provided more entertainment than education for their diverse reading publics, and were read as such, at least by some. At the same time, the popular accounts in the colonial press provided new knowledges about indigenous peoples in the antipodes; they promoted new forms of bourgeois subjectivity and nationalism in early Victorian Britain; and they grounded new theories of racial superiority which underwrote the colonial regimes. All of these factors continue to influence relationships of power and the global politics of difference today. How one interprets the past is a substantial and pressing concern.

In each of these popular accounts of Eliza Fraser's 'captivity', written according to the well-established conventions of the captivity genre,[4] the

Captain's death is a key element. It signals an historical, rhetorical and visual crisis in the various textual and visual representations, particularly those directed to a British audience. A ship's captain represented colonial authority in the antipodes. In the absence of King and Country, he personified all that was 'British'. When he died this authority, both actual and symbolic, was lost. Not only was Mrs Fraser vulnerable to sexual exploitation because deprived of the protection of a husband, she also was literally nowhere, in an in-between space without law, order, civility, sense or meaning. In both symbolic and political terms the Captain's death presages the most unfathomable of situations: a loss of control, loss of order, loss of the Father's Law, an unutterable horror—beyond language. 'It was dreadful beyond words' reported one survivor. 'To describe the feelings of these poor souls / is past the art of men' ran the ballad.

Yet, this event (the Captain's death, reported as 'murder') is reiterated again and again in the variants to the tale which appear in the colonial press. With his passing there was nothing to prevent survivors from descending into the chaotic and threatening world of 'the primitive'. These sensational tales of native barbarity recreate what at least some shipwreck victims expected to encounter and what the reading public at home imagined would ensue: that is, in the absence of Law, that the inhuman practices of the savages—including cannibalism, the burning at the stake, and the sexual violation of the innocent white woman—would swamp the shipwrecked victims. This is, indeed, what the stories and illustrations (but none of the official first-hand accounts of survivors) suggest followed in the wake of the Captain's death. Examined from a modern-day critical perspective, one can conclude that the sensational stories were not about cannibalism or barbarity or the blood lust of primitive peoples but about the unrepresentable fears of the colonial readers themselves. Preoccupations with native barbarity displace other unspeakable anxieties, anxieties about the loss of identity, the loss of control, and the consumption and incorporation of the colonial body. What is at stake here is the British Empire, its safety abroad, and its construction of itself as an emerging identity in the decade of the 1830s.

Interpretations of cannibalism

The conclusion above is one which, in broad outline, would concur with the investigations of a number of commentators whose texts expand on this theme. They include Michael Taussig's *Shamanism, Colonialism and the Wild Man: A Study in Terror and Healing*, Maggie Kilgour's *From Communion to Cannibalism: An Anatomy of Metaphors of Incorporation*, Peter Hulme's *Colonial Encounters: Europe and the Native Caribbean, 1492–1797*, and Jon Stratton's *Writing Sites: A Genealogy of the Post Modern World*.[5] Each of these texts focuses on the colonial fantasy of cannibalism and its discursive and political effects in the course of its study. Each is anti-positivist and indebted to some variety of post-modern theory, broadly defined. And each is intent on investigating not 'what really happened' but rather the importance of language, text, representation and discourse to the construction of Western subjectivity and politics of Empire.

Of the critical texts mentioned above, Peter Hulme's is the earliest and has been one of the most influential in the field of postcolonial studies. Indebted to the work of Edward Said and Michel Foucault, *Colonial Encounters* traces the ways in which colonial discourses of otherness manage colonial relationships and provide the justification to occupy new territories, either for possession (as in the case of Australia) or trade. Although primarily an analysis of key texts of colonialism and not centrally concerned with cannibalism, this trope becomes the leitmotif of his chapter on *Robinson Crusoe*. The book is clearly politically engaged, especially in regard to the issue of land. Hulme claims that cannibalism is the key trope through which 'the topic of land is dissimulated by the topic of savagery, *this move being characteristic of all narratives of the colonial encounter* [emphasis in original]' (3). His study, like the others, acknowledges the earlier, groundbreaking work of Werner Arens in his controversial book *The Man Eating Myth* (1976). His words resonate with the most pressing political concerns of Aboriginal people in present day Australia. Fundamentally, for both Aboriginal and non-Aboriginal people, what was and remains at issue is land, and the acquisitive, expansive drive for possession—at whatever cost—which lies at the heart of the colonial endeavour. In the words of Gilbert Murray:

> unnatural affection, child murder, father murder, incest and the violation of the sanctity of dead bodies—when one reads such a list of charges against any tribe or nation, either in ancient or in modern times, one can hardly help concluding that somebody wanted to annex their land (quoted in Bowman 14).

We will return to the implications of this statement in the light of Hulme's investigation, and those of the other critics of cannibalism, later in the essay.

Anthropologist Michael Taussig's analysis concerns the encounters between Westerners and the Andean Indians of South America, and the terrors of cannibalism for Europeans involved in the colonization process both abroad and at home. In *Shamanism, Colonialism and the Wild Man* he draws on his extensive ethnographic knowledge to investigate the social and psychic dynamics of colonial encounters, particularly for Westerners. In regard to the fantasies of cannibalism he maintains that Europe is always complicit with its own fears, sensing behind the mask of the cannibal the face of the colonizer. Colonialism itself produces a terror in the hearts and minds of the colonizer, which becomes displaced into a terror *about* the other. Paradoxically, as Taussig suggests, colonialism produces at its heart a fear of what colonialism itself is—an overwhelming force that devours the body politic of indigenous peoples (127). It arises within structures of knowledge and operations of power endemic to the West.

Maggie Kilgour, from the perspective of a literary theorist, would concur with Taussig's ethnographically-based observations. In *From Communion to Cannibalism* she performs a philosophically-engaged discursive analysis of the literature on cannibalism. Drawing on Lacanian and French feminist psychoanalytic models, she argues that European readers sublimated their fears and desires through a displacement of cannibalistic fantasies on to indigenous peoples. For her, colonial literature represents a bid for symbolic superiority over others. Cannibal tales attempt to make 'the other' knowable in order to eliminate ambivalent fears in the self about difference and alterity, or the threat that 'one' could be invaded or absorbed by others.

Although their approaches are more complex than this brief summary allows, Taussig and Kilgour both employ Lacanian psychoanalytic paradigms to explain the popularity of cannibal stories for a European audience. They stop short, however, of claiming a universal psychic structure for both European and indigenous peoples, something that Gananath Obeysekere, whose work will be discussed shortly, does attempt. Their work situates myths of cannibalism and other tales of terror within Western discourses as they contribute to the constitution of the Western psyche, Western politics, Western fears and desires.

Jon Stratton invokes Lacanian psychoanalytic, deconstructive and post-Marxist frameworks in his study, *Writing Sites*. His analysis links the myth of cannibalism to the rise of capitalism, labelling it a particularly capitalistic fantasy, a myth of excessive consumption. Following on from Werner Arens's earlier study, Stratton traces the modern origins of the West's fascination with cannibalism back to the sixteenth century, beginning with Columbus's voyage to the Caribbean. Columbus records in his journal that 'Caniba' was a word the natives of Espanola used to describe unwitnessed accounts of the practices of their neighbours, the Carrib people, who reputedly ate the flesh of their enemies, drank their blood and castrated them. Columbus's journeys usher in the age of European capitalism; his myth of cannibalism allows 'us' to name 'the other' (whom 'we' will soon exploit) in order to formulate the limits of humanity and civilization. Subsequent travellers tales, *Robinson Crusoe* prominent among them, extend these discursive strategies through which the West recognizes difference, a process productive to capitalism.

Stratton explores another paradox central to the myth of cannibalism: that of the relation between centre and periphery. The centre, here the European sites of Western capitalism, claims that the periphery, or the locus of 'the other', lacks (in Lacanian terms) and therefore must be controlled (symbolically, psychologically and also politically); whereas, in fact, the periphery produces a surplus (through labour) which guarantees the European centre as a site of presence. Myths of cannibalism, then, become major markers in a game of Empire as it struggles to assert political dominance and cultural homogeneity over the rest of the world—and to incorporate the other into the self. For Stratton, the myth of cannibalism is a 'myth of excessive consumption sited at the edge of exploration, of capitalistic desire' (166).

Although they are highly divergent in approach, there are aspects of these critical perspectives which complement and reinforce each other. The critical texts provide a number of schematics of interpretation which enable further investigations of our theme. They address not only the colonial encounter as it is represented in the texts of Empire, but also the personal, psychological, cultural and political anxieties produced by and productive of the twin impulses of capitalism and colonialism in the West. On one level, the terror which feeds and is fed by the fantasies of cannibalism allowed colonial readers to contain their fears of personal and national bodily disintegration; on another, it allowed for the sublimation of personal and national desires for unlimited capital expansion. These studies analyze the links and slippages within the discursive realm as it constitutes the personal and the political.

There is another, perhaps more politically engaged but also more problematic, critical impulse amongst scholars who study the effects of colonialism, including the fascination with cannibalism. In general terms, this approach involves a revisionist strategy emerging out of an anti-colonialist critique. Its intention is to restore indigenous people to history as subjects in their own right within the colonial encounter.[6] We can locate Gananath Obeysekere's work on cannibalism within this field. Although he, too, like the critics referred to above, engages in an analysis of textual representations, his intention is to get beyond the self-reflexivity of Western scholarship and restore the presence of the indigene to the historical event—not as an object caught in the colonizer's gaze, but as an active subject in the encounter. He reads against the grain of history to restore some sense of reciprocal subjectivity to colonizer and colonized alike. His politicized critique never allows the reader to forget that the fantasized terror of others which Europeans generated in their colonial texts conceals the real terror of the victims. Obeysekere's study of Captain Cook's encounters with the Hawaiians reminds us that the colonial mission of domination and conquest was accomplished 'through theft, coercion, suffering, bloodshed and the deaths of others on a scale that the imagination cannot encompass' (Rose 1994, commenting on Obeysekere 1992).

In his article 'British Cannibals', Obeysekere examines cannibalism with the proposition that it is a primal fantasy within the psychic structure of both European and indigenous peoples. On the basis of his meticulous analysis of explorers' journals, seamen and travellers' diaries, settlers' tales, records of ethnographic expeditions, oral tales and sensational accounts in the popular press, he posits a universal psychic structure which, he claims, can explain the fascination with fantasies of cannibalism for both Western and non-Western, or so called 'civilized' and 'primitive' actors. One might locate this dimension of his argument within Kleinian object-relations theory. That is, as a result of early mother-child bonding, all human beings desire attachment to the mother and engage in fantasies of oral gratification to maintain the bond. At the same time, due to unconscious fears of re-incorporation into the maternal body resulting in the loss of an integrated self, they reject this attachment to the mother. These anxieties, which are only partially resolved in infancy, lead to adult fantasies and inferences of cannibalism which are shared and reinforced by both parties in the colonial encounter.

On the basis of evidence from seamen's diaries and journals written during Cook's voyages of discovery, Obeysekere suggests the Hawaiians believed that the British were cannibals. He reasons that the British arrived on the islands in an emaciated condition, they were prepared to fight the natives as enemies, and they mimed cannibalistic behaviours when they asked the natives if they, like other indigenous peoples, ate their enemies. The terrified natives, fearing and witnessing British atrocities, suspected that cannibalism was a habit of the British. When the British mimed eating of the flesh to determine whether cannibalism was a habit of the natives, the natives mimed it back. Obeysekere calls it 'one form of terror against another' (1992a, 646).

Obeysekere studies encounters in Hawaii and New Zealand rather than Australia, but his investigations have relevance for Australia as well. There are a number of parallels between the data he studies and the evidence available from the 'Stirling Castle' episode. One can detect similar preoccupations, at least in regard to British attitudes, beliefs, behaviours and imaginings—and similar outcomes in regard to the destruction of indigenous cultures. Obeysekere, like the critics mentioned above, is also curious as to why cannibalism was such a recurring trope in colonial discourse. He reports that instances of cannibalism appear in colonial narratives even in areas where the practise of anthropophagy was not known to exist. His explanation is: it was what the British public wanted to hear; it was what the voyagers most expected to find; and it was what they most feared (1992a, 635). Certainly there is evidence in the Eliza Fraser stories that Captain Fraser fell victim to these assumptions. Further, in the unequal power dynamics on board the longboat after the wreck of the 'Stirling Castle', the crew (like Obeysekere's natives) resorted to psychological terror (threatening to draw lots) to bring the Captain to order. In addition, the popularity of the tales satisfied the emergent colonial desires of the British and American reading public.

Obeysekere's analysis is motivated by overtly political, moral and ethical concerns. His careful reading of the historical documents from an anti-colonial perspective enables Western readers to move away from merely reflecting on themselves. He performs a necessary corrective in his attempt to restore a 'dimension of reflectiveness and rationality' to indigenous peoples in order for Eurocentric scholars and readers to engage ethically and morally with the non-European victims of colonialism (1992b, 95). Much as I respect Obeysekere's endeavours and support his politics, I do not think such a reconstruction is possible, at least not on his terms or, more specifically, on the humanist psychological structures which support his study of 'British Cannibals'. In the discussion which follows I want to raise a number of issues which, although they are attached to Obeysekere's critique, are not meant to diminish his considerable achievement. The problem lies not in Obeysekere's desire to render a presence to 'the other' but in the terms in which it is done. I want to investigate these terms which relate to wider philosophical dilemmas provoked by, but by no means limited to, his work.

Obeysekere's approach raises a number of critical questions: Where is the subjectivity of the indigene to be found in the texts of colonialism? And what kind of subject is being brought to life in the critique? Reconstructions of history assume that there is a 'real' beyond discourse that can be reclaimed through careful historical analysis. To make this possible, it relies on modernist notions of universal humanity. The problem is that the indigene within the text is one already captured and constituted within the colonial gaze, language and understandings. Revisionist re-readings are still additional readings of Western texts: responses from Western speaking positions, with recourse to notions of Western identity politics, even though, in Obeyesekere's case, as a Sri Lankan, he carries the legacy of former colonial subjugation. Colonized subjects cannot be retrieved from a Eurocentric past and restored to their pre-colonized existence, their pre-discursive positions. At the same time, they are constituted within modernity by the processes of colonial subjugation. This is the core of the dilemma.

Western frameworks: modernist philosophy and psychoanalysis

There is no doubt that Aboriginal people at the time of the shipwreck of the 'Stirling Castle' lived full and complex lives, and that those lives were shattered, as much by the circulation of colonial tales in the popular press like those emanating from 'Stirling Castle' episode as by subsequent white exploration and settlement in Queensland. But their existence at the time of the shipwreck was not inscribed within those modern Western philosophical, epistemological and psychological frameworks on which Obeyesekere's reading partially depends. Their realities cannot be discovered there.

As Debbie Bird Rose explains, in an essay written in defence of Obeyesekere's work, when two separate cultures come into contact, they bring with them their own concepts of humanity, their cosmologies, understandings of 'strangers' and structures of intersubjectivity, which simultaneously shape the event (46). Obeyesekere allows indigenous actors a legitimate voice, and from an anthropological perspective, he also recognizes their alterity, their difference from us. But he renders them like us in his evocation of our common primal bonds, our 'cannibal complex'. This is my worry about his work. People living within traditional Aboriginal society experienced (and still experience) the self as intimately and indivisibly connected to the land, to kinship relations and to the Dreaming. Within this existence there is no concept of personal autonomy arising out of subject-object dichotomies, no division between the self, networks of kinship relationships, connections with the land and the spirit world. Instead, there is a sense of sacred inter-connectedness, and the continuity of relationships which sustain life within the Dreamtime.[8]

Colonialism deprived Aboriginal people of their land, and that loss brought about a loss of identity, a loss of the intimate connection with the sacred, the Dreaming. In both metaphoric and materialist terms, when Aborigines lost the land, they starved—physically and spiritually. When the British took possession of the land, they gained access to more than its natural resources. Their acquisition fed their bodies, their physical and cultural existence, their colonial and capitalist enterprise. These acts of possession consumed not only the means of physical survival for Aboriginal people but their ontological existence as well. Colonialism forced the entrance of Aboriginal people into 'our' world, as 'our' others, when it politically and symbolically severed their physical and spiritual connections to the land, at least within a Western political and ontological economy.

In his careful analysis Obeyesekere searches for evidence to enable multiple perspectives, and multiple subjects, to be countenanced when reflecting on historical events. But when he grounds his reading on universal psychic structures he adopts, for European and indigenous people alike, a modernist perspective on existence, one which is the product of Enlightenment philosophies. Foucault and a multitude of cultural critics who follow in his wake offer a cogent critique of the Enlightenment project (Foucault 313-20). That critique understands that modern man is an invention of modern thought. The Kantian revolution of the eighteenth century brought about our present (vulnerable, contested and rapidly passing) understanding of Man within modern philosophy. Kantian metaphysics pre-supposes a knowing and transcendent subject as the origin of thought and meaning. That subject recognizes itself as both the subject and object of knowledge, with knowledge being exterior to the self. Within Kantian and post-Kantian philosophy, we come to know ourselves through subject-object relations. This dichotomous nature of being makes no allowance for relations of the subject to the divine, or in Aboriginal terms, the Dreamtime. As George Vassilacopoulos explains:

> We can broadly differentiate modernity from the pre-modern by noting that the former has been shaped by dichotomies, the most significant of which is that between the subject and the object, whereas the latter embodies the primordial unity of the human, the natural, and the divine. The historical emergence of modernity gave rise to a new social paradigm in which pre-modern unity was to be destroyed or marginalised. This destruction was achieved by eliminating one of the members of the tripartite unity of human-divine-natural, the divine. For pre-modern awareness the divine played the role of an all-encompassing integrating force.[9]

In this sense, Aboriginal subjectivity prior to the arrival of the British in Australia can be understood as 'pre-modern'. Indeed, present-day Aboriginal people, although constituted within the discourses of modernity, maintain affinities with the Dreaming which cannot be encompassed within modernist frames of reference.

Modern subjectivity is bound up in and constituted by subject-object, self-other relations. Within a modern consciousness, the 'other' is both a threat to identity and necessary to define the terms and limits of that identity. Within the politics of colonization, the colonized subject becomes the 'other' who is needed to legitimize national identities and structures of power and domination. That 'other', as the object of knowledge within a colonial framework, cannot be confused or conflated with actual Aboriginal people involved in the recorded historical events of the time. When that 'other' is granted subject status in a revisionist history, that subject cannot be incorporated into a universal humanist framework, as Obeysekere proposes in his assumptions of common, human psychic bonds.

The unconscious and the uncanny

These reflections lead us into an investigation of the nature of the unconscious and its relation to what Freud called 'the uncanny'. If one accepts the unconscious as historically constituted rather than as a universal psychogenic construct, it can be understood as coming into being within the conceptual framework of subject-object, self-other dichotomies. Given that the specific investigation of this paper concerns cannibal tales that render indigenous peoples as 'other', Freud's concept of the uncanny is relevant. These tales, recurring throughout the history of colonialism from the sixteenth century to the present, can be seen to represent not only repressions of anxieties of the self which are projected on to others but also emanations of the uncanny for Western readers. The uncanny, according to Freud, arises at the boundaries where the self and the other collapse. He associates it with memories of home and of the mother's genitals at birth, memories which produce fears and anxieties about the loss of (the illusion of) autonomous identity. He defines it as 'that class of frightening which leads back to what is known of old and long familiar' (220). For Freud, the uncanny is what the unconscious represses, elsewhere associated with the primitive. But it is also the double of the canny, the familiar. Thus, he argues that 'the uncanny is in reality nothing new or alien, but something which is familiar and long established and which has become alienated from it only through the processes of repression' (225).[10]

The uncanny, the vampire, the cannibal and national identity

A number of present-day critics have begun to explore these notions of the uncanny in relation to nineteenth century Gothic literature, and, in particular, to vampire stories (eg., Gelder 1994; Donald 1992). It does not take a great leap of the imagination to recognize the close connections between vampiric and cannibalistic tales and attendant fantasies. Both Ken Gelder and James Donald relate the Gothic tradition of nightmares and horror stories of violence, uncertainty and terror to anxieties about national identity. Gelder suggests that vampire stories arise in periods when national identity is unstable and under threat. In the nineteenth century those fantasies were about the loss of control of the imperial body. If the colonial enterprise in the 1830s involved a desire to incorporate others, by the 1880s, with the rise of imperialism, attended by the popularity of vampiric fiction, the other returned to incorporate the colonizers: an uncanny return of the unfamiliar as familiar. Vampire stories challenge the borders of identity, representing the fears of a reverse colonization, a revenge against colonization when the vampire returns to colonize the colonizers (Gelder 12). And it is not only the perverse nature of the self-as-other which is contained in the spectres of these tales, but the loss of the sacred as well.

As Foucault maintains, the modernist self demands the separation of reason from unreason. Man in modern culture associates unreason with madness, sexuality, death, the diabolical, the primitive, the instinctual, but also the sublime, the Maternal body, jouissance, and the sacred (Donald 112). In the early nineteenth century these associations worked to produce a number of classes of 'otherness'—both at home, in Britain, and overseas, in the far reaches of Empire. Indigenous people, convicts, the poor, the mad, the passionate all fell into various categories of unreason. They became the others against whom the middle class formed itself as the marker of culture. To protect reason from unreason, colonial culture invented bureaucracy, laws, social practices and procedures and extensive disciplinary regimes to keep 'the other', and the anxieties which these multiple spectres of otherness produced for the man of reason, at bay.

In terms of colonialism, the fantasies of cannibalism are linked to unreason, and located in the fantasized bodies of Aboriginal people. They are seen to threaten the body politic both from within and without. They are uncanny—both familiar and unfamiliar at once. To the reader, these fantasies seem to be both radically different and also terrifyingly familiar. They play on the boundaries of the me and the not-me, the real and unreal, reason and unreason. The other is alien, different, strange—but also like the self. The fantasies are familiar because they are close to what 'I' am; that is, what has been occluded by subject-object, self-other relations in the formation of modern subjectivity. In other words, fantasies about the other which circulate in popular culture, like the fantasies of cannibalism prevalent in colonial tales of shipwreck, are *modern* fantasies arising out of *modern* anxieties about the instability of the self. They are not about 'the other' except as that other is interior to the self. Furthermore, the fantasies are always ambivalent, producing not only horror, but also fascination; not only fear, but also desire. As James Donald explains, 'the dialectic of repulsion and fascination in the monstrous reveals how the apparent certainties of representation are always undermined by the insistent operations of desire and terror' (119).

Mladen Dolar, whom Gelder discusses in his *Reading the Vampire*, suggests that 'the uncanny is at the core of psychoanalysis' (Dolar 7; see also Gelder 51-3). Dolar pushes the argument further, making pertinent observations relevant to our colonial critique. Dolar's assertion about the uncanny is linked to our earlier discussion about the destruction of the sacred as an integrating force of modern life and the role of the divine, or the sacred, within Aboriginal ontology. Dolar maintains that the unconscious arises out of the particular and specific rupture brought about by the Enlightenment which desanctified the pre-modern and then equated it with the uncanny, or the sacred untouchable place. Modernism excludes the sacred, rendering it '*unplaceable*' (Gelder 52). But this does not preclude the possibility of its return to haunt modern society.

Cannibal tales recur with uncanny frequency to remind us not only of our exclusion of the demoniac but also of the sacred from modern life. These critical discussions bring us back to the heart of the matter, that which I have represented here in terms of two different approaches to the myth of cannibalism: one emerging from politically motivated, positivist and materialist strategies, the other employing more discursive, but nonetheless politicized, strategies of analysis (although I realise that 'politicized' does not have the same resonance as 'the political' in the modernist sense). Post-modern perspectives provide new modes of understanding the cultural complexities of difference in a not yet postcolonial era but they cannot prescribe a cure or propose a program of action to correct the ills of the present. A question remains: can the post-modern be political, and on what terms?

Conclusion

I began this essay in an attempt to investigate the colonial fascination with cannibalism. This led to an investigation of two divergent critical models, one broadly post-modern and discursive, the other more traditionally positivist and more overtly politically engaged. One approach focused on the Western psyche, Western discourse and its imaginings. The other attempted to recover the place of the indigene and restore his or her voice to history. Both strove to come to terms with the colonial fascination with tales of cannibalism. I suggested that the methods and assumptions of the former cannot be divorced from a politics of the present and that those of the latter might, in fact, run counter to their intended political motivations. These concerns led to considerations about the nature of modernity and its relevance to a revisionist history. I argued that there is no authentic indigenous presence to be found in the texts of history; but this is not to say that we cannot recognize the early colonial events as ones in which two separate and distinct cultures came in contact. This is because texts which represent indigenous people already inscribe them within Western philosophical frameworks which preclude a recognition of pre-modern, pre-contact and pre-discursive indigenous experience. Those frameworks, broadly associated with the Enlightenment project, include the formation of the subject within Kantian metaphysics and the Freudian unconscious, understood as an historical psychic structure. Together they posit a modern subject brought about by the processes which constitute identity through the split between subject and object, self and other, sameness and difference.

Fantasies of cannibalism are modern fantasies. They are about modern, white, Western humanity—not about non-Western peoples, although their circulation in popular literature brings non-Western lives into a Western discursivity. Specifically associated with the rise of capitalism and colonialism, these fantasies manifest Western fears of loss of control and anxieties about incorporation and devourment of the colonial body. Tied to colonialism, they mask the nature of the colonial project which, in fact, incorporated Aboriginal life into a European body politic, nearly to the point of its extinction. These fantasies can be linked to the rise of the middle class, to bourgeois consciousness, and to hierarchies of power including those constituted through racial, gendered and class differences. They gain popularity when the social fabric is threatened, when its desire for a unified self-identity and for a stable social order is frustrated—as it ultimately must be since the desire for sameness, identity and closure always co-exists with difference, heterogeneity and fragmentation. The boundaries between self-and-other are never secure. The body politic is never one. Not only will uncanny spectres of that which has been repressed or excluded return to haunt the subject and the nation as it struggles for control, but many forms of subjectivities, not all of them fully encompassed by modernist understandings, will constantly destabilize the prevailing social order. Aboriginal cultures destabilize the social order brought about by colonialism.

From a European frame of reference, Aborigines are both inside the body politic, and therefore subject to its control; and also outside, beyond the boundaries of 'mankind'. In times of social disorder within the Western nation-state, when identity is threatened, they become an alterior presence represented by the ultimate fear, ultimate threat of otherness, that trope of cannibalism. They represent to the Western imagination an excess of meaning outside of language and beyond representation, a surplus in an otherwise seemingly coherent system of identity. These discourses, intimately linked to other social institutions and practices, constitute social life. They both limit and also make possible social change.

Although my particular research began with the consideration of a captivity story from the 1830s, my investigations into the nature of modernism and the place of colonized subjects within it continue to have relevance today. Even tales of cannibalism have not been exhausted. Cannibal stories are still alive in Queensland and are capable of being employed, successfully, as a winning political strategy. As in the nineteenth century, these present-day horror stories about otherness arise within conservative discourses of a threatened Eurocentric culture to quell anxieties and fears about loss of control, about fragmentation of the social order. They express an insecure people's desire for a unified self-identity. Pauline Hanson's political victory in 1995, and the subsequent election of a national Liberal government in Australia, came at a time when social diversity (and the pressing claims of migrants, women, students, the unemployed and Aborigines—particularly Aborigines) threatened dominant Eurocentric notions of national unity.

The resounding Liberal victory in Australia came about after 13 years of a Labour government. That government was committed to honouring cultural diversity, supporting Aboriginal self-management and restoring land rights to Aboriginal people. Within six months of taking office, the new government, elected by a massive majority, had turned its back on these commitments, instituting new policies and regulations to bring Aboriginal people under strict state control. Promises of racial reconciliation have been dashed. For the moment, at least, national and personal fears about national and personal difference have swamped the Australian political system, resulting in a return to former conservative and paternalistic policies and mechanisms of control. Once again a nation founded on the legacies of colonialism is attempting to subdue the terrors of otherness by consuming the (still) colonized 'other'—contemporary Aboriginal people and their cultures. It mistakes its own fears for the face of the other.

If we ignore or reject post-modern perspectives, how can this turn-about be understood? And if we do employ them, how can the resultant understandings fail but be political? The state and national Australian elections in 1995/6 'make sense' within the terms of this critique. All that seemed to have been gained under the former Labour government appears to have been lost. The anxious desire of Eurocentric Australians for identity and closure has momentarily won the day. Old structures of power, modes of knowledge and policies of domination have been reasserted. The dilemma for those who would wish it otherwise is that there is not one clear political direction which might rectify the situation. Post-modern critique offers no sure program for social change, although it is a part of the processes through which such change can come about. It understands that the impasse both is contained by and exceeds 'the political', and offers a corrective to the humanist project which would mistake 'the other' for the self.

The present impasse is not the end of the story. Towards the end of Michael Taussig's book he returns to Kant. He points out that the fundamental breakdown of knowledge systems was anticipated by Kant in *The Critique of Pure Reason* (Taussig 462). Our knowledge cuts us off from other ways of knowing. That knowledge is always undermined by ambiguity and contradiction. It produces a sickness in the culture of control. That sickness is the space of death—but it is also the space of healing. Evidence of death and healing are (always) already evident within the political and social fabric of the Australian nation. The necessity of maintaining Australia's economic ties with its Asian neighbours is a force which promises to moderate the political fervour of the likes of Pauline Hanson and the psychic fears of difference within the nation which have been tapped by her racist rhetoric. Those economic considerations, supported by the cultural diversity of Australia's post-war culture, may present a new platform for Aboriginal and Torres Strait Island peoples in Australia, one on which they can press their claims for land rights and reconciliation. Political, economic and psychic contradictions and ambiguities confound traditional Western systems of knowledge; they also rent the social fabric, allowing for new, postmodern (and possibly healing) forms of heterogeneous nationalism to arise and take shape in neo-colonial nations grappling with the economic, social and psychic contradictions inherent in the Australian nation, and possibly others within the emergent postcolonial world.

Notes

1. See Obeysekere 1992. The desire to restore the 'other' to history as a subject is also one taken up by Malek Alloula (1986).
2. In my book, *In the Wake of First Contact*, I question the reliability of this detail of what empirical historians take to be an actual occurrence. See Chapter 2, 'Eliza Fraser's Story: Texts and Contexts', 29-65.
3. Berkhofer's study remains a useful text although it is limited by its thematic delineation of stereotypical traits. See also Terrie Goldie (1989), who traces from

a more current, postcolonial perspective the major rhetorical tropes which mark the indigine in colonial literature. Of his five categories: sex, violence, orality, mysticism and prehistoric atemporality, only the mysticism is missing here.

4. The best study of the genre remains Richard Slotkin's (1973).
5. For a more detailed examination of these issues see Schaffer 1996 Chapter 5, 'Cannibals: Western Imaginings of the Aboriginal Other', 106-26.
6. See, for example, Malek Allouha (1986), and the discussion of this work by Rey Chow (1993).
7. Similar dilemmas are explored in the exchange between Myra Jehlen and Peter Hulme in response to her article 'History before the Fact: or, Captain John Smith's Unfinished Symphony' (1992). See Peter Hulme, 'Making No Bones: A Response to Myra Jehlen', *Critical Inquiry* 20 (August 1993), 179-86 and Myra Jehlen, 'Response to Peter Hulme', Critical Inquiry 20 (August 1993), 187-91.
8. For discussions of Aboriginal identity, culture and religion see Attwood and Arnold (1993), Stanner (1979) and Swain (1993).
9. George Vassilacopoulos, 'The Historical Nature of the Unconscious', unpublished manuscript prepared as a draft chapter for a study of Hegel's philosophy.
10. I am grateful to Ian McLean for directing me to this passage which he discusses in a different light in his forthcoming work on colonial art in Australia.

Works Cited

Alloula, Malek. (1986) *The Colonial Harem*, trans. M. and W. Godzich. Minneapolis: U of Minnesota Press.

Anderson, Benedict. (1991) I*magined Communities: Reflections on the Origin and Spread of Nationalism.* London: Verso.

Arens, W. (1979) *The Man-Eating Myth: Anthropology and Anthropophagy.* Oxford: Oxford UP.

Attwood, B. and J. Arnold, eds. (1993) *Power, Knowledge and Aborigines.* Melbourne: LaTrobe UP.

Berkhofer, Robert F., Jr. (1978) The White Man's Indian. New York: Knopf.

Bowman, David. (1991) 'Yes, and Lasseter's Reef Lives On', *Australian Society* (September): 14-15.

Buchanan, Neil and Barry Dwyer. (1986) *The Rescue of Eliza Fraser.* Noosa, Queensland: Noosa Graphica.

Chow, Rey. (1993) *Writing Diaspora: Tactics of Intervention in Contemporary Cultural Studies.* Bloomington: Indiana UP.

Curtis, John. (1838) *The Shipwreck of the Stirling Castle.* London: George Virtue.

Dolar, Mladen. (1991) 'I Shall be with you on your Wedding Night: Lacan and the Uncanny', *October* 58 (1991): 5-23.

Donald, James. (1992) *Sentimental Education: Schooling, Popular Culture and the Regulation of Liberty.* London: Verso.

Foucault, Michel. (1973) *The Order of Things: An Archeology of the Human Sciences.* New York: Vintage/Random House.

Freud, Sigmund. (1955) 'The Uncanny', *The Standard Edition of the Complete Psychological Works of Sigmund Freud*, Vol. XVII, trans. James Strachey. London: Hogarth Press.

Gelder, Ken. (1994) *Reading the Vampire.* London: Routledge.

Goldie, Terrie. (1989) *Fear and Temptation: The Image of the Indigene in Canadian, Australian and New Zealand Literatures.* Kingston, Ontario: McGill UP.

Hulme, Peter. (1986) *Colonial Encounters.* London: Methuen.

Jehlen, Myra. (1992) 'History Before the Fact: or, Captain John Smith's Unfinished Symphony', *Critical Inquiry* 19 (Summer 1992): 667-92.

Kilgour, Maggie. (1993) *From Communion to Cannibalism: An Anatomy of Metaphors of Incorporation.* Princeton: Princeton UP.

'Narrative of the Capture, Sufferings, and Miraculous Escape of Mrs. Eliza Fraser'. (1837) New York: Chas. Webb & Sons.

Obeyesekere, Gananath. (1992a) 'British Cannibals: Contemplation of an Event in the Death and Resurrection of James Cook, Explorer', *Critical Inquiry* 18 (Summer 1992): 630-54.

Obeyesekere, Gananath. (1992b) *The Apotheosis of Captain Cook: European Mythmaking in the Pacific.* Princeton: Princeton UP.

Pratt, Mary Louise. (1992) *Imperial Eyes: Travel Writing and Transculturation.* London and New York: Routledge.

Rose, Debbie Bird. (1994) 'Worshipping Captain Cook', *Social Analysis* (Winter, 1994): 43-9.

Sanday, Peggy. (1986) *Divine Hunger: Cannibalism as a Cultural System.* Cambridge: Cambridge UP.

Schaffer, Kay. (1996) *In the Wake of First Contact: The Eliza Fraser Stories.* Melbourne, Cambridge and New York: Cambridge UP.

Slotkin, Richard. (1973) *Regeneration through Violence: Mythology of the American Frontier 1600–1860.* Middletown, Conn.: Wesleyan UP.

Stanner, E.W.H. (1979) *White Man got no Dreaming: Essays, 1938–1973.* Canberra: Australian National UP.

Swain, Tony. (1993) *A Place for Strangers: Towards a History of Australian Aboriginal Being.* Cambridge: Cambridge UP.

Stratton, Jon. (1990) *Writing Sites: A Geneology of the Postmodern World.* Sydney: Harvester.

Taussig, Michael. (1986) *Shamanism, Colonialism and the Wild Man.* Chicago: U of Chicago Press.

Vassilacopoulos, George. 'The Historical Nature of the Unconscious', unpublished manuscript.

'Wreck of the Stirling Castle'. (1837) London: J. Catnach of Seven Dials.

GENDER, HISTORY AND IDENTITY

in Writing by Australians of Aboriginal Descent

Chris Weedon

Fiction, Poetry and the Struggle Against the Legacies of Colonialism

Desolation

You have turned our land into a desolate place,
We stumble along with a half-White mind.
Where are we?
Who are we?
Not a recognized race...
There is desert ahead and desert behind.

Uncle Worru in The Dreamers (Davis 1982, 109).

In contemporary Australia people of Aboriginal descent face struggles on many fronts: for land rights, education and the recognition and development of Aboriginal culture; against marginalization, discrimination and the day-to-day experience of racism. All these issues have their roots in two hundred years of White colonialism. Kevin Gilbert, the Aboriginal poet, writer and activist describes this history in the following terms:

> The history of the Aboriginal people of Australia since White settlement has been predominately one of *genocide* and the *decimation* of indigenous peoples and cultures. The last two hundred years have seen a range of destructive White policies and practices towards Aboriginal people: appropriation of land, indiscriminate shooting, rape, imprisonment on reservations and missions, forcible removal of children from their parents, denial of citizenship, pass laws and other infringements of basic human rights (Gilbert 1978, 238).

Two hundred years of White power and cultural imperialism in Australia have seen the forced imposition of Eurocentric and sometimes racist cultural forms, meanings and values on the indigenous peoples. Until recently the value of Aboriginal histories and cultures was denied, sacred sites were treated as just another piece of available land, traditional rites and culture were appropriated as material for the entertainment of tourists and traditional Aboriginal people were seen to inhabit a timeless primitive zone outside of history.[1] In recent decades, Aboriginal writers have attempted to contest the negative inscription of Aboriginality within mainstream Australian culture. Fiction, drama and poetry by Aboriginal people, both in English and in Aboriginal languages, have played a central role in the struggle for positive identity and self-determination.[2]

The publication of fictional texts in English by Aboriginal writers is a fairly recent phenomenon. The first complete published work by an Aborigine, David Unaipon's *Native Legends*, appeared in the 1920s. Yet it was not until the 1960s that Aboriginal writing began to be published regularly. The first volume of Aboriginal poetry, *We are Going* by Oodgeroo Noonuccal (Kath Walker), was published in 1964; the first Aboriginal novel, *Wild Cat Falling* by Mudrooroo Narogin (Colin Johnson), appeared in 1965; and the first publication of an Aboriginal play, Robert Merritt's *The Cake Man* was in 1978. (Kevin Gilbert's *The Cherry Pickers*, composed in 1968, was possibly the first written Aboriginal play, but it was not published until 1988.) In addition to written texts, a number of traditional (oral) tales and reminiscences from 'tribal' cultures have been collected, translated and published.[3] Some Aboriginal writing is published by mainstream publishers. Yet even here it often relies on subsidies and is not widely available, even in Australia.[4]

In this essay I am concerned with examples of English language Aboriginal writing from Western Australia. Most of these texts deal with the experience of urban and camp life, often coupled with historical perspectives which offer accounts of why urban and fringe-dwelling Aborigines have come to be in the position in which they now find themselves.[5] The writing is concerned both with domination: the effects of colonization, White racism and cultural imperialism on Aboriginal people and culture(s); and with resistance: with how Aboriginal people can fight at the level of culture for a new sense of value, history and identity.

As Glenn Jordan and I have argued at greater length elsewhere,[6] recurrent themes in Australian Aboriginal novels, short stories, poetry and drama include the brutality of racism; the quest for identity (which often means the recovery of history); the difficulties of growing up and living as a 'mixed-race' person in a racist society; the condition of spiritual and material poverty resulting from cultural imperialism; and the problem of links between the past and present—which is often conceived in terms of issues of knowledge and power. Aboriginal fiction explores these themes in the context of representations of the different situations of Aboriginal tribal and urban people against a backdrop of 200 years of oppression—on desolate reserves, in fringe dwellings on the outskirts of country towns, in poverty-ridden urban areas. In this essay I look in more detail at one particular theme in Aboriginal writing: the relationship between gender, history and identity.

Gender, History and Identity

The Aboriginal experience of colonization was in many ways a gendered one. Not only did traditional Aboriginal culture work with defined gender roles and relations, the colonizers, too, arrived with specific attitudes and expectations about women and men. The particular circumstances of colonization and frontier life involved not only practices of genocide but also the rape and sexual enslavement of indigenous women.

There are many references to the pre-colonial period and the coming of White settlers in Aboriginal poetry. Most often pre-colonial Australia is depicted as a place where Aboriginal people could live natural lives with pride. The coming of the colonizer and the effects of colonization on Aboriginal culture, identity and material life receive a much fuller fictional treatment in Mudrooroo's novel *Dr Wooreddy's Prescription for Enduring the Ending of the World* (1983), which depicts the earliest period of White colonization. The text offers an alternative history of White settlement which renders the *num*, the White colonizers, strange and non-human. In addition to depicting the process of genocide, the novel offers an analysis of the psychic and cultural effects of colonialism. These include a gradual shift in understanding White settlement in terms of Aboriginal belief systems to a familiarity with White meanings and ways of seeing the world.

Both women and men in the text are depicted as at the same time victims of genocide and agents of resistance. Yet the role of women is different from that of men. Women are both victims of White rape and those members of the Aboriginal communities who attempt to come to some sort of *modus vivendi* with the colonizers, introducing their men-folk to White foods, clothing and White ways. This theme of collaboration for survival finds echoes in many texts dealing with contemporary Aboriginal life, where, in their desperation to assimilate, women are often accused of denying their children access to their Aboriginal heritage.[7]

The novel tells the story of how the central female character Trugernanna—who is based on an historical figure—and her husband Wooreddy co-operate with the self-styled missionary, Robinson, in his project of contacting the Aboriginal people of Van Diemen's Land (Tasmania). Robinson promises them land away from White people where they believe that they will be able to return to their traditional ways of life.

In the face of widespread genocide, this seems an attractive prospect. Yet Robinson's real aims include denying them the right to traditional life-styles and culture, 'civilising' and 'Christianising' them. For much of the narrative, Robinson treats Trugernanna as an innocent 'child of nature', fighting against the sexual feelings that she arouses in him. He relies on her and Wooreddy for survival and then betrays them. They are rounded up with the last remnants of the Aboriginal peoples of Tasmania to die of Western diseases on a small island off the mainland coast. Their story is among other things one of trust denied.

Whereas *Dr Wooreddy's Prescription for Enduring the Ending of the World* includes depictions of limited armed resistance to White settlement, Mudrooroo's earlier novel, *Long Live Sandawara* (1979)—set in the present and in the last decades of the nineteenth century—focuses on resistance. Here women play a limited role in the narrative, as helpmates to their warrior men, and we learn little of women's experience of the brutal practices of colonization. It is predominantly in the work of Jack Davis and of women poets and writers that these issues come to the fore.

Many texts by women poets deal with the mission period when colonial policies acutely affected women in ways different from men. At the core of women's specific oppression, as in the earlier period of colonization, is White rape and sexual abuse of Aboriginal women. Yet mixed-race children, the consequence of this widespread practice, and of consensual sexual relations between White men and Aboriginal women, became a central focus of colonial attention.

From about 1905 until the early 1970s the Australian government pursued an 'assimilationist' policy which dictated that the children of Aboriginal mothers and White fathers were to be taken away from their Aboriginal mothers and the communities of their birth. Aboriginal mothers of 'mixed-race' children had no legal rights to these children; their White fathers rarely acknowledged their existence. As a result of this policy 'mixed-race' children were forcibly removed from their families and placed in White-run orphanages and missions where use of Aboriginal languages and culture was prohibited. On the missions, outside contact with Aboriginal people was severely restricted or forbidden, children were often cruelly treated and they were to be 'assimilated' whatever the cost.

BLACK ACTOR:
The police would just arrive and take the child and put him [or her] on a reserve or a mission where he [or she] could learn to live White, to assimilate. While the children played in the Settlement

compound—huge wire fences, concentration camp fence—the old
women would come up and call them over, hold their little hands
through the compound fence and tell them who they were, who their
mothers were, what their skin was, and what their totems and
dreamings were. The children were caught, belted by the authorities,
and told not to mix with those dirty blacks (Davis 1982, 42).

Jack Davis's play *Kullark*, from which this quotation comes, spans three
periods of Aboriginal history: the years of White settlement 1829-34, the
Moore River Native Settlement in the 1930s and 1945, and a country town
in the south-west of Western Australia in 1979. If scenes and documentation
from the early years of White settlement depict the process of genocide, the
scenes from the Moore River Native Settlement show the brutality of
attempts to assimilate 'mixed-race' children by removing them from their
Aboriginal families, forbidding the use of Aboriginal languages and denying
access to Aboriginal culture and traditions.

The emotional and psychological effects of this policy are a repeated
theme in poetry by women of Aboriginal descent:

A Letter To My Mother

I not see you a long time now
White fulla bin take me from you, I don't know why
Give me to Missionary to be God's child
Give me new language, give me new name
All time I cry, they say—'that shame'
I go to city down south, real cold
I forget all them stories, my Mother you told
Gone is my spirit, my dreaming, my name
Gone to these people, our country to claim
They gave me white mother, she gave me new name
All time I cry, she say—'that shame'
I not see you long time now, I not see you long time now

Eva Johnson (in Gilbert 1988, 24).

The effects of this policy form perhaps the most important motivating factor
in Sally Morgan's highly successful mixture of autobiography and life history
My Place (1987) which traces the history of three generations of the author's
'mixed-race' Aboriginal family. Using an autobiographical mode, Sally, the
eldest daughter of the third generation, relates her own quest to discover her

origins, drawing on the life histories of her mother, Gladys, her great-uncle Arthur and her grandmother Daisy, known as Nan. The text depicts the profound effects on individual lives and identities of successive racist attitudes and policies towards Aboriginal people.

Although technically a mixture of autobiography and life history, *My Place* is written very much like a novel. Its plot is the search for a suppressed family history, Aboriginal heritage and identity. The text focuses on history as it affects the everyday lives of the characters, their sense of self-worth and emotional life. The four narrators create between them a plural history which offers different gendered perspectives on past events.

The fear of having their children taken away and raised in state institutions is depicted as the key structuring force in both Gladys's and Daisy's lives. The felt need to hide all signs of their Aboriginal origins makes Gladys tell her children that they are ethnically Indian, and it causes Daisy to hide her Aboriginal features from her grandchildren's school friends. Indeed, in racist Australia, to be Australian is to be White and to be Aboriginal is to be less than human:

> The kids at school had also begun asking us what country we came from. This puzzled me because uptil then, I'd thought that we were the same as them. If we insisted that we came from Australia, they'd reply, 'Yeah, but what about your parents, bet they didn't come from Australia' (Morgan 38).

My Place offers numerous examples from the three life histories of how the history of White racism affected and continues to affect identity. For example, Sally's mother, Gladys, tells of how her experience at a children's home taught her to be ashamed of her ethnic origins, language and culture. Arthur, Gladys and Daisy speak of their experiences of forced labour on the stations backed up by police repression. They tell of women taken away from their communities and trained for domestic service. They recall 'mixed-race' children taken from their mothers and brought up in homes on missions where darker children were separated from lighter children and all were forbidden to speak 'native' languages. Arthur remembers seeing people in chains and hearing of Whites shooting Blacks for sport. He recalls internment during the war and denial of citizenship. Gladys tells of how Aboriginal people were under the control of the Native Welfare Department and made to carry permits in order to travel.

The widespread experience of Aboriginal women in this period—that of having their children taken away—points to another fundamental aspect of their experience of colonization, namely rape. Perhaps the most tabooed question to emerge from the different narratives which constitute *My Place* is that of incest. In this instance, the implication is that the White owner of the homestead fathers both Sally's grandmother and her mother.

When Sally discovers that she is Aboriginal, this raises profound questions of identity:

> What did it really mean to be Aboriginal? I'd never lived off the land and been a hunter and gatherer. I'd never participated in corroborees or heard stories of the Dreamtime. I'd lived all my life in suburbia and told everyone I was Indian. I hardly knew any Aboriginal people. What did it mean for someone like me? (141).

It is to answer these questions that Sally probes her family history and searches for her lost Aboriginal relatives.

The reclamation of Aboriginal history and identity, which is the central focus of My Place, is achieved through the process of story telling. Unlike the representations of a lost past found in many texts by men in which we find proud images of tribal elders and armed fighters, women's writing, much of which to date is poetry, stresses the importance of the sense of continuity, history, place—but also loss—that story telling can give. This theme emerges clearly in another poem by Eva Johnson:

Remember?

Born by river
Gently rested on a lily pad
Woman—tired eyes
Wading beside filling string bag with lily roots,
        fish, small tortoise, buds
Woman—singing
Around fire, night time sitting
With kin—sharing food
        cooked in hot ashes
Children laughing.
                Mother singing
        baby on breast
Women telling stories, sharing, giving
Songs, spirit names, teaching
IN LANGUAGE.

No more river—Big dam now
String bag empty
    Supermarket now
Women sitting in big houses
        sharing, singing, remembering
    Mother crying, baby clinging
Women telling stories,
    new stories, new names
       NEW LANGUAGE

                    Eva Johnson (in Gilbert 1988, 25-6).

It is story telling which can forge links between past and present and help Aboriginal people reclaim a history and come to terms with change and loss. While much of this poetry, like the plays of Jack Davis and the fiction of Mudrooroo and Archie Weller, often remembers a somewhat idealized pre-colonial past,[8] it looks to the values of this past for a better future. Story telling—whether in the form of fiction, drama or poetry—acts to reclaim alternative positive values and a history not only of oppression but of resistance to it. Both can offer the bases for a positive sense of history and identity which can ground resistance to cultural colonization and racism in the present.

Notes

1. For more on the primitivist construction of Aboriginal people and other people of Colour see Jordan and Weedon 1995 (chapters 9, 10 and 14).
2. For a history of Aboriginal resistance to colonization see Lippmann 1981.
3. Examples of transcribed and translated Aboriginal texts include Paddy Roe, *Gularabulu: Stories from the West Kimberley*, ed. Stephen Muecke (1985); Elsie Roughsey, *An Aboriginal Mother Tells of the Old and New* (1984); Bill Neidjie, *Story About Feeling* (1989); and Jordan Crugnale, ed., *Footprints Across Our Land: Short Stories by Senior Western Desert Women* (1995). See also Kevin Gilbert, ed., *Inside Black Australia: An Anthology of Aboriginal Poetry* (1988).
4. Australian Aboriginal writing has been published by both small presses and mainstream publishers, but in both cases usually with the help of assistance from central and state government.
5. See work by Jack Davis, Kevin Gilbert, Oodgeroo Noonuccal, Mudrooroo Narogin and Archie Weller.
6. See Jordan and Weedon 1995 (489-539).
7. For fictional instances of women's role in the denial of Aboriginal heritage, see, for example, Mudrooroo's novel *Wild Cat Falling* (1979), Archie Weller's collection of short stories *Going Home* (1986) and Sally Morgan's *My Place* (1987).

8. For examples of idealizations of a pre-colonial past see, in particular, the work of Archie Weller.

Works Cited

Crugnale, Jordan, ed. (1995) *Footprints Across Our Land: Short Stories by Senior Western Desert Women*. Broome, Western Australia: Magabala Books.

Davis, Jack. (1983) '*Kullark*' and '*The Dreamers*' [two plays]. Sydney: Currency Press.

Davis, Jack. (1970) *The First-Born and Other Poems*. Sydney: Angus & Robertson.

Davis, Jack and Bob Hodge. (1985) *Aboriginal Writing Today*. Canberra: Australian Institute of Aboriginal Studies.

Gilbert, Kevin. (1978) *Living Black*. Ringwood: Penguin Books Australia.

Gilbert, Kevin, ed. (1988) *Inside Black Australia: An Anthology of Aboriginal Poetry*. Ringwood, Victoria: Penguin.

Gilbert, Kevin. (1988a) *The Cherry Pickers*. Canberra, Australia: Burrambinga Books.

Johnson, Colin: see Mudrooroo Narogin.

Jordan, Glenn and Chris Weedon. (1995) *Cultural Politics: Class, Gender, Race and the Postmodern World*. Oxford: Blackwell.

Lippmann, Lorna. (1981) *Generations of Resistance*. Melbourne: Longman Cheshire.

Merritt, Robert. (1978) *The Cake Man*. Sydney: Currency Press.

Morgan, Sally. (1987) *My Place*. Fremantle, Western Australia: Freemantle Arts Centre Press and London: Virago.

Narogin, Mudrooroo [Colin Johnson]. (1979) *Wild Cat Falling*. 1st pub. 1965. Sydney: Angus & Robertson.

Narogin, Mudrooroo [Colin Johnson]. (1979) *Long Live Sandawara*. Melbourne: Quartet Books.

Narogin, Mudrooroo [Colin Johnson]. (1983) *Doctor Wooreddy's Prescription for Enduring the End of the World*. Melbourne: Hyland House Publications.

Neidjie, Bill. (1989) *Story About Feeling*, ed. Keith Taylor. Broome, Western Australia: Magabala Books.

Noonuccal, Oodgeroo [Kath Walker]. (1981) *My People—A Kath Walker Collection*. 1st pub 1970. Milton, Queensland: Jacaranda Press.

Roe, Paddy. (1985) *Gularabulu: Stories from the West Kimberley*, ed. Stephen Muecke. Fremantle, Western Australia: Fremantle Arts Centre Press.

Roughsey, Elsie. (1984) *An Aboriginal Mother Tells of the Old and New*. Ringwood, Victoria: Penguin.

Rutherford, Anna, ed. (1988) *Aboriginal Culture Today*. Vol. X, nos. 1 & 2 of *Kunapipi*. Sydney, Coventry and Geding Sovej: Dangaroo Press.

Walker, Kath: see Oodgeroo Noonuccal.

Weller, Archie. (1981) *The Day of the Dog*. Sydney: Allen & Unwin.

Weller, Archie. (1986) *Going Home—Stories*. Sydney, London and Boston: Allen & Unwin.

'POOR GREEN ERIN':

German Perspectives of the 'Irish Question' in the mid-19th Century

Eoin Bourke

When a certain set of images of a culture—let us call it *X*—begins to congeal into a stereotype in the consciousness industry of another culture—call it *Y*—then you will usually find that that stereotype has less to do with the observed culture *X* than with the observer culture *Y*, and that the set of images has a function internal to *Y* and subservient to its particular political and economic needs and interests at that point in time. Or, to put it in terms of imagology, the stereotyping helps to design a hetero-image of a kind that will promote the desired auto-image. A straightforward example is that in nineteenth-century Europe the Social Darwinist image of the African as an incompletely evolved human had nothing to do with African reality and everything to do with European colonialist aspirations. It was important to imperialist interests to construct an *a posteriori* case for subjugating other cultures once that process had got underway, and the argument found was that one's own race was biologically more advanced and therefore a dominator by birthright. Or, closer to home, the image projected by *Punch* in the 1840s of Paddy the Irishman as a fanged and salivating ape-like figure was meant to imply, at a time when Daniel O'Connell was stepping up his campaign for the repeal of the Union, that the Irish were genetically unfit to conduct the serious and intellectually taxing business of self-government.

The colonialist hetero-images invented for such purposes throughout Europe were strikingly similar to one another despite the actual dissimilarity of the cultures being subjugated. Moreover, the very same defects that were attributed by Europeans to Africans, Indians, native Americans, Irish and other outside cultures were applied internally to Jews. Favourite allegations, directed with unimaginative repetitiveness at various peoples, were those of fecklessness, moral depravity and treacherousness, implying therewith that the colonists were industrious, upright and loyal. Pseudo-scientific treatises sought to link very diverse peoples in racial terms to explain their common deficiencies. The physician John Beddoe purported to establish a high degree of 'nigrescence' (cf. Curtis 1973, 19ff) in the Irish, and an article in *Harper's Weekly* set out with the help of physiognomy studies to prove that the low-type Irish were racially related to the Africans through Iberian connections. The fact that the Irish 'had never been out-competed in the healthy struggle of life, and thus made way, according to the laws of nature, for superior races', was only due to their isolation from the rest of the world (Curtis 1984, 55).

One way of seeking a corrective to the virulent stereotyping of the Irish that took place in the media of mid-nineteenth-century Britain is to examine the travel writing and commentaries undertaken in a third culture which was neither an interested party in the binary colonial relationship nor involved in a colonizing project of its own. Germany was at that time such a culture. Up to the 1820s there had been extremely little attention paid to Ireland, and knowledge of the country was sparse until Hermann von Pückler-Muskau's best-selling *Briefe eines Verstorbenen* (Letters of a Deceased Man) of 1830 triggered off a veritable avalanche of commentaries. By 1844 an author named Ludwig Schipper had proclaimed that the civilized world had never debated any topic more intensely than Ireland's relationship to England.

However, one finds on reading the commentaries that even supposedly neutral German voices frequently have an agenda of their own which predisposes them towards either the colonizer or colonized. The aged Goethe of 1829, for instance, had long since cast off and indeed eschewed his own former *Sturm und Drang* rebelliousness and become firmly monarchist, and accordingly gleaned his image of Ireland purely from such organs as the London *Times*. To Johann Peter Eckermann he recounts an Irish Bull that he had read: 'An Irishman is lying in bed. Someone comes dashing in and shouts: "Run for your life! The house is on fire!", whereupon the Irishman replies. "Why should I? I only rent the place".' Goethe, who had never been to either Britain or Ireland, was much too anglophile to recognize in the cultivation of the Irish joke a colonialist strategy, namely the attempt to create the impression that the Irish were too addlebrained to take on the task of self-government.

Goethe, though areligious, was influenced strongly by his Protestant socialization in his attitude towards the prospect of Catholic Emancipation. Apart from a certain aesthetic interest in Catholic ritual he considered the Papacy to be a deformed and baroque heathenism, capable of crucifying Christ a second time were He to return. While this critique of the *institution* of the Catholic Church was not without foundation, Goethe was wrong in transferring his image of a conspiratorial clericalism to all believers and hence to most Irish people. 'In the case of the Catholics', he said in April 1829:

all precautions are useless. The Holy See has interests that we would never dream of and underhand ways and means to implement them of which we have no notion. If I were now sitting in Parliament I would not prevent Emancipation either, but I would place on record that when the first head of an eminent Protestant rolls as a result of Catholic suffrage, then one should think of me.

A remark he made some days later demonstrates his susceptibility to a further colonialist strategy—that of presenting the colonizers in the role of innocent victims of harassment at the hands of the colonized:

Just as it was unfortunate that Ireland up to now had to bear its tribulations alone, now it is unfortunate that England is being drawn into it. That is the problem. Moreover, Catholics are just not to be trusted. You can see how grave the situation of two million Protestants has been in the face of the superior strength of five million Catholics till now in Ireland, and how, for instance, poor Protestant farmers who were surrounded by Catholic neighbours have been suppressed, harassed and persecuted. The Catholics cannot agree among themselves, but they always band together when there is a Protestant to be contended with. They are like a pack of hounds that bite one another but, as soon as a stag shows itself, are immediately at one with each other and go for it in a mass.

Although these remarks are not entirely without a basis in fact in view of the agrarian attacks carried out by secret societies in the early decades of the century, the picture of an unfortunate England 'being drawn into' the Irish problem is a staggering inversion of historical truth, and the image of the lowly hounds savaging the noble stag is worthy of the most vituperative anti-Irish propaganda of *Punch* in the 1840s. Goethe's comments betray both a pro-Establishment bias and a refusal to enquire into the political and economic causes of social evils—two attitudes that were to contrast strongly with those of *Vormärz* writers some years later. For the Jewish poet Heinrich Heine, to whom Catholicism as an institution was no more acceptable than to Goethe, it was nevertheless self-evident that the British Parliament should vote for Emancipation 'on the grounds of a natural sense of justice as well as of political shrewdness'. His reaction to the news of King George IV's filibustering and the House of Lords' obstructionism in 1828 was to call for an armed intervention by the peoples of Europe in support of 'poor green Erin'. Another Jewish writer, Ludwig Börne, referring to the Penal Laws, commented on the grief with which Germans witnessed 'how a government that once had the courage to deprive four million of its subjects of their freedom on the grounds of their religion—and indeed suddenly, unprepared and at one blow—that this same government has not the courage to redress that injustice with the same speed but rather proceeds with a circumspection which would have been more praiseworthy at the time it committed the injustice in the first place'. Börne added that religious suppression was not the only cause of Irish distress but rather what he called 'the old abscess of old states', that is, the unequal distribution of property, which he said was pushed to the limit in Ireland, as well as the fact that the landlords lived in the main cities 'where they devoured the marrow of the land'.

Pro- and anti-Irish feelings did not always split so cleanly along the lines of progressive and conservative thought as it did in the case of Heine and Börne on the one hand and Goethe on the other. The conservative Prussian political scientist Friedrich von Raumer exercised some quite trenchant criticism of England, calling its rule over Ireland intolerant and barbaric, and saying that 'the King, the House of Commons and House of Lords have consecutively or simultaneously committed outrages against Ireland'. The progressive publicist Karl Gutzkow ascribed the vicissitudes of Irish history to the gullibility of 'Pad' with his Irish Bull in the face of Papish emissaries, for 'Pad', he said, had always yielded too lightheadedly to the machinations of 'the nearest priest with a foreign accent'. As in the case of Goethe, Gutzkow's anticlericalism, which was at that time entirely justified in the German context, made him suspect the long arm of Rome wherever Catholics strove for anything. To recognize that England was in severe breach of its own democratic principles as far as Ireland was concerned was a difficult step for some German progressives because they had traditionally upheld Britain as the 'stronghold of freedom' in their own struggle for democratization. To embark on a true analysis of the 'Irish Question' led inevitably to a relativization of England as a political model, whereas it enabled conservative thinkers like Raumer to proffer Prussian statism as an alternative model.

Even the Young Hegelian Friedrich Engels started out in his *Condition of the Working-Class in England* from a viewpoint very close to that of Thomas Carlyle, stating that the Irish national character only felt at home wallowing in filth, and that the Irish were too slovenly, fickle and besotted to pursue any lengthy activity to its conclusion. His liaison with Mary Burns was probably instrumental in changing his opinion radically. While in the *Condition of the Working-Class* he had stated that Irish poverty was not to be ascribed to British oppression but rather to the Irish national character, he was to write four years later of the brave and fiery Irish whose forced emigration to England would accelerate the advance of British democracy. He wrote from Ireland in 1856 that 'one can regard Ireland as the first

English colony, and as one which is ruled in the old way because of its proximity, and here one notices that the so-called freedom of English citizens is based on the suppression of the colonies'. Karl Marx had always known that, as he put it, John Bull had to make slaves elsewhere in order to be free at home. He and Engels documented how Irish land was systematically cleared by means of evictions in order to replace smallholdings of tillage by large-scale grazing to supply the English markets with wool and meat. Marx remarked that, between 1846 and 1866:

> 1,032,694 Irish people were replaced by about one million cattle, pigs and sheep. [...] In no other European country has an alien regime carried out this direct form of expropriation of the natives. The Russians confiscate only for political reasons, the Prussians buy out property in West Prussia.

Perhaps the most reliable commentators are eye-witnesses who came to Ireland without any particular agenda, because with their lack of a basis for stereotyping they were capable of a fresh appraisal of Irish conditions. When the bankrupt dandy Prince Pückler arrived in 1828 more or less by coincidence, his mind was a clean slate. He had travelled to England in the attempt to find a dowager duchess to solve his acute financial problems, and failing to do so, continued his journey on through Wales and Ireland. He was appalled by the squalor he saw. 'The dirt, poverty and ragged dress of the common man', he exclaimed, 'is beyond belief!' Of the city of Galway he said that the outlying districts were of a kind incomparable to anything yet seen. 'Pigsties are palaces in comparison and I often saw numerous groups of children (for the fertility of the Irish people is equal to their misery) as naked as on the day they were born and wallowing about in the slime of the street with the ducks'. In Athenry, which he said was more poverty-stricken than any Polish village, he was pursued across ruins and brambles by a huge crowd of half-naked beggars who tried every possible flattery on him, including the cry 'Long live the King!' 'When I threw a handful of coppers among them, soon half of them, young and old, lay in the mud grappling bloodily while the others rushed off to the shebeen to drink their gains'.

Pückler was also the astonished witness of faction-fighting in Galway and Kenmare:

> While I lunched in the tavern I once more had the opportunity to watch several such set-tos. First a mob forms, screaming and shouting, and becomes more and more dense, then in the batting of

an eyelid a hundred shillelaghs are swishing through the air and one hears the thumps, usually applied to the head, banging and cracking away until one party has gained victory. As I found myself at the source, I solicited the help of the inn-keeper to buy one of the most splendid samples of the weapon, still warm from the battle.

At the same time, Pückler, like all of the travel writers after him, pointed out the extraordinary joviality of the Irish, so seemingly misplaced in view of their wretched conditions:

The people always seem to be in good spirits and sometimes demonstrate in public such fits of gaiety that border on the lunatic. Whiskey is often to blame: I saw one half-naked youth performing the national dance on the market-place with such abandon and for so long that he became fully exhausted and collapsed unconscious like a Mohammedan Dervish to the vociferous cheers of the crowd.

One might have expected the socialite Pückler to remain on this superficial level of bemused observation, but the longer his stay in Ireland lasted, the more political became his commentary, whether in the form of pungent asides such as ascribing the newly built Military Road in the Wicklow Mountains to the fact that 'the Government has the watchfulness of a bad conscience about Ireland', or in the form of indictments of bigotry, which Pückler, unlike Goethe and Gutzkow, almost consistently directs against the Protestant upper class. Although Pückler, the owner of a large estate in Lusatia, never questioned landlordism as such, he came more and more to criticize its excesses in Ireland, haranguing Lord Powerscourt for being 'one of those absentees who by the hands of ravenous and merciless agents strip the people of their last rag and rob them of their last potatoes to enrich the courtesans of London, Paris and Italy'. He was appalled at the race hatred of some Tory members of the landed gentry, quoting one Co. Galway Orangeman 'immersed in bile' who wished for nothing more than an Irish rebellion so that the blood of five million Catholics would flow, for according to this gentleman only the wholesale extermination of that race would bring peace to the island. Pückler also stood colonialist stereotyping on its head by remarking on the general lack of education of the smaller Anglo-Irish landlords when compared to the indigenous peasantry. Of the former he said, 'the men speak of nothing but hunting and riding and are somewhat ignorant. Today, for instance, a landlord from the vicinity [of Athenry] searched long, patiently and in vain for the United States on the map of Europe'. In a footnote it is added that 'all Catholic children in Ireland are carefully instructed and can at least read, whereas the Protestants are often extremely ignorant'.

Pückler, who himself was a secular thinker, was outraged at the system of Church taxes whereby Catholic peasants were forced to pay the tithe to the alien Established Church, and he details the machinations of the Anglicans to collect tithes even where there was no Protestant parish.

> In Kilcummin there is not a single parishioner, and the service, which according to law must be performed once a year, is enacted in the ruin with the help of a Catholic clerk [...]. But not a whit less must the non-attending parishioners pay the uttermost farthing of their tithes and other dues; and no claims are so bitterly enforced as those of this Christian Church—there is no pity, at least none for Catholics. A man who cannot pay the rent of the church land he farms, or his tithes to the parson, inevitably sees his cow and his pig sold, (furniture, bed etc. he has long lost), and himself, his wife, and probably a dozen children (for nothing propagates as well as potatoes and misery) thrust out onto the road, where he is left to the mercy of that Providence who feeds the fowls of the air and cloths the lilies of the field. Quelle excellente chose qu'une religion d'état!

The ethnographer Johann Georg Kohl was also a newcomer to Ireland in 1842 and seemed to have had little idea of what to expect. He, too, was shocked by what he called the endless abnormalities otherwise unknown in Europe. He had never seen so many ruined houses and wondered why they had not been cleared away. Although widely travelled, he had never encountered such desolate living conditions. 'Paddy has enough houses in which there is no sign of a window but only a single square hole in the front which functions as a window, chimney, front-door and stable-door, for light, smoke, people and pigs all saunter in and out of this one hole'. He saw with his own eyes the truth of the claim that the Irish lived with pigs in the parlour. 'It might not sound pleasant to everyone's ears but it is a simple fact that the Irishman feeds his pig just as well as his children. Without exception it is accepted into the living-room and lives there doing what it likes, or has a little corner for itself just as the children have theirs'.

Kohl is amazed at the total indifference to dress that is evident even among the better-off farmers:

> Irish rags and tatters have something special about them. For in no other land are they so worn-out, so riven, even down to the original

threads and dissolving into dust on the body. At the elbows and other angular parts of the body the clothes disintegrate like the petals of a dying rose. The borders of the jackets hang down in tresses. The outside is indistinguishable from the inside, the top from the bottom, the sleeves from the waist. In the end the legs and arms no longer find their usual way into the garments. Every morning the costume is draped differently, and it could seem miraculous that such a heap of rags held together by threads can be arranged around the body if it were not all the same whether the trousers is used as a jacket or the jacket as trousers.

Kohl's German sense of practicality was offended by the fact that the peasants, while harvesting or cutting turf, wore a completely inappropriate dress coat with swallow-tails, with one of them usually missing and the other 'dangling sadly like a widow in free space'. Their head-dress consisted not of a watertight cap, as a German might expect, but rather of a 'comically collapsed and deformed silk top hat that had, God knows how often, dissolved to pap in the rain and had afterwards dried back into shape'.

Kohl, however, had not set out to reinforce anti-Irish stereotypes but rather, being the thorough person he was, tried to find rational explanations for what he observed. The fact that the peasants, as he put it, 'climbed their dung-heaps in French-style dancing-costumes' had to do with the dumping of surplus masses of cut-price frock coats from England. The pig, he said, was of the utmost importance as a financial fall-back in case the rent could not be found. The empty houses and ruins were to be ascribed to the cruel evictions by landlords and middlemen and the enforced emigration of the poor. The dwellings were dilapidated and the fields badly cultivated because the frequently absenteeist landlord gave no support to improving them.

> Also the duration of leasing contracts is a very important matter. Very many Irish peasants are only 'tenants at will', i.e. they have their lease only as long as it suits the landlord to leave it to them. These people cannot develop any great interest in improving their land because they can never be sure that they will not be driven from it at any moment.

Here Kohl spells out the reason why Ireland could never develop its own indigenous domestic culture of cuisine, dress and craftsmanship: because many country dwellers had no fixed abode and therefore never found the leisure and space to nurture such a culture.

Like Pückler, Kohl was struck by the value placed by the peasantry on education. Although he considered a rumour he heard that Kerry was full of shepherds and labourers who could understand Latin an example of Irish hyperbole, he did meet a ragged Kerryman who cherishingly carried a manuscript around with him which contained ancient Irish poems as well as a translation into Irish of a scientific treatise by Aristotle: 'I often found such old manuscripts in the hands of the common people of Ireland'. On visiting a hedge school in County Kerry, he wrote:

> the schoolhouse was a mud cottage covered with grass and without windows or comforts. The small schoolchildren sat wrapped in their tatters at the open low door of the cottage and held their little books in the direction of the door to catch the scanty light that penetrated the darkness. [...] The teacher, dressed in the Irish national costume described above, sat in their midst. Outside the door lay as many pieces of turf as there were children within. Each boy had brought a piece of turf as tribute and remuneration for the teacher. [...] He taught the little ones the English alphabet. The boys looked very sprightly, fresh and bright-eyed while engaged in their studies, and when one considers their poverty, their diet and their clothing, then it seems extraordinary that this is the case with all Irish children, at least those in the open countryside.

In Bantry, Kohl encountered a beggar named Mary O'Sullivan who was decked out like a madwoman and wielded a stick at passers-by to cajole them into giving alms. Kohl bravely accepted her invitation to visit her hovel. Mary's sister, niece, small son and daughter sat on the floor with the pig and ate a half-cooked potato from the pot. In the half darkness Kohl could make out the contorted and moaning figure of a 20-year-old youth with deformed fingers and 'imbecilic look' occupying the only bed. Kohl, thinking that this poor creature had it good, considering that he could not contribute to the household, asked the mother with German bluntness whether she still loved him, whereupon she stroked the crippled hand and retorted, 'why wouldn't I? Isn't he my own flesh and blood, God bless him? I'm the only one that understands his language. Every morning I give him mashed potatoes and, when I have it, some meal pap and milk'. Kohl's utilitarian thinking had received a dent. 'When one considers the conditions of such destitute people', he pondered, 'who hardly have enough to stay their own hunger and have to demand of their own children labour and earnings and usually cast out and curse the superfluous consumer, then this woman's love can be called a phenomenon'.

Not all travel writers were so willing to delve behind surface impressions or to question prejudices. In his book *Reisen in Irland* written in 1845, the North Friesian Knut Jongbohm Clement adheres to the then emerging race theory that 'healthy' races were destined to oust others perceived as weak and inferior, a theory which had begun to replace the old threadbare argument of moral superiority even before Gobineau's writings on the inequality of races and Darwin's on natural selection. No longer did one have to use the excuse of christianization in order to colonize; rather, one saw colonization as an inevitable fact of life because one's own race was biologically programmed to prosper at the expense of others. Clement found himself at the intersecting point between the two rationalizations—in other words, his ideas of racial hierarchy had a religious dimension. To his way of thinking it was no accident that in Ireland the dominating 'Germanic' race of English was Protestant, and the Celtic underdogs were Catholic. The conditions in Ulster confirmed this for Clement: 'Out of the darkness of Donegal with its old mountains one enters Tyrone and Derry and leaves more and more the wilderness and poverty and everything Irish and Papist behind one'. Ulster, he says, had become Ireland's leading province by dint of Protestant discernment and diligence, and its cities founded by Englishmen and Scots had blossomed as a model for the rest of Ireland. The three cities of Londonderry, Belfast and Newry 'grew up, rapidly and strongly, like Germanic Man under his pure and natural heaven'. Only in the North of Ireland did Clement find a literate and thinking people. Otherwise a pall of intellectual murkiness and ignorance, he claimed, lay over Ireland like the cover of darkness; crime was rampant, people and cottages were smothered in dirt, the fields in weeds; the land was full of disease, smallpox, the pockmarked and the blind. At the few points where Clement registered the signs of orderliness and diligence, as in Co. Waterford or South Co. Wexford, he presumed the influence of Danish or even Friesian blood, as Celtic blood alone would have been incapable of it.

Clement surpassed himself on the subject of pigs:

out of every house there gazes a pig with its front trotters firmly on the threshold with the father of the family often beside him, as if the piglet wanted to say: I am the man of the house here. A recent traveller described the Irish as often having dark blue eyes and black hair. When I was there that was not yet the case—on the average their eyes resembled those of a pig, and their glance was swinish. I am not joking or mocking: Paddy and Pig look at each other so often, it is no wonder that their eyes become similar.

A lover of statistics, he was horrified that everyone he asked about the population size of their town neither knew nor cared. He also found Irish cuisine beneath contempt: 'How much culinary art can be expected of a people who live mostly from ungarnished potatoes'. He was nauseated by 'the dead flies in the meals, fly's eggs, fly's legs in the milk, hairs in bread and butter, the yellow stains on sugar and the hundred thousand filthy hands and yellow unwashed faces, the rags which threatened to fall from the body at any moment and gleamed with snot and other dirt', the sauces 'flavoured with pickled flies'.

In the following comments on the people of Limerick, Clement showed how deep the roots of today's racism are: 'the crudest of all, it seems to me, were from Limerick and its environs, drovers, hucksters, peasants and Irish striplings, who were as nimble as they were brazen, just like the Hebrews and Canaanites, with whom the Irish are distantly related'. The idea of a hierarchy of races implied that the liberation of 'inferior' races from the yoke of imperialism had little point since such races would never be capable of rising to the task of free self-determination. 'If ever the Irish should succeed', Clement wrote, 'in extricating itself from the English clench, it is hardly likely that they will ever cast off their old Paddy habits and develop a completely new kind of person, for the Celt, the Slav and the Jew are unchangeable in their ancient ways'.

In the case of Clement and Jakob Venedey, their contrasting perspectives split down religious lines. Venedey, an exiled liberal from the Catholic Rhineland, was a great admirer of the Irish, not least because Daniel O'Connell supported Rhenish independence from Prussia. This was undoubtedly the reason why Venedey was followed by British agents the length and breadth of Ireland. Not that he was entirely uncritical: he, too, was astounded by the dirt of the slum-dwellers of Dublin—'the children look as if they have never been washed, and the old people as if water costs money'—as well as their indolence, which he compared to Italian *far niente*: 'one only has to observe the idle in the street corners or on the thresholds to see how they relish doing nothing'. To illustrate this national pastime he tells the Irish joke: '"Pat, what are you doing?" a master asks his worker. "Nothing, Your Honour!" he answers. "And you, Jack?" he asks another. "I'm helping Pat!" is the reply'. But like Kohl, Venedey goes beyond stereotyping to seek explanations for seemingly abnormal behaviour. He, too, ascribes the lethargy he observes not to inbred or racially determined sloth but rather to the exploitative labour and tenancy conditions. In Manchester, Liverpool and Birmingham, he says, the Irish could work the English into the ground:

The Irishman is a clever man and will not work like an animal where he cannot reap. He is a most diligent day labourer when the day's work yields him a day's wages, be it ever so little. But the moment he senses that he is working for someone else whom he hates, and that with good reason, then he sits down and looks on.

Pückler's book on Ireland, written 15 years previously, had led Venedey to expect the witnessing of much street-fighting, but the historic phase of faction-fighting was largely a thing of the past when he arrived. In his six weeks in Ireland he only experienced one brawl. This made him aware, in contrast to Clement, that a so-called 'national character' is not a thing hewn in stone. He ascribed the change, probably accurately, to the salutary effect of Fr. Matthew's Temperance Movement. 'Whiskey was to the Irish what "firewater" had been to the American Indians. But the newly awakened sense of national identity among the peasantry made them conscious that it was one of the sources of their slavery'. They were on their way towards invalidating the clichéd image of the Irishman who was constantly drunk and therefore incapable of self-government. Venedey observed a certain unsettling of those who benefited from such stereotyping. He quotes from the speech of an anti-Repeal Protestant politician in Dublin who obviously felt more at ease with the image of the brawling, chaotic Catholic nature:

'Remember that there are times when the Devil finds it expedient to wear a white cloak. Has Ireland's time come? A temperance movement is no doubt a very plausible undertaking. And yet it is clear that it has instilled a military regularity into the masses and has lent their behaviour a measure of self-control and order that has turned them into dangerous opponents of English rule. Who, then, can truthfully state that the Temperance Movement is the good thing it is made out to be?'

As far as religious differences go, Venedey never lost sight of his liberal principles. One would wish that what he had to say about denominational schools would be taken to heart today by those Church leaders in present-day Northern Ireland who still insist on segregation: 'Tolerance in schools will destroy the intolerance outside them. It is impossible for blind hatred to prevail among people who have gone to school together, sat beside one another and grown up together in work and play'. At the same time he was aware that the social confrontations were not only of a religious nature. When he told a Catholic farmer somewhat patronizingly that in Germany

130

there were Catholics and Protestants who lived in harmony with one another, the farmer asked whether the Protestants were Anglo-Saxons and the Catholics Irish. The Germans were as incapable as the English, Venedey concluded, of understanding what went on in Ireland, because in neither Germany nor England were the two religious groups simultaneously two different ethnic groups. He noticed in the North of Ireland a kind of caste system: 'the Catholics are the miserable leftover of the indigenous population once driven from their land and trade, the Protestants the descendants of the English and Scots brought here to anglicize the country'. Among the Protestants of the North of Ireland he, like Clement, detected a distinct popular culture, but came to different conclusions. 'The English character is predominant—the people look more earnest, tidier and unhappier'. He described his inn-keepers in Belfast as having faces 'as surly, severe and grave as a bad conscience. It was not possible to get them talking, while in the rest of Ireland one only had to knock on the door for it to be opened and to breach the surface ever so slightly to tap an eternal spring'.

In Belfast, 'England's watchtower over Ireland', he felt ill at ease. The Orange marches seemed to him to be particularly provocative:

> If the English had set out to invent an institution to keep alive forever the Irish people's memory of the wrong that England had done against them and to perpetuate the idea that the one group were the vanquished, the other the victors, the one the slaves, the other the masters, they could not have invented anything better than those Orange Lodges.

He saw them as part of the British tactic of 'divide and rule' to counteract the earlier co-operation between progressive Presbyterians and Catholics— the United Irishmen of 1798—and their common aim of an independent Ireland. The second strategy was still cruder: the dissolution of the Irish Parliament by the Act of Union, against which Daniel O'Connell was now campaigning. In the North of Ireland, he said, the revolutionary ideas of the enlightened Presbyterians had been replaced by the politics of stagnation based on prejudice, 'whereby on the one hand the immediate interests of the majority call for doing nothing, for political negativity, while on the other the passions of a minority pour oil on the fire. [...] Ireland's future, however', wrote Venedey with prophetic insight, 'rests on the reconciliation of the Old and New Irish, and if this does not come about by one means or another, Ireland—the *whole* of Ireland, North and South—will enter upon an epoch of destruction and barbarity'.

Probably the most damning eye-witness account of Britain's role in Ireland came from another Jewish commentator who visited Ireland in 1850: the radical democrat Moritz Hartmann, who himself had felt the brunt of Prussian hegemony by being exiled for his part in the 1849 resurgence in Baden. 'One of the saddest monuments in Dublin', he wrote, 'is the former House of Commons, where once at least a shadow of liberty resided and now England rules with its money. For the House of Commons has been transformed into a bank'. Among the poor of Dublin, Hartmann was witness to conditions which far outstripped even that of the Jewish ghettos of Germany. The contrast between the splendid edifices of the English ruling class and the slums lying between them was crass: on one spot the Royal Hospital Kilmainham where English soldiers lived out their comfortable old age, and right beside it shanty towns of single-roomed mud cabins without windows, settlements that one would not have considered possible near a large city, inhabited by emaciated, brutish figures no longer capable of happiness: 'born rachitic, they grow up starving and die from consumption'. Hartmann ascribes these conditions not to the idleness of the Irish but rather the alienating effect of the English *laissez-faire* economic system:

> The Irishman is no *lazzarone* by nature; he works willingly to earn his daily bread. But he likes to do it while enjoying life and revolts against the brutalizing stress and strain that the Englishman demands. [...] Because of the way England and the modern world has arranged production, millions have to vegetate and perish at the plough, the machines and in the mines so that some few can live in wealthy leisure. Nature, wherein lies truth and to which the Irishman is very close, rebels in him against this exploitation and stultification.

The suffering that England had inflicted for centuries, according to Hartmann, had become incurable and could no longer be cut out like a tumour; instead it would go on corroding and destroying, perhaps even England itself. But meanwhile the English were still conquerors in Ireland. 'Everywhere one perceives in Dublin a conquered city: soldiers, a rarity in London, are here innumerable; at every turn one encounters redcoated hordes. Everywhere there are barracks of enormous size, and the castle in the centre of the city is a veritable fortress'. Hartmann analyzes the semiotics of suppression in describing even the architecture, monuments and street-names as instruments of the imperialist strategy of denying the indigenous culture:

Even the streets and the houses show how an English character has been forced upon the conquered city to persuade it that the history of England and the glory of England is also its history and glory. Most of the streets, with the exception of the oldest, bear famous English names. Moore Street is the only one that has an Irish name of more recent times. Otherwise one reads Grafton Street, Cumberland Street etc., the latter being named after the high-born gentleman who led the bloody orangemen in hunting down Irishmen. [...] In the magnificent Sackville Street stands Nelson upon his column, and from the Phoenix Park a pyramid with the names of Wellington's battlefields dominates the city. Ireland would have preferred to see both heroes conquered rather than victorious. But what's the use? England treats Ireland the way a bad parent brings up a child: it is *forced* to swallow the food it doesn't like.

Hartmann predicted that such war memorials would be blown up as soon as the revolution broke out, and that the time would come when the so-called glory of expansionist empire-building would be looked upon with contempt, adding that truly noble peoples were never conquerors. The first prophecy came true, if somewhat delayed, with the blowing up of Nelson's Pillar in 1966, the second with the world-wide protests against the Columbus celebrations of 1992. The thought that the British Empire was not so glorious after all has meanwhile reached unexpected quarters. While Lady Thatcher remains blissfully untouched by it, Sir Patrick Mayhew, the then Northern Irish Secretary, has been heard to say in recent times that England's historic relationship with Ireland has not always been 'edifying'.

Works Cited (mainly in translation)

Curtis, L. Perry. (1973) *Apes and Angels: The Irishman in Victorian Caricature.* Newton Abbot: David & Charles.

Curtis, Liz. (1984) *Nothing but the Same Old Story—the Roots of Anti-Irish Racism.* London.

Börne, Ludwig. (1826) 'Irländische Erzählungen', in *Sämtliche Schriften*, ed. Inge and Peter Rippmann. 2 vols. Düsseldorf, 1964, 2: 468-70.

Clement, Knut Jongbohm. (1845) *Reisen in Irland oder Irland in historischer, statistischer und socialer Beziehung.* Kiel.

Eckermann, Johann Peter. (1986) *Gespräche mit Goethe in den letzten Jahren seines Lebens*, in Johann Wolfgang Goethe, *Sämtliche Werke nach Epochen seines Schaffens.* vol. XIX. Munich.

Gutzkow, Karl. (1835) 'O'Connell', in *Oeffentliche Charaktere.* Frankfurt/Main, 1973: 165-88.

Hartmann, Moritz. (1850) 'Briefe aus Dublin', in *Streifzüge und Wanderungen—Reisebilder von Gerstäcker bis Fontane*, ed. Gotthard Erler. Rostock, 1978: 61-115.

Heine, Heinrich. (1828) *Englische Fragmente*, Ch. IX: 'Die Emanzipation', in *Werke und Briefe in zehn Bänden*, ed. Hans Kaufmann. Berlin, 1961, 3: 469-76.

Kohl, Johann Georg. (1843) *Reisen in Irland.* 2 vols. Dresden/Leipzig.

Marx, Karl & Friedrich Engels. (1975) *Irland—Insel im Aufruhr*, ed. Richard Sperl. [Engels's and Marx's collected comments on Ireland are to be found in English translation in their *Ireland and the Irish Question*, ed. R. Dixon (Moscow, 1971).]

Pückler-Muskau, Hermann von. (1830) *Briefe eines Verstorbenen. Ein fragmentarisches Tagebuch aus England, Wales, Irland und Frankreich, geschrieben in den Jahren 1828 und 1829.* Munich.

Raumer, Friedrich von. (1836) *England im Jahre 1835.* Leipzig.

Schipper, Ludwig. (1844) *Irlands Verhältnis zu England geschichtlich entwickelt, und O'Connells Leben und Wirken.* Soest.

Venedey, Jakob. (1844) *Irland.* 2 vols. Leipzig.

GENDER, GENIUS AND IRELAND

at the Turn of the Century

Penny Boumelha

It is by now virtually a commonplace to observe that much of the late nineteenth-century justification for English colonialism rested upon devices which served to render justification apparently irrelevant: that is to say, when political history could be represented as the fulfilment of a scientific law, the manifestation of an inherent biologically-founded nature, it was transferred outside the arena of the apologia. In the case of Ireland, this inevitability of colonialism was underpinned by a set of powerful (though, of course, not uncontested) racial theories which, at their crudest, locked into perpetual opposition two fundamentally different racial strains, variously conceived as Celt and Saxon, Celt and Teuton, Alpine and Teuton, and so on. The precise number, nomenclature, and defining characteristics of these racial groups and their sub-groups may have remained matters of dispute, but their existence and their determining power over the course of human history was very widely accepted, both by the colonial power and in at least some forms of oppositional Celticist or nationalist discourse.[1] But the credibility of such explanatory fables in turn rested in part upon the possibility of identifying, documenting, and quantifying the somatic variations between such supposed racial groups, and the desire to make the intrinsic difference of the Celt visible and measurable is as urgent an ideological task, in this period, as the finding of somatic determinations upon perceived gender differences in intellect, temperament, and ability. In both cases, the evidence was constructed from the sciences of physiognomy, craniometry, comparative anthropology, quantitative ethnology, and (a term that I find particularly appealing) 'transcendental anatomy', or the argument that psyches differ in close correspondence with variations in physical organisation.[2]

To say that there is at work here an *analogy* between discourses of gender and race risks falling short; others have analyzed the mutual reinforcement of colonial rule and male dominance which, in Joseph Valente's words:

[i]n figuring the conquerors as the exponents of a principle coded and celebrated as masculine (encompassing an aggressive will to historical progress, technical mastery and rational transcendence...) and the conquered as the embodiment of a principle stereotyped and discounted as female (encompassing a passive repose in organic

135

cyclicality, affective immanence and domestic concerns…), …has inscribed a vicious symbolic circle in which sexual and socio-economic dominance reflect and authorize one another (189).[3]

The racializing of gender and the gendering of race investigated by Nancy Stepan yielded a method of argument and a conception of evidence that served to bestow significance upon sets of comparable physical data—cranial capacities, for instance, or jaw angles—whose meaningfulness would otherwise be seriously open to doubt (Stepan 1990, 40-2).[4] What is at stake, then, is not a simple paralleling of gender and race, but rather a sense that each version of difference grounded explanation of the other. The analogy served to produce particular forms of femininity and of the primitive that pointed up the necessary constitution of the English male as guardian, governor and guarantor.

Having sketched in very briefly this interpretative context, I want now to narrow my focus and look at the functioning of the gender/race analogy in a specific area of debate: the particular inflection taken by the concept of genius under the pressure of late nineteenth-century somatic determinism. Probably the leading English theorist of *genius* at the time was Francis Galton, still regarded as an important precursor of genetics, whose book *Hereditary Genius* defines the term as meaning 'those qualifications of intellect and disposition which…lead to reputation' of the kind commanded by 'a leader of opinion…an originator' (33). Galton supported his argument for the heritability of genius by some solid empirical research; he took as a kind of index of natural ability the *Dictionary of Men of the Time* (1865), and investigated the appearance there of so many men related by family, discounting any element of social determination upon their success on the grounds that true genius is of such power that mere social circumstance could not have repressed it (6-8, 34-6). Throughout Galton's work, and elsewhere in the related debates, the term '*man* of genius' is commonly used—the only time I have noted the use of a non-gendered term is when Galton goes on to gloss 'a person who is a genius' as 'a man endowed with superior faculties' (viii). Nor can it be supposed that the term can readily be taken as gender-inclusive, to judge from the range of quotations commonly used in the course of the argument, such as Goncourt's 'There are no women of genius; the women of genius are men' (quoted in Ellis 1904, 420); from the percolation of the debates into other kinds of writing, as in Lord Henry Wotton's proposition, in *The Picture of Dorian Gray*, that "'no woman is a genius… Women represent the triumph of matter over mind, just as men represent the triumph of mind over morals'" (42); and finally, from the care taken to differentiate between men and women in consideration of the term, as in the Italian theorist Lombroso's ratio of 70 male geniuses to 30 female (142), or Allan's less generous estimate of 1000 to 1 (ccvii). More extreme is the proposal of Möbius, in 1901, that artistic genius be regarded as a secondary sexual characteristic of the male, something like a beard (*Stachyologie*, quoted in Ellis 1904, 377); and still more, Otto Weininger's contention that 'genius declares itself to be a kind of higher masculinity, and thus the female cannot be possessed of genius' (111). The idea that women lack genius extends far beyond the commonplace that there have been no female Shakespeares, to take a newly materialist form in this late nineteenth-century version of the debate. As I shall go on to argue, women are debarred by anatomy, primitivism and their reproductive role in the processes of evolution from possession of genius.

The main impetus for the reconsideration of genius appears to have come from the new science of eugenics (first proposed by Francis Galton in his *Hereditary Genius*), in which a pre-genetic understanding of the transmissibility of physical and mental characteristics feeds directly into a social programme of so-called 'race improvement'. Galton's tracking of families of genius is not intended as a pleasant genealogical diversion, but as the basis of a planned approach to selective breeding in order to maximise the stock of mental and physical ability, as well as of solid civic virtue, in the imperial population. For Galton, there is always a distinct racial or national—sometimes even regional—dimension to eugenics. He is confident, for instance, that, 'The natural ability of which this book mainly treats, is such as a modern European possesses in a much greater average share than men of the lower races' (1892, x). His account, in the somewhat tendentiously named *English Men of Science*, of eminent scientists includes a detailed investigation of other ethnic and local origins: one out of every ten on his list, he informs his reader, is Anglo-Irish, and a further one (equivalent to ten per cent) includes, in his own terminology, the Anglo-Scotch, Scotch-Irish, pure Irish, Welsh, Manx, and Channel Islanders. Out of 100 men of science, six were born in Cork, Belfast, or Dublin (as compared to the twenty-one born in London). Looking more closely at their achievements, he concludes that those he regards as being of 'pure race' have higher standing in proportion to their numbers, while the lowest achievers are the Anglo-Irish and the Anglo-Welsh (16-19).

It is worth pausing briefly over this idea of the 'pure race' and its capacity for greater achievement. In his recent book *Colonial Desire*, Robert Young has examined at some length the significance of the nineteenth-century debate between theories of race that posit monogenesis (that is, a single originating human species within which is to be found a range of anatomical and mental differences constructed as racial), and those that argue for polygenesis (or a plurality of distinct human species corresponding to racial differences). Despite the diluting effect on this controversy of Darwinian evolutionary theory, the polygenetic hypothesis gained ground with the support of the new ethnological sciences. The debate is not only about the fantasy of origins, as Young points out; also at stake are possible human futures and the social policies that might serve to bring them about or ward them off (46-50, 64-8). For the straightforward polygenist, interracial sexual unions, like all attempts to breed across species, can result only in infertile offspring; for the committed monogenist, miscegenation produces fertile but ever more degraded offspring whose existence subverts and threatens the distinctions that maintain racial (and, by implication, national and cultural) differences.

In this context, Galton's concern with the quantification of racial purity takes on significance as being representative of a wider debate. Much space is given, in contemporary debates over race, to considering the question of the degree of purity or otherwise of the races in whatever taxonomy is being established at the time. To the Anglo-Saxonists' racial fable of a proud and independent people of common Anglo-Saxon ancestry, some Celticists in Ireland and elsewhere opposed a legend of racial purity of their own; they were in agreement on the idea that racial mixing through sexual relationship and breeding had led—*could* lead—only to degeneration and eventual extinction.[5] Galton's discrimination between the likely incidence of genius in the 'modern European' and 'men of the lower races' places in a revealing context the frequent association of the Irish—in their predominant contemporary construction as 'Celts'—with others whose placing on the 'tree' of races (a common figure) is less ambiguous: for John Beddoe, a type of Irish Celt is linked with what he calls 'Cro-Magnon' or 'Africanoid' man (10); Charles Dilke, rather earlier in 1868, sees the Chinese as 'the Irish of Asia' (191), and, congruently, J.W. Jackson contends that the 'Irish intellect' manifests 'a certain Orientalism' (68); while Darwin had argued for a link between the Irish peasantry and the Maori (185), and they are in a surprising number of places compared—chiefly in their alleged incapacity for self-government—to the Hottentots (Curtis 1968, 58-9, 63, 72, 136; Curtis 1971, 17). These associations between colonized peoples may depend on the angle of the jaw or the shape of the cranium, the pigmentation of the skin, as in Beddoe's 'index of nigrescence' (5), or (in Dilke's argument) the disposition to 'inveterate' migration, but the variety of forms of evidence does nothing to conceal a common construction of them all (including the Irish Celt) as somatically primitive (see Curtis 1968, 46). There was no universal agreement as to which particular anatomical characteristics *were* 'primitive', but there was a high degree of consensus that, whatever they were, they were shared by 'the lower races', the Celt, and women. Beddoe, for example, identifies 'an Irish type…which I am disposed to derive from the race of Cro-Magnon' but which too often evaded his craniometrical techniques: 'Though the head is large, the intelligence is low, and there is a great deal of cunning and suspicion'. Physical characteristics of the Gaelic type include narrow cheek-bones, a narrow and receding chin, long slitty nostrils, and prognathism (or a bulging jaw), found in roughly 20% of his Irish subjects as compared with only 6% of his English. Ireland is 'apparently [the] present centre' of prognathism, which, surmises Beddoe, had 'Africa as its possible birthplace' (10-11). Just this last characteristic—the protruding jaw—is taken by Havelock Ellis to be a point of similarity and a shared measure of inferiority between white women and the lower races, and he also argues that the dolichocephalic head-shape, shared by women, criminals, degenerates, the insane, and the prehistoric races, is a mark of their primitive stage of brain development (1904, 92). Women and the Irish share, then, an ideologically-laden association with the 'primitive' and 'prehistoric' which distinguishes them from (in Galton's phrase) the 'modern European', constructed as male and as having at least the potential for genius.

This is not to say, though, that genius is regarded as an unmixed blessing. It is not difficult to unearth stereotypical representations of 'the Celt'—and the Irish, according to most, are the purest-blooded of Celts—which contain strongly positive elements, often of the kind that might most suggest the possibility of at least artistic genius.[6] There were, of course, dissenters from the whole idea of a Celtic race: Thomas Huxley, in one of a series of popular lectures arranged by the National Sunday League in 1870, insisted that attempts to establish the differences between Saxon and Celt were 'a mere sham and delusion', the Irish being just as mixed, ethnically, as the people of Devonshire (9); and Grant Allen asserts with his usual forthrightness that the idea of a 'Celtic' race is merely a convenient identification for the turbulent, radical, and unconquered peoples of Britain (152-3). Nevertheless, there is a striking consensus about the nature of the Celt: for Renan, imaginative, shy, sentimental, and deeply religious (4-10); for Arnold, following him, visionary, imaginative, emotionally and spiritually profound, and sentimental (343-7, 351, 355, 360); for Beddoe, witty, eloquent, imaginative and sensitive (245-6, quoting from Maclean 220). And so on. To set against these surely estimable qualities, however, are others of particular relevance both to the colonial endeavour and to the gender-race analogy: Celts, says Curtis, were often considered to be unfit for self-government, incompetent in business, scientifically obtuse, intemperate and violent (1968, 13). For Arnold, they are vague and timid, impatient and unstable (343-5); for Beddoe, they are quick-tempered and melancholy (245 6). In brief, then, they combine (as Jackson puts it) 'effeminateness' and childishness (63); an 'essentially feminine race', they are—in common with women, children, lunatics and primitives—constitutionally incapable of political effectivity or the will to self-government (Renan 8).

So it is that the mere presence of some of what Arnold names the 'constituents of genius' (346) is in itself not enough to redeem a race—or for that matter, a sex—from primitivism. One of the explanations offered for the relative absence of genius among women depends upon the theory of differential variability, of which Havelock Ellis was a major exponent. At its simplest, what this means is that the distribution of deviation from the mean of intelligence is held to be considerably greater among men than among women. Whereas Galton simply assumed that talent was normally distributed across the male population (1892, 23-8), others held that there was, in Ellis's arresting phrase, a 'tendency of men to be abnormal' (1904, 412). He devotes a chapter of his book *Man and Woman* to tracking by sex variations in what, in contemporary terminologies, were seen as congenital defects: hare-lip, club-foot, supernumerary nipples, left-handedness, albinism, idiocy, moral insanity, disposition to suicide, and criminality, in all of which, he suggests, men predominate (358-72). In what strikes me as a kind of back-formation of argument, he later proposes that genius, being uncommon, can appropriately be seen as a congenital deviation from the norm which will therefore prove to be more commonly found in men than in women:

> All sorts of monstrosities and deformities on the physical side are more common in men. It is not surprising that the same should be true of intellectual mutations, and that there should be more genius among men as well as more idiocy. It has never seemed to me that in admitting this conclusion I was departing from the doctrine of sexual equivalence I have always held. Many fallacious and sometimes contradictory arguments have, however, been brought by women against it, so far at least as genius is concerned, for I have not observed that the champions of women have shown much enthusiasm regarding their equality in idiocy (1934, 171-2).

From Ellis's siting of genius among the 'monstrosities and deformities on the physical side', it becomes evident that the notion of inherited and

140

heritable genius gives a new force to the commonplace that genius and madness are near allied. If genius is regarded as a form of inspiration or of intense focus upon one activity, then, says Galton, 'it is perilously near to the voices heard by the insane, to their delirious tendencies, or to their monomanias. It cannot in such cases be a healthy faculty, nor can it be desirable to perpetuate it by inheritance' (1892, x). Lombroso goes further, suggesting that 'Many lunatics have parents of genius, and…many men of genius have parents or sons who were epileptic, mad, or, above all, criminal' (145). From this he concludes that 'genius is a true degenerative psychosis belonging to the group of moral insanity…' (333). The key term here, I believe, is 'degenerative'; the theorisation of genius is beset by the fear that deviation from the norm always leads in the direction of physical debility and/or mental deterioration. This proved a source of comfort to some feminists, who could see in the very average-ness of the female evidence of sounder evolutionary qualities. Anna Garlin Spencer, for example, argued that:

> Speaking generally, the feminine side of humanity is in the 'middle of the road' of life. Biologically, psychologically and sociologically, women are in the central, normal, constructive part of the evolutionary process. On the one side and on the other, men exhibit more geniuses and more feeble-minded, more talented experts and more incompetents who cannot earn a living; more idealistic masters of thought and action and more 'cranks' and ne'er-do-weels [*sic*] who shame their mothers.

The degeneration of the species is one of the cultural obsessions of Northern Europe in this period, and it is among the contradictory ironies of the thesis that genius—most associated with the innovative, creative and experimental forms of intelligence—should also be one of the agents by which degeneracy saps the powers of will and critical intelligence. The historian of medicine George Drinka has argued that where what he calls 'the degenerate myth' and 'the genius myth' meet is in the contemporary construction of modernity. The suggestion here is that the demands of modernity—embodied in the pace, anonymity and exposure to the masses of urban life—produce dangerous overexcitations of the nerves, leading to excessive sensibility, hyperaesthesia, and a general instability of nervous (and therefore cerebral) function. Whether these manifest themselves in the form of the genius or the enervated degenerate, they are in any case transmitted through heredity, and there is no clear somatic distinction to be drawn between the heightened nervosity of the idiot, the hysteric, the epileptic or the genius (53-9, 251-2). The noted French physician Moreau produced a diagrammatic representation of this in his celebrated image of the 'tree of idiosyncratic hereditary nervous states', in which we find exceptional intelligence, tics, neuralgia, music, imbecility, deafness and rickets all represented as branches or twigs from the same common stock of nervosity. [7]

But if racial degeneration is the threat to and within the modern civilization of genius, it remains to examine the role in such theories of those somatically debarred from the full development of genius. The relation between intellectual or creative genius and reproduction was in any case an issue in dispute, and in the case of the woman's potential for genius, matters are complicated by the assumption that the reproductive, and therefore evolutionary, role of the female is more clearly defined (see Allan cxcv-ccxix, and Ellis 1904, 421-5). In a curious way, it came to be argued that, since the woman's evolutionary role finds its justification always in the future, her intellectual qualities are directed primarily towards the maintenance of the knowledge of the past. W.K. Brooks, for example, writes in 1883 that:

> if the female organism is the conservative organism, to which is intrusted the keeping of all that has been gained during the past history of the race, it must follow that the female mind is a storehouse filled with the instincts, habits, intuitions, and laws of conduct which have been gained by past experience. The male organism, on the contrary, being the variable organism, the originating element in the process of evolution, the male mind must have the power of extending experience over new fields…(Brooks 160; quoted in Russett 95).

In such a view, the demands of genius—innovative and experimental—are at odds with the conservative and accumulative evolutionary function of the woman's mind.

Once again, there can be detected here an interdependence between the feminization of the Celt (always presumed male but, as has been widely documented, gendered effeminate) and the primitivization of the woman (usually presumed English but racially coded prehistoric). Matthew Arnold had contended that, 'The skilful and resolute appliance of means to ends which is needed both to make progress in material civilisation, and also to form powerful states, is just what the Celt has least turn for' (345), partly because of his (to continue Arnold's masculine) tendency to cling to the past. The English historian Lord Acton concurs, arguing—in terms strikingly similar to those I have quoted from Brooks on the subject of women—that, 'The Celts are not among the progressive, initiative races, but among those which supply the materials rather than the impulse of history, and are either stationary or retrogressive' (240). Ireland—a 'barbarous fossil', as Jackson calls it—is inherently conservative, attuned to the 'instincts, habits, intuitions, and laws of conduct' (59) of the past, and so the Irish are organically incapacitated, by and large, from the exercise of that masculine genius which conquers new areas of experience and serves in the formation of states.

Of course, in most versions of the argument, neither the Irish nor women are *wholly* ineligible for genius, but its likely appearance is statistically minimized. I have already alluded to estimated ratios of male to female geniuses and there are, in fact, quite numerous references in racial theories to 'Irish genius', but I would suggest that their presence is somewhat ambiguous, drawing on the historic development of the term away from a primary (and never wholly lost) association with location towards a primary association with intellectual organization. Discussions of the 'genius of the Irish' tap into the point at which the idea of locality and the idea of intellectual capacity meet, in the notion of a somatically-determined national character. The genius of a people could, after all, be to be without genius; as Coventry Patmore proposes, 'whole nations and generations [have] existed without producing a single noticeable instance of it' (99).

I have been arguing, then, that the detailed and specific use of an analogy between race and gender serves to debar, in the main, both Irish male and English female alike from that form of genius, associated with modernity and progress, which not only justifies colonialism and male dominance, but makes them inevitable. Physical data from physiognomy, craniometry and quantitative ethnology assign both femininity and the Celt to the pre-historic, the retrogressive, and the past; intellectual and psychic organization assign the future (however clouded by fears of degeneracy) to the English male. Where evolution and history merge, there is no more to be said.

Notes

I should like to thank Cheryl Hoskin for her assistance with research for this paper.

1. Robert Knox (1850) proposed four races (Saxon, Celt, Slavonian and Sarmatian) but nominated the Celt as the principal enemy of the Saxon. David Mackintosh (1865) drew further contrasts between the Anglo-Saxon and the Celt. Ernest Renan's 'The Poetry of the Celtic Races' (1854) advocated the worth and purity of the Celtic race while pitting the Celt against the Teuton. Renan is echoed by Matthew Arnold's 'On the Study of Celtic Literature' (1867) in his contrast

between the Celt and the Saxon (German) races. For further examples of the Celt/Saxon theory and its employment in both colonial and Celticist discourse, see L.P. Curtis Jr. (1968).

2. Knox, *The Races of Men,* as described in M.D. Biddiss (1986).

3. See also Catherine Hall (1992), especially Part III, 'Race, Ethnicity and Difference': 203-94; C.L. Innes (1993), Chapter 1: 'Mother Country: The Feminine Idiosyncrasy': 9-25; and Sabina Sharkey (1993).

4. Cranial capacity and jaw angles were used extensively for comparative measurement, for example by John Beddoe (1885), Francis Galton (1892), and Havelock Ellis (1904).

5. The term Anglo-Saxonism was first used by Curtis in his *Anglo-Saxons and Celts,* to describe 'the belief that the glory of English civilization…was no accident or freak of nature but the result of a set of skills and talents which were the unique inheritance of a people…conventionally known as Anglo-Saxons' (8). Renan and Arnold proposed a racial purity for the Celts, elements of which could be traced in the population of Britain. Spencer and Galton both maintained that hybridization between disparate races led to degeneration. See Nancy Stepan (1982, 105). A useful summary of the cultural debate on hybridity in the nineteenth century can be found in Young (6-19).

6. See, for example, Arnold (298, 345, 346); Renan (2) and Jackson, (68-9).

7. Degeneracy was first promoted as an important concept in heredity by Benedictin Morel in 1857, and quickly gained acceptance in European psychiatry and anthropology. See Russett (1989, 68-70, 218); also Drinka (47-53). Count Gobineau had previously proposed a racial theory of degeneration through hybridization in his *Essay on the Inequality of Human Races* (1853–5); see his *Selected Political Writings,* (27, 58-60); also Young (99-109).

Works Cited

Acton, Lord. (1862) 'Goldwin Smith's *Irish History*', in *The History of Freedom and Other Essays,* eds. John Neville Figgis and Reginald Vere Laurence. London: Macmillan, 1907.

Allan, J. McGrigor. (1869) 'On the Real Differences in the Minds of Men and Women', *Journal of the Anthropological Society 7*: ccvii.

Allen, Grant. (1894) 'The Celtic Fringe', in *Post-Prandial Philosophy.* London: Chatto and Windus.

Arnold, Matthew. (1867) 'On the Study of Celtic Literature', in *Lectures and Essays in Criticism,* ed. R.H. Super. Ann Arbor: University of Michigan Press, 1962.

Beddoe, John. (1885) *The Races of Britain: A Contribution to the Anthropology of Western Europe.* Bristol: J.W. Arrowsmith.

Biddiss, M.D. (1976) 'The Politics of Anatomy: Dr Robert Knox and Victorian Racism', *Proceedings of the Royal Society of Medicine* 69: 245-50.

Brooks, W.K. (1883) *The Law of Heredity.* Baltimore: John Murphy.

Curtis, L. Perry, Jr. (1971) *Apes and Angels: The Irishman in Victorian Caricature.* Newton Abbot: David & Charles.

Curtis, L.P., Jr. (1968) *Anglo-Saxons and Celts: A Study of Anti-Irish Prejudice in Victorian England.* Bridgeport: Conference on British Studies at the University of Bridgeport.

Darwin, Charles. (1875) *The Descent of Man, and Selection in Relation to Sex.* 2nd ed. London: John Murray.

Dilke, Charles Wentworth. (1869) *Greater Britain: A Record of Travel in English Speaking Countries during 1866 and 1867.* 4th ed. London: Macmillan.

Drinka, George Frederick. (1984) *The Birth of Neurosis: Myth, Malady, and the Victorians.* New York: Simon and Schuster.

Ellis, Havelock. (1904) *Man and Woman: A Study of Secondary Sexual Characters.* 4th ed., rev. and enl. London and Newcastle: Walter Scott.

Ellis, Havelock. (1934) 'The Question of Genius in Women', in *My Confessional: Questions of Our Day.* London: John Lane.

Galton, Francis. (1892) *Hereditary Genius: An Inquiry into its Laws and Consequences.* 2nd ed. London and New York: Macmillan.

Galton, Francis. (1874) *English Men of Science: Their Nature and Nurture.* London: Macmillan.

Gobineau, Count de. (1853-5) 'Essay on the Inequality of Human Races', in *Selected Political Writings,* ed. Michael D. Biddiss. London: Jonathan Cape, 1970).

Hall, Catherine (1992) *White, Male and Middle-Class: Explorations in Feminism and History.* London: Polity Press.

Huxley, Thomas. (1870) 'The Forefathers and Forerunners of the English People', *Pall Mall Gazette* 10 January, 1870: 9 [rpr. as 'Professor Huxley on Political Ethnology', *Anthropological Review* 8 (1870): 197-204, with printed responses thereto].

Innes, C.L. (1993) *Woman and Nation in Irish Literature and Society,* 1880-1935. New York: Harvester Press.

Jackson, J.W. (1869) 'The Race Question in Ireland', *Anthropological Review* 7: 68.

Knox, Robert. (1850) *The Races of Men: A Philosophical Enquiry into the Influences of Race Over the Destinies of Nations.* London: Henry Renshaw.

Lombroso, Cesare. (1891) *The Man of Genius.* London: Walter Scott.

Mackintosh, David. (1865) 'The Comparative Anatomy of England and Wales', *Anthropological Review* 4.

Maclean, Hector. (1866) 'On the Comparative Anthropology of Scotland', *Anthropological Review* 4.

Patmore, Coventry. (1893) 'Simplicity', in *Religio Poetae,* etc. London: George Bell and Sons.

Renan, Ernest. (1854) 'The Poetry of the Celtic Races', in *The Poetry of the Celtic Races, and Other Studies.* London: Walter Scott, 1867: 1-60.

Russett, Cynthia Eagle. (1989) *Sexual Science: The Victorian Construction of Womanhood.* Cambridge: Harvard UP.

Sharkey, Sabina. (1993) 'Gendering Equalities: The Case of Irish Women', *Paragraph* 16.i: 5-22.

Spencer, Anna Garlin. (1972) *Woman's Share in Social Culture* [reprint of 1912 edition]. New York: Arno Press.

Stepan, Nancy Leys. (1990) 'Race and Gender: The Role of Analogy in Science', in *Anatomy of Racism*, ed. David Theo Goldberg. Minneapolis and London: University of Minnesota Press.

Stepan, Nancy. (1982) *The Idea of Race in Science: Great Britain 1800-1960*. London: Macmillan.

Valente, Joseph. (1994) 'The Myth of Sovereignty: Gender in the Literature of Irish Nationalism', *ELH* 61.

Weininger, Otto. (1906) *Sex and Character*. London: Heinemann.

Wilde, Oscar. (1891) *The Picture of Dorian Gray*, ed. Donald L. Lawler. New York and London: W.W. Norton.

Young, Robert J.C. (1995) *Colonial Desire: Hybridity in Theory, Culture and Race*. London and New York: Routledge.

COLONIAL DISCOURSE AND DOMESTIC FEMININITY:

The British and Irish Ladies' Society, 1822–1828

Alison Twells

Expressing a wish that West African people could be 'put in the way of forming better dwellings', Hannah Kilham reflected on the domestic lives of people in Ireland: 'many of the *poorer* Irish cabins I have seen', she wrote, 'are like little palaces in comparison with some of these African huts' (Biller 183). Kilham's description of Irish homes in this passage bears little relation to her experience of them: her journal and reports of her visit to Ireland in 1822–23 provide account upon account of the poor state of the domestic lives of the Irish people. In comparing African and Irish domestic situations in this way, Kilham emphasises what she sees as Africa's uncivilized state, and in so doing constructs a hierarchy of civilization determined by notions of domesticity.

This article explores aspects of the philanthropic relationship between British and Irish women in the early nineteenth century. It focuses on the activities of the British and Irish Ladies' Society, the organization that sent Kilham to Ireland in 1822–23 to enlist the support of middle- and upper-class Irish women in the domestic reform of the Irish poor. Drawing on ideas of the family shaped by evangelical theory and political economy, Hannah Kilham deployed a language of domesticity in order to articulate Ireland's 'difference'. My argument is that the focus on domestic reform was central to the process by which middle-class English women were able to create a powerful role for themselves within missionary culture and the colonial enterprise. Representing poor Irish women as in need of her civilizing influence, Hannah Kilham's writing can be seen to represent a 'feminization' of the colonial voice.

I

The emergence of a missionary culture in Britain had its origins in the evangelical revival of the late eighteenth and early nineteenth centuries. Alongside the expansion of church and chapel congregations, the 1790s saw the formation of the first national missionary and philanthropic societies, most significantly the Baptist, London and Church Missionary Societies, the Sunday School movement and the Society for Bettering the Condition of the Poor.[1] Over the next twenty years local auxiliary societies were formed, becoming a central feature of the development of a public evangelical culture in towns throughout Britain. Hannah Kilham's home town of Sheffield typified such developments: by 1816 a small but active group of evangelical men and women had established a network of societies organized around the Society for Bettering the Condition of the Poor, Aged Female Society, Bible Society, Sunday School Union, Girls and Boys Lancasterian Schools and branches of the London, Wesleyan Methodist and Church Missionary Societies.

The new patterns of religious belonging to sweep Britain during these years, while enabled by important theological developments (Bebbington 1989), were intimately bound to broader processes of cultural formation. As Davidoff and Hall have shown, evangelical belief and practice were central both to the construction of middle-class culture and identity and to the claims of its members for greater power and authority. The notion of the religious family, the recodification of gender roles in terms of the separate but complementary spheres of men and women, and the evangelical redefinition of status as the product of effort and piety rather than the fortune of birth were central to the middle-class self-representation as more civilized, progressive and worthy of power and authority than either the idle and immoral aristocracy or the ignorant and irreligious working class (Davidoff and Hall, 1987).

The missionary society, and the voluntary society more generally, has been seen by historians as central to the negotiation of differences within the middle class, and thereby to the development of a coherent middle-class culture and identity (Morris 1983). Women as well as men were involved in the public activities of such societies: as Prochaska has argued, women were much more than 'behind-the-scenes' subscribers and supporters; they participated as public lady visitors; they were responsible for the distribution of tracts, pamphlets, Bibles, occasional material relief and plentiful advice concerning domestic economy to poor women in their neighbourhoods (Prochaska 1980). Indeed, as Davidoff and Hall have shown, philanthropy was central to middle-class women's negotiations with men concerning the extent and nature of their public role. Identified by both evangelical theology and political economy as the locus of morality and influence, women emphasized the moral benefits to society of their involvement in public missionary activity, representing their responsibility for the education and reform of poor women in their neighbourhoods as an extension of their domestic role, thereby exploiting the contradiction in evangelical formulations of women's role which emphasized social subordination alongside spiritual equality (Davidoff and Hall 108-48).

Taking as the main objects of their mission the rural poor and urban working class within Britain and the 'heathen' overseas, missionary men and women promoted domestic reform on a global scale. In this they were inspired not only by evangelical theology but by new formulations of the relationship between the family, gender roles and society popularized by the newly-developed 'Science of man'. In the theories of 'stadial development' offered by the Scottish enlightenment thinkers of the mid-late eighteenth century, the status of women was identified as a main signifier of social progress; it was thus the location of the domestic woman in her appropriate sphere that placed late eighteenth-century European society at the apex of civilization (Meeks 1973; Bryson 1945). Such ideas influenced social practice, as missionary men and women adopted the role of educator and dispenser of new civilized modes of cultural and familial organisation.

Hannah Kilham's missionary career offers an insight into the ways in which middle-class women were able to participate in the reshaping of relationships and identities of class, gender and ethnicity in this period. Born into an Anglican family in Sheffield in 1774, Hannah Spurr converted to Wesleyan Methodism during the Great Yorkshire Revival of the early 1790s, going on to join the breakaway Methodist New Connexion in 1797 and marrying its leader, Alexander Kilham, the following year. In 1804 Kilham, a widow of five years and recently bereaved of her infant daughter during a small-pox epidemic, joined the Society of Friends, preferring the quietude of a Quaker religious practice which allowed her to focus on her personal devotion. Drawing on a more middle-class constituency and supporting women's active participation in religious life, Quakerism also provided a ready environment for her launch into Sheffield's newly-emerging philanthropic circles. A founder member of the Society for Bettering the Condition of the Poor in 1803, Kilham became involved over the next few years in the newly formed Society for Visiting and Relieving Aged Females, Sheffield Bible Associations and the Girls' Lancasterian School which opened in 1813.

Kilham kept up-to-date with missionary developments overseas, subscribing to the *Missionary Register*, the quarterly journal founded by the CMS in 1813 for the purpose of publicizing missions and stimulating popular interest in missionary activity. In 1816, inspired by the visit to Sierra Leone of the CMS secretary Edward Bickersteth, she began writing books for use in mission schools in the colony, thus fostering her wish to travel to West Africa as a missionary. In pursuit of this goal, Kilham began to learn two West African languages, taught by two sailors from the Gambia whom she had sought out on the banks of the Thames; in return, they were given a Christian education. Kilham's attempts to persuade the Quaker hierarchy to allow her to travel to West Africa were unsuccessful: in addition to the traditional theological reservations concerning the value of missions, the male leadership saw it as unsuitable for a single woman to make the journey. [2] In 1822, in a bid to allay her disappointment at not going to Africa, Kilham accepted an invitation by the British and Irish Ladies' Society to visit Ireland.

Although lacking in the exotic attractions of mission work in West Africa, Ireland was nonetheless seen as a worthy object of British Christian concern. British missions to the Irish had emerged as part of the general increase in missionary activity from the late eighteenth century. These included the Hibernian Church Missionary Society, established in 1799; the Hibernian Bible Society and Hibernian Sunday School Society, both of which aimed to extend Protestant education to Ireland; the Irish Evangelical Society (1814), which aimed to train students for the dissenting ministry; and various tract societies, which distributed tracts and religious books and, in the case of the Scripture Readers' Society (1822), employed people to visit houses to read extracts from the Scriptures to the lower orders. As Maria Luddy has argued, Protestant philanthropy existed alongside and sometimes in conflict with a much larger philanthropic provision by Catholic female religious and laywomen (Luddy 1995). The British and Irish Ladies' Society can be located within the proselytizing Protestant tradition.

II

The British and Irish Ladies' Society originated as the women's section of the interdenominational 'London Committee', founded in 1822 in response to reports of great distress among the poor in Ireland following the failure of the potato crop. Composed of high-standing women, the BILS saw its role in corresponding with ladies in Ireland, encouraging them to form relief associations at county and district levels and to support them through subscriptions and donations. The popularity of the Society can be seen in the 135 societies that were formed in 1823; during 1824 this increased to 254, thus establishing a network of female-controlled societies which extended over 29 counties and which had considerable autonomy from the parent body. [3]

As its full title suggests, the 'British and Irish Ladies' Society for improving the condition and promoting the industry and welfare of the female peasantry in Ireland' was particularly concerned with domestic reform among poor women. The aims of the Society, as stated in its *First Report*, were:

> to visit the dwellings of the poor, and obtain a knowledge of their situation, under certain heads. To aid the sick by the loan of linen, obtaining medical advice, etc. To encourage industry, and attention

to domestic duty; to encourage parents to send their children to school; to assist the poor in any other way that their circumstances may appear to require (BILS 1823, 8).

The 'other ways' included distributing spinning wheels, flax, wool, flannel and nets for fishery to women and children; establishing shops and a Repository in London for which women would produce their goods and then buy requisite items at a subsidised rate; supplying lime for white-washing cottages; and 'supplying means for distributing presents among such as may distinguish themselves by the clean, orderly and decent appearance of the children' (BILS 1823, 8).

Such practices, combining the systematic collection of information concerning the lives of the poor and the provision of means of employment with a system of material relief and moral education, reveal a mixture of evangelical benevolence and scientific philanthropy (Yeo 1996). Supplying Irish women with the means to improve their livelihoods involved more than enabling them to produce clothing and other articles 'requisite for their health and comfort'; it would also stimulate a 'moral reaction', inculcating a spirit of industry and moral independency which, it was believed, would transform family life: 'whatever tends to create industry and civilisation among the females', declared the *First Report*, 'will be found to influence the whole family' (BILS 1823, 26). Within this model, the cause of poverty is located not merely in the moral failure of the individual, but in the absence of useful employment: 'habits of industry' go hand in hand with 'a sense of virtue and piety' and 'cleanliness and attention to domestic duty' (BILS 1823, Regulations).

Hannah Kilham's *Thoughts for the House*, four sheets of 'maxims' offering advice on domestic management and family life, were written for women in Ireland (BILS 1825). Illustrated with engravings of rural households engaged in useful employment—spinning, knitting, bonnet- and basket-making—in clean, spare, well-aired homes, the *Thoughts* focus on the themes of industry and morality, exhorting women to send their children to school and to concentrate on making a good home: 'It is by doing useful things, a little and a little', claims one, 'that a man will in time make a barren spot beautiful and a woman make her house tidy, clean, snug and pleasant'; 'When the mother of a family is conscientious, kind, cheerful, neat, orderly and diligent, she will be doing good to the whole house—every day'. Drawing on her *Family Maxims*, written for the Sheffield poor in 1813, the basic principles of *Thoughts for the House* were later reproduced in Kilham's language books for West African children, suggestive of her belief in the universal applicability of the benefits of domestic reform (Kilham 1813, 1823, 1827).

The ladies of the BILS subscribed to a view of human nature as shaped by environmental conditions. In this they contested the popular belief among the English that such misery was natural to the Irish and that no improving measures need be taken:

> They will consider how many degrading habits usually spring from a state of external misery—how it leads to a poor man's forgetfulness of himself as an accountable being, whilst it absorbs the mind in a sense of present suffering, or in the endeavour to preserve a more animal existence... May not that despondency, dependence and idleness, which some have described, and that sort of indolent content with the rags and dirt surrounding him, which others have so forcibly depicted as characteristic of the Irish peasant, be traced back to the miserable habits in the midst of which he is born and bred... (BILS 1824, 17).

The 'apathy and listlessness', the 'despondency, dependence and idleness' of the 'indolent' Irish peasant were all the product of domestic mismanagement. Even drunkenness, Kilham claimed, turning around the formulation of later temperance advocates, was the product of domestic failure, the result of 'their wretched condition at home' (Biller 145).

The ladies' own influence as members of a higher class and as Protestants was an important element in their view of social progress. In Kilham's words, it was 'the influence of the ladies over the female peasantry in their respective districts' that would not only stimulate 'ideas of comfort and cleanliness', but 'confer...benefits of a higher nature...by the improvement of moral principle and the repression of mean, degrading and vicious habits'. She anticipated 'every real advancement in the moral feeling, on the part of the future mothers of the families of Ireland' which was 'calculated to have the most extensive and desirable effects on the habits of the rising generation' (BILS 1823, 39-40). Interestingly, the ladies themselves were not beyond benefitting from their involvement in philanthropy. Writing from Dublin, Kilham emphasized the positive effects on the 'young ladies of Portarlington', hitherto 'accustomed only to the ample abodes of their relatives and friends', who were shocked to discover people living 'in a state so wretched—worse fed and lodged than their own dogs and horses' (Biller 153-4). Such discoveries supported the evangelical critique of the indulgent and idle lives of the ladies of the aristocracy and fashionable elements within middle-class society.

In addition to providing employment for women, the education of children was seen by the BILS as a crucial factor in Ireland's improvement. Writing in the *Second Report*, the ladies commented on 'the docility and gentleness of the children', seeing in their natural dispositions evidence of the 'superior people [their] parents might have been, if they had had but a tolerable education' (BILS 1824, 29-30). Three years later, the Society had established its own Model Infant School at Longford, with the intention that its focus on the education of children in domestic and useful skills and, in true Lancasterian fashion, the training of young women as teachers, should be replicated elsewhere in the country. As outlined in *An Address to the School Mistress of the Longford Infant School*, the emphasis was placed on the children's future roles as manual labourers, housewives and servants: both sexes were to be given instruction in reading, Scripture and the skills of knitting, plaiting and basket-making; the boys were also to garden, whilst the girls hemmed, sewed and stayed behind after lessons to clean up (BILS 1823, 29-30). Thinking it 'more likely to be hurtful than useful to children who are to labour for their bread' (BILS 1827, 53), it was considered inappropriate to place too much emphasis on intellectual pursuits: it was as skilled and virtuous labourers and domestic workers that Ireland's children were to be instruments of national regeneration.

III

Hannah Kilham represents women's involvement in missionary activity as the natural result of the impact upon their senses and sensibilities of their observation of misery. Writing from Limerick in January 1823, she uses optical imagery to represent her need, having seen, to act:

> It is impossible to convey by any description the just idea of the wretchedness that exists among the poor in the old part of this city. It can only be known by going into dwellings, and seeing it with our own eyes; and having seen and felt with the sufferers, I could not, without violating the claims of humanity, and the sacred sense of individual duty, forbear attempting in some way to convey the feeling (Biller 149).

In addition to justifying women's excursion into the public world, Kilham represents the philanthropic relationship as a straightforward act of Christian benevolence.

Far from representing a simple altruism however, inscribed within the missionary relationship was the expectation of a return, of an engagement within a broader cultural project.[4] The Reports of the BILS are full of 'success stories'. In the *First Report*, two lady visitors from Limerick give a typical and enthusiastic account of the personal transformation of a woman whose cabin they described as 'dyed with smoke, and hung with spider's webs' and so dirty that 'the colour of the floor had evidently not been seen for a long time past'. Their suggestion that they could provide the necessary lime for white-washing was received 'languidly', the occupant stating that she would prefer to be given the price of the lime with which she would buy potatoes. However, when they offered her a spinning wheel, 'her countenance brightened up in a moment, and she earnestly replied 'Ah! If you'll lend me a wheel, *and let me spin*, I'll whitewash and do anything you please!' She promptly applied to the Board of Health for white-washing materials, expressing her desire that her home should be clean before the ladies called again (BILS 1823, 48).

Subsequent Reports are full of similar joyful accounts of the 'wretched and disconsolate' becoming 'cheerful smiling faces'; women who had become more clean and self-respecting; those who would now willingly walk miles to each other's houses in order to spin and whose motivation enabled them to work through the night. The accounts tell of 'crippled' girls making gloves, of beggars 'reclaimed' to take their place among the best of the spinners (BILS 1824, 28). 'A spirit of industry has been excited', proclaimed the contribution from Waterford, 'and the generality of our poor women seem as if awakened from a long dream of depression, indolence and wretchedness' (BILS 1824, 28). An account from Carlow reported that 'where inmates were idle', cabins were 'filthy', but were 'clean and comfortable where they were employed'; 'so true is it, that cleanliness and industry go hand in hand…' (BILS 1827, 5). Hannah Kilham endorsed such accounts in her journal: 'I am informed that in the city of Cork there is already an evident effect from the visits of the ladies, the poor being stimulated to cleanliness' (Biller 148). 'It is cheering', she wrote following a day's visiting with the Countess of Clare, 'to see the industry, cleanliness and comfort that could be found in a cabin' (Biller 150).

Such 'seeing' always occurs through the eyes of the ladies who are not only of another class but are Protestant and, in the case of Kilham, English. The Society rarely gives any indication of alternative views of their activities. This is despite evidence of instances of antagonism. The *First Report* of the BILS, talking of the 'gratifying and encouraging' reception met with in most places, acknowledges that they 'were unfortunately restrained from extending to many parts of the country, by the prevalence of insubordination among the lower class of people'. Similarly, Hannah

Kilham refers to their not being totally welcomed by the peasantry: in a footnote to her Report she exhorts visitors not to be deterred by 'the apparent listlessness in the peasantry' (BILS 1823, 48). Other indication comes by way of praise for the ladies for risking their own health by 'going all weathers, to stand the whole day in an indifferent cottage, to give out work with their own hands'. 'Listlessness' and 'indifference' can be read in this context as being as much about resistance to missionary practices and assumptions as any direct 'insubordination' (BILS 1823, 22). Indeed, the account of the woman from Limerick, discussed above, who was prepared to whitewash her cottage if provided with spinning materials, is suggestive of a very different agenda and of ways in which the people receive and transform the concerns and messages of their cultural 'superiors'.

While Kilham's work in Ireland,—and the response to it—was in many ways similar to her work in England, the attempt to impose domestic femininity shaped by Protestant evangelicalism has, in the context of the colonial relationship, other dimensions. In her writing, Ireland's homes are characterized by a particular wretchedness, a depravity on a scale unknown in England. Contrasted with English homes, they are taken as indicators of a lower level of civilization. Kilham wrote in her journal:

> I do not conceive it possible for any language or picture of destitution to have conveyed to any mind the impressions received from the actual sight of the peasantry, as they at present exist. The wretched cabin built by the hard-strained efforts of extreme poverty, is destitute of almost everything that could mark any attainment of civilized life (Biller 163).

The focus of missionary women on processes of domestic improvement as a means of civilization suggests the centrality of gender to the construction of colonial discourse in this period. The BILS missionary project—that of turning cabins into homes—placed British missionary women at the heart of the missionary/colonial enterprise: Hannah Kilham's writing, representing Irish women as in need of their civilizing care, can be interpreted as representing a feminization of the colonial voice.

Notes
1. The Missionary Societies were formed in 1792, 1795 and 1799 respectively, and the Society for Bettering the Condition of the Poor in 1796. For a general discussion of the evangelical revival, see Gilbert 1976.
2. Although an evangelical wing was developing within the Society of Friends, there was much resistance to missionary zeal, originating in the belief that the

universality of the inner light militated against the need to evangelize the Gospel. Kilham placed herself on the evangelical wing, arguing that slavery had obscured the inner light for the African people. See Anon, 'An Address made by a member of our Society to instruct some African Negroes', which is likely to have been written by Kilham.

3. The Society attracted a similar social elite in Ireland: patrons included the Countess of Kingston, Lady Colthurst, Countess of Clare, Viscount Adare, etc, while the positions of district secretaries and treasurers were occupied by members of the business elite and lesser gentry. See Luddy (183-4).

4. For a recent discussion of the philanthopic relationship, see Kidd 1996.

Works Cited

Bebbington, David. (1989) *Evangelicalism in Modern Britain: A History from the 1730s to the 1980s*. London: Unwin Hyman.

Biller, Sarah, ed. (1837) *Memoir of the late Hannah Kilham*. London.

British and Irish Ladies' Society. (1823) *First Report of the British and Irish Ladies' Society*.

British and Irish Ladies' Society. (1824) *Second Report of the British and Irish Ladies' Society*.

British and Irish Ladies' Society. (1827) *Fifth Report of the British and Irish Ladies' Society*.

Bryson, Gladys. (1945) *Man and Society: The Scottish Inquiry of the Eighteenth Century*. Princeton, NJ: Princeton UP.

Davidoff, L. and C. Hall. (1987) *Family Fortunes: Men and Women of the English Middle Class, 1780–1850*. London: Hutchinson.

Gilbert, A.D. (1976) *Religion and Society in Industrial England: Church, Chapel and Social Change 1740–1914*. Longman.

Kidd, Alan. (1996) 'Philanthropy and the "social history paradigm",' *Social History* 21.ii: 180-92.

Kilham, Hannah (1813). *Family Maxims*.

Kilham, Hannah. (1823) *First Lessons in Jaloof*.

Kilham, Hannah. (1827). *African Lessons*.

Luddy, Maria. (1995) *Women and Philanthropy in Nineteenth Century Ireland*. Cambridge: Cambridge UP.

Meeks, Ronald. (1973) *Social Science and the Ignoble Savage*. Cambridge: Cambridge UP.

Morris, R.J. (1983) 'Voluntary Societies and British Urban Elites, 1780–1850', *The Historical Journal* 26.i: 95-118.

Prochaska, F. (1980) *Women and Philanthropy in Nineteenth-Century England*. Oxford: Clarendon Press.

Yeo, Eileen. (1996) *The Contest for Social Science in Britain: Relations and Representations of Class and Gender 1789–1914*. London: Rivers Oram Press.

'EATER AND EATEN':

The Great Hunger and De-Anglicization

Laura O'Connor

James Joyce's riveting Christmas dinner scene in *A Portrait of the Artist as a Young Man*, and the portrayal by Conor Cruise O'Brien and others of William Butler Yeats's 'passion and cunning' in exploiting the political vacuum left after Charles Stewart Parnell's deposition and death in 1891, has established Joyce and those associated with the Irish Literary Revival—W.B. Yeats, Lady Gregory, John Millington Synge and Gaelic Revivalist Douglas Hyde—as acknowledged legislators of Irish cultural nationalism. In 'Ireland after Parnell' (1922), Yeats recalls his 'sudden certainty that Ireland was to be like soft wax for years to come…at the first lull in politics' (*Autobiographies*, 199). Post-Parnellite rancour had turned the Irish past into a 'melodrama…of villain and victim', and, 'preparing the way without knowing it for a great satirist and master of irony [i.e. Joyce]', Yeats's 'conviction [grew] that we should satirize rather than praise' in order to transmute the colonial melodrama into art (*Autobiographies*, 206-7). The historical evidence for the substitution of cultural nationalism for constitutional politics is compelling: in 1892 the newly-founded National Literary Society was the forum for Douglas Hyde's 'The Necessity of De-Anglicising the Irish Nation', the salvo that launched Gaelic Revivalism and clarified the cultural task of the Yeats-led Irish literary movement in English which was organized around the Irish National Theatre (1899) and the Abbey Theatre (1904). This paper examines the overtly Parnell-centered historiography of a lecture on 'Modern Ireland' that Yeats gave in America in 1931–2 and a poem composed by 'rhyming passages from [the] lecture', 'Parnell's Funeral' (1934), in order to uncover an alternative famine-centered periodization of history in their anatomy of 'Irish satiric genius' and metaphors of cannibalism.

The contemporary wave of famine-centred historiography marking the 150th anniversary of the famine, much of it deeply influenced by subaltern studies, can be seen as a revisionist response to how Irish history has been periodized and thematized around the emergence of the Irish nation-state, with Parnell and constitutional politics centre-stage, and other histories made peripheral to it. The title of F.S.L. Lyons's classic textbook, *Ireland Since the Famine*, indicates the status of the famine in Irish historiography until recently: universally acknowledged as a watershed, but occluded as an

157

object of inquiry. Yeats's historiographical exercise is an attempt to trace 'the origin of what seems to me most unique and strange in our Irish excitement' and 'fanaticism'—his own susceptibility to it is betrayed by his flirtation with fascism at that time—'for the sake of my own peace of mind'.[1] He identifies 'Four Bells, four deep tragic notes' that close the sixteenth, seventeenth, eighteenth and nineteenth centuries: the Flight of the Earls (Gaelic clan leaders), the Battle of the Boyne, the United Irishmen movement, and Parnell's death. His historical knowledge is limited to the aftermath of the Battle of the Boyne which secured the ascendancy of the Anglo-Irish, Yeats writes, and his interest lies in the cultural nationalist epoch that followed the post-Parnell fourth bell. Though the first bell, the destruction of the Gaelic social order, and the untolled catastrophe of the Great Famine (1845–50), are muffled in Yeats's chronology, his search for the root of Irish fanaticism in self-cannibalizing Irish satiric genius discloses a history of Gaelic ethnocide. This subaltern history of a coming to terms with memories of Gaelic ethnocide provides a genealogy for de-anglicizing cultural nationalism that supplements the received version of cultural nationalists supplanting politicians. The supplementary history reveals a de-anglicizing motive behind the pre-eminence of satire in early twentieth-century Irish writing.

The 'furious hatred' unleashed by the Parnellite split resulted in 'young men turning away from politics altogether, taking to Gaelic, taking to literature' and generated a 'movement of imagination that was, I am convinced, a direct expression of the national self-contempt that followed the death of Parnell' and of which Joyce is the most famous exemplar (MI, 258, 263). 'From that national humiliation, from the resolution to destroy all that made the humiliation possible, from that sacrificial victim I derive almost all that is living in the imagination of Ireland today', Yeats continues, citing Joyce's Christmas dinner scene as the foundational moment when Irish satiric genius became introverted. 'Parnell's Funeral' tells us that while strangers murdered Emmet, Fitzgerald, and Tone, 'popular rage / *hysterica passio* dragged Parnell down / None shared our guilt, nor did we play a part / Upon a painted stage when we devoured his heart'. Who is the 'we' who devoured Parnell's heart? The first part of the poem portrays 'we' as a mob similar to the marauding 'pack' in Yeats's early Parnell-poem, 'To a Shade' (1913). 'We' becomes an honorific group in the second part of the poem, however, which conspicuously excludes Free State politicians DeValera, Cosgrave, and O'Duffy from the elite ranks of 'we cannibals': 'Had DeValera eaten Parnell's heart / No loose-lipped demagogue had won the day, / No civil rancour torn the land apart. / Had Cosgrave eaten Parnell's heart, the land's imagination had been satisfied / Had even O'Duffy—but I name no more— / Their school a crowd, his [i.e. Parnell's] master solitude; / Through Jonathan Swift's dark grove he passed, and there / Plucked bitter wisdom that enriched his blood'. Passing through Jonathan Swift's dark grove to pluck blood-enriching bitter wisdom is a rite of initiation into 'Irish satiric genius'—satyric genius spelt with a y, as it were—that transfers hatred of England to Ireland and releases a passion for reality: 'we had passed through an initiation like that of the Tibetan ascetic, who staggers half dead from a trance, where he has seen himself eaten alive and has not yet learned that the eater was himself' (VP, 835).

Yeats draws on this metaphor of self-devouring again in 'A General Introduction for my Work' (1937) which contains an apologia for not writing in Irish—'Gaelic is my national language, but it is not my mother tongue'—and states that he has constituted himself as a poet out of love-hatred of English, a medium of Irish ethnocide:

> The 'Irishry' have preserved their ancient 'deposit' through wars, which during the sixteenth and seventeenth centuries, became wars of extermination... No people hate as we do in whom that past is always alive, there are moments when hatred poisons my life and I accuse myself of effeminacy because I have not given it adequate expression. It is not enough to have put it into the mouth of a rambling peasant poet. Then I remind myself...that I owe my soul to Shakespeare, to Spenser and to Blake, perhaps to William Morris, and to the English language in which I think, speak, and write, that everything I love has come to me through English; my hatred tortures me with love, my love with hate. I am like the Tibetan monk who dreams at his initiation that he is eaten by a wild beast and learns on waking that he himself is eater and eaten (*Essays*, 518-9).

Consumed by an insatiable atavistic hatred toward English, the language through which all he loves has come and beyond which he cannot get, Yeats learns on waking from his nightmare of annihilation by the beasts of culture and tribal loyalties that he himself is both 'eater and eaten'. The first phase of modern Irish literature began 'when dialect was being reshaped as literature' by Lady Gregory and Synge, and when Synge, reacting 'either against our [i.e. Lady Gregory's and Yeats's] tendency to select too obviously what was noble, or against popular Catholic idealism' selected brutality or violence for his theme (MI, 261-2). Synge and Joyce realized Yeats's 'dream of enlarging Irish hatred', for Joyce 'selected all that was sordid and casual in the life of Dublin, and from the local hate he passed on to all that had remained unspoken in the European mind for generations' (MI, 263). He recalls the young Joyce as he first met him in Dublin, 'possessed with an extreme irritation, mounting to almost ungovernable rage against all that he saw and heard, even against the mere bodies and faces that passed him in the street' (MI, 263). Such Swiftian misanthropic fury is also found in Synge, who, when asked by Yeats whether he wrote from love or hatred of Ireland replied, 'That is a question I have never been able to answer' (MI, 263). The founders of 'Modern Ireland' are not politicians, but those writers whose hostility towards 'national self-contempt' unites them with Parnell's and Swift's *saeva indignatio*. Yeats mythologizes the young Joyce's Christmas dinner as an origin of Irish satiric genius by representing the famous literary scene as an inaugural totem meal.

Why is satire the preferred genre of we Irish, 'in whom that [ethnocidal] past is always alive' and why is it conceptualized as a form of self-cannibalism? A provenance for the 'eater and eaten' symbolism of the late nineteenth- and early twentieth-century 'taking to Gaelic, taking to literature' movement of imagination can be retraced to Yeats's first bell, the routing of Gaelic culture, a history that is outlined with devastating clarity in Edmund Spenser's *A View of the Present State of Ireland* (1596). If the English do not exercize the conqueror's prerogative and forcibly anglicize the Irish, Spenser argues, the Irish may ultimately gaelicize the new English settlers, as they had assimilated their Anglo-Norman predecessors. The question of who incorporates or assimilates whom is literalized as anxiety about who eats whom. Spenser recommends breaking Irish resistance by starving the non-compliant Irish into cannibalizing each other so that 'none of them fall by the sworde, nor be slaine by the soldyer, yet thus beinge kept from manvrance...they would quicklie consume themselues and devoure one another' (135). In the preface to his 1902 selected edition of Spenser's work, Yeats, (who professes to owe his soul to Spenser), writes that Spenser could 'commend this expeditious way from personal knowledge' gained while assisting Lord Grey in the decimation of Munster. He quotes Spenser on 'the proofs whereof':

'notwithstanding that [Munster] was a most rich and plentifull countrey...yet ere one yeare and a half they were brought to such wretchednesse, as that any stony harte would have rued the same. Out of every corner of the woodes and glynnes they came creeping forth on theyr hands, for theyr legges could not beare them; they looked like anatomyes of death, they speake like ghosts crying out of their graves; they did eate of the dead carrions…yet sure in all that warre, there perished not any by the sword, but all by extremitye of famyn, which they themselves had wrought' (quoted in *Essays*, 374).

The extraordinary shifting of blame onto the victim is a classic example of a colonial Caliban complex, where the violence of the colonizers is projected onto the violated colonized culture so that the incorporation of lands, extermination of peoples, and devouring of native resources are displaced onto so-called cannibalistic natives. The 'expeditious way' of Spenser's modest proposal lies not only in exonerating the crown from the 'extremitye of famyn, which [the Irish] themselves had wrought' but in grasping that destroying a culture and imposing a language requires a measure of native compliance. The extremity of famine would provoke the Irish to renounce their native culture and conform to that of the colonists so that, in effect, they would complete the ethnocidal process themselves.

The enforced anglicization, and the Gaelic ethnocide which was its corollary, undertaken during the Tudor conquest and formalized by the Penal Laws (1691–1829) culminated with the Great Famine (1845–50) which accelerated a shift from the gradual erosion of Irish to a repudiation of it by the Irish themselves. The trauma of famine and mass emigration— to which untold (untolled) numbers of Irish-speakers were lost[2]—resulted in 'the mass flight from the Irish language' that Seán De Fréine argues was a social self-generated movement of collective panic (83-4). Joseph Lee highlights the anomaly of Ireland's abrupt decline of bilingualism since the nineteenth century compared with other minor national European languages (662-77). Lee insists, as Hyde had done a century earlier, that the loss of bilingualism should be viewed as a choice, not as an unavoidable fate. The collective decision to extirpate Irish is epitomized by the notorious tally-stick. Children wore tally-sticks around their necks that were notched whenever they were overheard lapsing into Irish and they were beaten for each lapse. This process of national self-immolation, of beating Irish out of the next generation in a cultural equivalent of 'consuming themselves and devouring one another', belatedly fulfilled Spenser's linkage of starvation with anglicization.

Douglas Hyde's 'The Necessity of De-Anglicising Ireland' challenges the Irish to face their complicity with anglicization and Irish (Gaelic) ethnocide and to attempt to reverse it by restoring Irish as a spoken language. Dismayed that the Irish have 'ceased to be Irish without becoming English', he urges his compatriots to confront the contradiction of slavishly imitating the English whom they profess to hate (153-4). He recommends a restoration of the spurned native culture in a point-by-point reversal of Spenser's language and custom proposals without, however, proposing corresponding changes in the socio-political superstructure. Hyde's great achievement was to rally the Irish around overcoming internalized shame: 'We must arouse some spark of patriotic inspiration among the peasantry who still use the language, and put an end to the shameful state of feeling—a thousand-tongued reproach to our leaders and statesmen—which makes young men and women blush and hang their heads when overheard speaking their own language' (160). Though he focused popular attention on the psychic cost of Irish ethnocide, he is deafeningly silent on the trauma of famine. Yeats swiftly accepted 'de-anglicization' as a common goal for the National Literary Society, arguing that the achievement of US literature proved the possibility of creating a literature that 'shall be none the less Irish in spirit from being English in language'.[3] My point about the two De-Anglicizing movements that became known as the Gaelic Revival and the Irish Literary Renaissance is that while they did fill a post-Parnellite political vacuum, they were also attempting to come to terms with a history of famine and ethnocide that was rarely made explicit in public debate about 'national self-contempt', though the link between the famine and the 'death' of the Irish language remained a vital part of folk memory.

Yeats's first play, *The Countess Cathleen* (written and revised between 1889 and 1912), features a heroine who barters her soul to feed starving peasants. It is permeated with Yeats's class guilt about the famine and anxieties about nationalist ethics, particularly as they pertain to himself and Maud Gonne. Starvation is also the theme of *The King's Threshold* (1903) in which the poet Seanchan goes on hunger strike to protest his banishment from King Guaire's State Council and the insult to poetry it implies. In 1920, during the hunger-strike by poet and Lord Mayor of Cork Terence MacSwiney, Yeats added a tragic ending to *The King's Threshold* and memorialized MacSwiney as a mystic martyr along with the executed 1916 insurrectionists by publishing 'Easter 1916' after his death (*Variorum Plays*). Tom Paulin's essay on Yeats's timing of the publication of 'Easter 1916', 'Yeats's Hunger-Strike Poem', argues that Yeats's and Joyce's revulsion at England's intransigence towards MacSwiney was intensified by 'a tribal reflex' to the Great Hunger (141). A tribal reflex suggests a partly occluded consciousness and an overdetermined motive force, that locus of blindness and insight that has characterized the famine's status in Irish historical memory until recently. In the 1932 'Modern Ireland' lecture, Yeats links self-cannibalizing Irish satire with Catholicism, and with the messianic self-sacrifice of the 1916 insurrectionists that unleashed 'something terrible in Ireland, the mood of the mystic victim…Parnell had been the victim, the nation the priest, but now men were both priest and victim—they offered the nation a terrible way out of humiliation and self-detraction [and since then the hunger strike] has helped to make deliberate suffering a chief instrument in our public life' (MI, 266). Irish satiric genius combines the primitive satire of ritual self-scapegoating that Yeats associates with Catholic martydom and the satiric powers of the Gaelic *file* (seer-poet) and the *non serviam* secular satire that was epitomized for him by the eighteenth century Anglo-Irish Protestant tradition of Swift, Berkeley, Burke, and their solitary heir, Parnell.

Yeats wrote 'Parnell's Funeral' during a barren period by 'rhym[ing] passages from a lecture'.[4] It is an effort to jump-start poetry, a writing exercise on a par with the Steinach operation Yeats had the same year. Satirize me! the poet-speaker begs, as if he wants to be spanked into poetry:

Come fix upon me that accusing eye.
I thirst for accusation. All that was sung,
All that was said in Ireland is a lie
Bred out of the contagion of the throng,
Saving the rhyme rats hear before they die.
Leave nothing but the nothings that belong
To this bare soul, let all men judge that can
Whether it be an animal or a man.

Satire alone speaks true: 'All that was sung, / All that is said in Ireland is a lie / … Saving the rhyme rats hear before they die'. This 'rhyme rats hear before they die' alludes to Elizabethan satire of the legendary exterminatory powers of Irish satirists. The epilogue to Ben Jonson's *Poetaster* declares that the author will 'Rhyme them to death, as they do Irish rats, / In drumming tunes'. The closing peroration of Sir Philip Sidney's *Defense of Poetrie* forbears to wish disdainers of the art 'to be driven by a poet's verses (as Bubonax was) to hang himself, nor to be rhymed to death, as is said to be done in Ireland'. More famously still, Shakespeare has Rosalind declare in As You Like It that 'I was never so berhymed since Pythagoras' time, that I was an Irish rat, which I can hardly remember' (3.ii.176-7).[5] The double allusion juxtaposes contrary notions of satire—an Irish tradition that maintains a connection with magical satire and a secular English tradition of intellectual scepticism that is intrigued by the Irish tradition it satirizes—that comprise the dual satiric tradition of Irish writers in English. The contraries are more complex than the credulity/scepticism polarity might suggest, since they are deeply embedded in the power conflicts between both cultures over the past millennium.

That a healthy scepticism exists in the Irish tradition is evident in the middle Irish prose romance *Imtheacht na Tromdháimhe* [Proceedings of the Great Bardic Company] that popularized the legend of Irish pesticidal satire, since it is itself a satire of the poets' tyrannical hold over a public that fears their fatal satiric powers. Peevish and arrogant, the seventh century poet Seanchán finds fault with King Guaire's hospitality and, outraged that mice have nibbled his egg, satirizes and kills them. Seanchán is placed in a food chain of biting satirists and exterminators (he threatens to slay the cats for not killing the mice [or rats]) which satirizes his satiric trade and underscores an economy whereby the poet sings for his supper, and bites the hand that feeds him when he dislikes the fare. Seanchán is reputed to have recovered the epic *Táin Bó Cuailgne* after it had been lost to living memory by fasting over Fearghus MacRóich's grave until Fearghus appeared and recited it to him (Ó hÓgáin 384-7). Yeats links Seanchán, who embodies the vagrancy and continuity of the Gaelic tradition, to Hanrahan, the hero of his *Stories of Red Hanrahan* (1892–1905) who is based on Gaelic poet Eoghan Rua Ó Súilleabháin (c.1748–84) and is a significant mask for Yeats:

> [Hanrahan] resolved to begone westward, for Gaelic Ireland was still alive…and as the English tongue and English manners died behind him, he became a new man; for was he not the last of that mighty line of poets which came down unbroken from Sancan Torpeist (whom the Great Cat well nigh ate), and mightier Oisin, whose heart knew unappeased three hundred years of daemonic love?[6]

Hanrahan's journey follows the de-anglicizing pilgrimage westward to their roots in the *Gaeltacht* undertaken by revivalists.

Yeats concludes the 'Modern Ireland' essay with the claim that the 'poetic theme is found, like sanctity, through desire and humiliation' (MI, 268); and the thirst for accusation and desire to be reduced to 'nothing but the nothings that belong / To this bare soul' in 'Parnell's Funeral' seeks the mystic state in which the poetic theme can be found. Though the urge to shed cultural accretions is not the purpose of the hunger-strike cursing ritual in *The King's Threshold* (Seanchán's fast protests the social decorum due the poet), it becomes a major focus of the play's interest. The play[7] explores the effects of starvation on Seanchán's mind and the impact of the cursing ritual on his society. Yeats's interest in occultism and symbolist *deréglèment* informs his treatment of how Seanchán wastes away into a 'bare soul' or 'poetic theme', but it is the specific Irishness of that bare soul and poetic theme that engages him. The desire for contact with a race memory that motivates the de-anglicizing pilgrimage westward is evident in the play's close:

> *Youngest Pupil.* O Silver trumpets, be you lifted up
>   And cry to the great race that is to come.
>   Long-throated swans upon the waves of time,
>   Sing loudly, for beyond the wall of the world
>   That race may hear our music and awake.
> *Oldest Pupil [motioning the musicians to lower their trumpets].*
>   Not what it leaves behind it in the light
>   But what it carries with it to the dark
>   Exalts the soul; nor song nor trumpet-blast
>   Can call up races from the worsening world
>   To mend the wrong and mar the solitude
>   Of the great shade we follow to the tomb.

Seanchán enters a Swiftian-Parnellite dark grove of bitter wisdom, that Yeatsian *anima mundi* where the dead living in their memories dream the living into passionate life through inherited instinct. 'The "Irishry" have preserved their ancient "deposit" through wars...of extermination' (*Essays*, 518): the play's closing assertion of continuity between a remote ancestral and an as yet unborn 'Irishry' affirms that the '"Irishry"...in whom that [ethnocidal] past is always alive' has a future because its 'deposit' or past refuses to die. That Yeats's attempt to join 'that mighty line of poets which came down unbroken from Sancan Torpeist' from whom he is divided by language should result in a hunger-strike play suggests the importance of the link between the 'taking to Gaelic, taking to literature' movement of imagination and the attempt to deal with a history of ethnocide through starvation.

A major preoccupation of *The King's Threshold* is the magical efficacy of the cursing ritual, especially the way in which the poet's cursing power increases as his strength ebbs. Yeats's interest in what makes hunger strikes so compelling will be appreciated by those who remember the impact on public opinion of the 1981 H-Block hunger strikes in Belfast. Hunger strikes engage the power of the curse to redirect the victim's defilement onto the victimizer, a power that seems to exceed the force of rhetoric to become magic. For example, though Margaret Thatcher denounced the hunger strikes as blackmail and remained intransigent about them, she shows the magical impact of the curse in her repeated rebuttal, 'murder is murder is murder'. The doubly tautological mantra, reminiscent of Lady Macbeth's darker utterances, is a kind of talismanic counter-curse. The presumably unconscious attempt to return the curse on the cursers through the three-pointed statement uncannily boomerangs back on itself. The power of the curse to cast the humiliation of colonization back on the colonizer is the subject of Caliban's famous rejoinder in *The Tempest*, a statement that has become a touchstone of Caribbean postcolonial literature: 'You taught me language, and my profit on't / Is, I know how to curse. The red-plague rid you / For learning me your language!' (I.ii.363-5).

The difference between how satire and knowing how to curse are held in public esteem reflects the cultural asymmetry between the sceptical English / magical Irish dual tradition. Satire channels aggression into a witty and erudite display of verbal mastery; cursing, by contrast, is viewed as an uncontrolled outburst of invective and a sign of cultural bankruptcy. Classic satire, the urbane wit of the coterie poet or intellectual, is placed by its privileged position at court or civic centres of power at an opposite pole to curses, which are proscribed as beyond the pale of civil discourse. Satirists distance themselves from the naked aggression of cursing by disclaiming personal malice and disavowing belief in the magical power of words. Though Elizabethan satires of Irish satirists (itself a projection, perhaps, of a Caliban complex onto that pestilential place) revel in their comparative sophistication, they also betray fascination with the annihilative energy on which satire depends. The elite engage in refined satire while cursing is the weapon of the outcast satirist. As a result of colonialism, the Elizabethans and their English successors were insider satirists and Seanchán's colonized Irish successors were outcast satirists, the essential difference between their genres being a matter of unequal power relations and social justice. The Seanchán/Elizabethan double allusion points a paradox, however: although the Elizabethans have the political power their Irish neighbours lack, Irish satiric power exceeds theirs.

People without other means of redress, whether for personal reasons or because civil and judicial institutions neglect to safeguard—or perhaps violate—their interests, resort to cursing to right their grievances. Outcast satirists or cursers have a satiric purpose—they intend to shame and to ridicule their target—but unlike their privileged counterparts, their cursing power increases proportionately to their grievance. The widow's curse was especially feared in Ireland, for example, in the belief that the frustration of her marginalized position added magical potency to her words. Patrick Power speculates that the social taboo on cursing in the presence of women may be motivated by an atavistic fear of women's superior cursing power stemming from their comparative social powerlessness, rather than from a chivalric desire to protect them from verbal violence. An oral Gaelic poem collected and translated by Lady Gregory, 'The Curse of the Boers on England', celebrates the superior cursing power of the underprivileged: 'O Lord, let there fall / Straight down on her [Queen Victoria's] head / The curse of the peoples / That have fallen with us...The Lord does not listen / To the curse of the strong' (76-9). In a context of injustice and power inequity, cursing can become oracular and bring about a dialogic inversion of power relations and discourse hierarchies.

'The poetic theme is found, like sanctity, through desire and humiliation': satire, with its intent to wound and wound back, is the pre-eminent genre of humiliation. Irish satiric genius draws on the power of the powerless to disturb the powerful by infusing language with vengeful desire. Yeats's version of Irish satyric genius is strikingly introverted. It is directed against internalized colonial oppression or 'national self-contempt' rather than the colonial oppressor. How does one satirize national self-contempt? One can excoriate philistines who would not give 'the right twigs for the eagle's nest' ('To a Wealthy Man...') or leaders who have not eaten Parnell's heart, but that begs the question of how one judges the right twigs for nation-building or sets about eating Parnell's heart. The first phase of transforming 'national self-contempt' began 'when dialect—['which is sometimes Gaelic in construction, Tudor in vocabulary']—was being reshaped as literature' in Irish English by Lady Gregory and Synge at the Abbey theatre while the Gaelic League was organizing to restore Irish (MI, 260, 262). The 'taking to Gaelic, taking to literature' movement to destroy all that made national self-contempt possible attempts to reconstitute the self and the nation by cannibalizing Irish and English culture. By intensifying his love-hatred of English, as he deliberately set out to do by rhyming passages from the satiric genius lecture, Yeats hopes to realize his goal of writing 'a vivid speech that has no laws except that it must not exorcise the ghostly voice' (Essays, 524). A different kind of constitutional nationalism, the painful task of reconstituting the self and a national culture out of a fraught linguistic heritage, is placed in the foreground by Yeats's anatomy of satiric genius.

Yeats is an influential historian of modern Ireland, and many of his poems are cited as authoritative accounts of major historical events. The 'Modern Ireland' lecture is of interest because its chronology of four bells overtly engages how national narratives are framed by periodization. I have suggested that the 'eater and eaten' theme sounds the untolled bell of famine and ethnocide, and that national self-contempt arose not only from post-Parnellite rancour but from painful memories of attempted ethnocide—and

Irish complicity with it—and of the Great Hunger. Like his Celtic aesthetic of the nineties, Yeats's satiric genius aesthetic is predicated on the fact that English culture has largely supplanted Irish culture, but both partly occlude the history out of which they derive. The evolution from a Celtic to a satiric aesthetic contains its own history of decolonization, moreover, as Yeats's attempt to pinpoint the beginning of contemporary satire in the Celtic movement shows. The guiding precept of the revivalists, Lady Gregory's 'We do our work to restore dignity to Ireland', had a 'tendency to select too obviously what was noble' (MI, 259, 261) that provoked a reaction, first from Synge and culminating with Joyce. To the writers of the thirties, it seemed that the revivalists had restored dignity to an excessive, and even stultifying, degree and had contributed (albeit unwittingly) to a form of official nationalism that was now being used to sanction censorship. The revivalists' spiritual aesthetic privileged the epic genres of poetry, folklore, and ancient sagas that exalted heroic values; the corporeal aesthetic of post-Independence writers preferred prose genres that debunked glamourized heroism. The change from colony to nation-state is paralleled by a shift from epic to satire. Yeats's attempt to trace 'the origin of what seems to me most unique and strange in our Irish excitement' and contemporary 'fanaticism' by analyzing Irish satire shows how the evolution of a literary genre contains a complex political history. By exploring the nature of the satiric impulse, and bringing to consciousness the half-suppressed memories of attempted ethnocide that trigger the tribal reflex, we can enrich our understanding of Irish national narratives.

Notes

1. See 'Modern Ireland: An Address to American Audiences', ed. Curtis Bradford, hereafter referred to as MI, 256; and the Variorum edition of the poems (VP) 832-5 for a commentary based on excerpts from the lecture.

2. The first census with language data is the post-famine 1851 census which records 1.5 million Irish speakers (23%), a figure commonly agreed to be an underestimate, though to what extent remains controversial (De Fréine 1977, 80-1; Wall 1969, 81-90). It is a figure haunted by the likely number of pre-famine Irish-speakers, estimated by Anderson at nearly 4 million, or half of the population, though the number may have been close to a third (Hindley 1990, 14-20).

3. Letter to *United Ireland* 17 December 1892, *Uncollected Prose* vol 1, 255-6.

4. 'A year ago I found that I had written no verse for two years; I had never been so long barren; I had nothing in my head, and there used to be more than I could write. Perhaps Coole Park where I had escaped from politics, from all that Dublin talked of, when it was shut, shut me out from my theme; or did the subconscious drama that was my imaginative world end with its owner? But it was more likely that I had

grown too old for poetry. I decided to force myself to write. In 'At Parnell's Funeral' I rhymed passages from a lecture I had given in America' (VP, 855).

5. See F.N. Robinson, *Satirists and Enchanters in Early Irish Literature*. Robinson makes a case for the similarity of Irish and classic satire on linguistic, thematic and functional grounds. On satire as pesticide he cites an amusing anecdote, Eugene O'Curry's 1855 report to the Royal Irish Academy on his failure to rhyme rats to death. O'Curry blames the rats' inability to understand his language; Yeats, whose 'boyhood indolence' was defeated by O'Curry's unarranged and uninterpreted history (*Essays*, 511), might have adduced other reasons for their immunity.

6. *The Secret Rose, Variorum Plays*, 198. The Great Cat or King of the Cats well nigh ate Seanchán for threatening the cats, but Seanchán was saved by St. Ciaran's intercession.

7. Yeats's sources for the play were Lady Wilde's *Ancient Legends* 159-63 and Edwin Ellis's *Sancan the Bard* (1895); see Ure 1963, 32.

Works Cited

De Fréine, Seán. (1977) 'The Dominance of the English Language in the 19th Century', in *The English Language in Ireland*, ed. Diarmuid Ó Muirithe. Cork: Mercier.

Gregory, Lady Augusta. (1903) *Poets and Dreamers: Studies and Translations*. New York: Oxford UP, 1974.

Hindley, Reg. (1990) *The Death of the Irish Langauge: A Qualified Obituary*. London: Routledge.

Hyde, Douglas. (1986) 'The Necessity of De-Anglicising the Irish Nation', in *Language, Lore and Lyrics*, ed. Breandán O'Conaire. Dublin: Irish Academic Press.

Lee, Joseph, J. (1989) *Ireland 1912–1985*. Cambridge: Cambridge UP.

Lyons, F.S.L. (1985) *Ireland Since the Famine*. London: Fontana.

O'Brien, Conor Cruise. (1965) 'Passion and Cunning: An Essay on the Politics of W.B. Yeats', in *In Excited Reverie: A Centenary Tribute to William Butler Yeats 1865–1939*, eds. A.N. Jeffares and K.C.W. Cross. London: Macmillan.

Ó hÓgáin, Dáithí. (1991) *Myth, Legend & Romance. An Encyclopaedia of the Irish Folk Tradition*. New York: Prentice Hall.

Paulin, Tom. (1992) *Minotaur: Poetry and the Nation State*. London: Faber & Faber.

Power, Patrick. (1974) *The Book of Irish Curses*. Cork: Mercier.

Robinson, Fred Norris. (1911) *Satirists and Enchanters in Early Irish Literature*. Harvard University.

Spenser, Edmund. (1934) *A View of the Present State of Ireland*, ed. W. L. Renwick. London: Eric Partridge.

Ure, Peter. (1963) *Yeats the Playwright*. London: Routledge & Kegan Paul.

Wall, Maureen. (1969) 'The Decline of the Irish Language', in *A View of the Irish Language*, ed. Brian Ó Cuív. Dublin: Oifig an tSoláthair.

Wilde, Lady Jane F. ['Speranza']. (1888) *Ancient Legends, Mystic Charms and Superstitions of Ireland*. Boston: Ticknor & Co.

Yeats, W. B. (1955) *Autobiographies.* Dublin: Gill & Macmillan.

Yeats, W.B. (1961) *Essays and Introductions.* New York: Macmillan.

Yeats, W.B. (1964) 'Modern Ireland: An Address to American Audiences, 1932–3', ed. Curtis Bradford. *Massachusetts Review* 5.ii: 256-68.

Yeats, W.B. (1981) *The Secret Rose, Stories by W.B. Yeats: A Variorum Edition*, eds P.L. Marcus, W. Gould and M.J. Sidnell. Ithaca, NY: Cornell UP.

Yeats, W.B. (1970) *Uncollected Prose by W.B. Yeats*, ed. John P. Frayne. 2 vols. New York: Columbia UP.

Yeats, W.B. (1966) *The Variorum Edition of the Poems of W.B. Yeats*, eds. Peter Allt and Russell K. Alspach. 3rd edn. New York: Macmillan.

Yeats, W.B. (1966) *The Variorum Edition of the Plays of W.B. Yeats.* ed. Russell K. Alspach, assisted by Catherine C. Alspach. New York: Macmillan.

Yeats, W.B. (1959) *Mythologies.* New York: Macmillan.

ALTER/NATIVES FOR THE COLONIAL BODY:

Matter and Memory in O'Faolain's
No Country for Young Men

Laura Doyle

In Allen Feldman's study, *Formations of Violence*, he quotes an IRA prisoner of the notoriously abusive H-Block in the Long Kesh prison who explained that 'The higher the beatings, the stronger we were. That was their weakness' (229). This prisoner articulates a paradoxical logic in which the body's weakness is its strength, because those who would dominate it come to depend on it as the means to their end and, moreover, condition the body to resist and survive. In this physical, political equation, the body, beaten or beating, is the middle term. The body is the point of contact between those who stand opposed to each other and it is this condition that Feldman describes as the 'material reciprocity [operating] within ideological exclusion' (1). The body as 'the terminal locus of power also defines the place for the redirection and reversal of power' (178). In other words, the interdependence of bodies—what the phenomenologist Maurice Merleau-Ponty calls their intercorporeality—means that physical domination can entail destabilization and even transformation of the dominating relation.

Not that this transformation is likely to be final and triumphant; on the contrary, the escalating violence in the Long Kesh prison that culminated in the 1981 deaths by hunger strike of Bobby Sands and eleven other men reveals the fatal relentlessness of these antagonistic physical exchanges. Consider the circle of abuse and resistance in what came to be called the 'Dirty Protest'. It began with the guards' denial of second towels for showers and their violently invasive body searches which led to the prisoners' refusal to shower which led to the guards' denial of bathroom privileges which led to the prisoners' shitting in the corners of their cells which led to the guards throwing the prisoners' sheets and mattresses into the piles of shit while searching for contraband which led to the prisoners throwing the excrement out the window which led to the guards boarding up the windows which led to the prisoners spreading the shit on the cell walls which led to the guards each day moving prisoners and cleaning and whitewashing cells—until in the end the guards smelled nearly as much as the prisoners, struggling to rid themselves of the stench before going home. In this cycle, dirt and shit invasively permeated the home lives of the guards as it did the cell lives of the prisoners. Guards and prisoners entered a body deadlock in an extreme instance of what Sara Suleri calls 'colonial intimacy'. As one prisoner put it, 'From the moment we hit the H-block we had used our bodies as a protest weapon. It came from the understanding that the Brits were using our bodies to break us' (Feldman 179). The body here belongs neither to one side nor the other but always to both; it is open to both, vulnerable to both, and by the same token, though not with equally empowering effects, accessible to both.

A number of twentieth-century novelists have attempted to render the often violent, sometimes mundane, yet almost always ambivalent struggles over this bodily middle term. I think of authors as different as Jean Rhys, William Faulkner, Tsitsi Dangarembga, J.M. Coetzee, and Isabelle Allende. In Ireland, James Joyce was among the earliest writers to trace the embodied colonial, sexual, and racial dynamics of his characters' lives in *Ulysses*, in a parodic rather than tragic mode. He does so in part (as I have argued elsewhere) by following the crisscrossing paths of their bodies walking Dublin's streets (Doyle 1994, Chapter 5). In moments of bodily brushings-past or embrace or collision in *Ulysses*, social oppositions are momentarily concretized, destabilized, and felt as questions rather than givens, a point I will exemplify shortly.

Here I wish to position Joyce as a precursor to the contemporary Irish novelist Julia O'Faolain. O'Faolain picks up where Joyce leaves off in registering the unsettling ripple effects of bodily encounter. In many ways, she writes the same story he does but from a woman's point of view. She is equally critical of certain strains of nationalism operating in the colonial situation; and like his, her critique particularly pinpoints the constricting hold of nationalism on sexuality and bodies. For both authors, in the end, bodies provide Janus-faced sites of reversal and slippage in the colonial economy.

'Colonial facts', Sara Suleri observes, 'are vertiginous' (3). In her pursuit of an 'idiom for alterity' that will do justice to these facts, she coins the term colonial intimacy. Insisting that there are 'necessary intimacies that obtain between ruler and ruled', she moves away from a simple binary and hierarchical model of power in order to open up questions about the 'highly unsettling…economy of complicity and guilt [that] is in operation on the colonial stage' (3). She draws attention to the subtle ways that the dynamics of coloniality 'fail to cohere around the master-myth' of otherness and instead 'move with a ghostly mobility' (3). In many ways Joyce and O'Faolain seem to shape their fiction exactly to reflect these complex, contingent colonial manoeuvers and a ghostly mobility thus haunts their work—in Joyce's case often at a linguistic level and in O'Faolain's more strictly at a mimetic one. In O'Faolain, in particular, historical memory and bodily matter merge as the source of potential, and potentially fruitful, disturbances in the colonial force-field.

In *Ulysses* we are treated to delicious moments of transgressive, mutual touch and seeing. My favourite is the scene in which Bloom, Cunningham, Power, and Dedalus share the funeral carriage. As the carriage turns a corner and their bodies sway, all of the dynamics of insiders and outsiders are quickly thrown into relief, and by the same token momentarily fall away when the motion 'united noiselessly their unresisting knees' (6.228). This touching of their intentionless knees offers us a glimpse of the body as 'ghostly' insofar as it seems to slip *across* the terrain of social oppositions. Knees touch whether temple or church is your place of worship. 'Material reciprocity' intrudes upon 'ideological exclusion', even if in the next moment, and for this very reason, exclusion returns with renewed force. Joyce delights in the impish effects of this material reciprocity.

Yet he is also sensitive to the renewed force of exclusion that can follow, which complicates, or adds ambivalence and a note of parody to, his insistent desire to pit material reciprocity against it. A mockery of both colonialism and of the most problematic ideologies of resistance to it accompanies his intercorporeal method. He understands how resistance to colonialism mirrors colonialism, how resistance can become a strange complicity, how the body can be turned against itself. In particular, he glimpses the *sexual* politics of anti-colonial resistance, which lends added force to his narration of the body's slipperiness in the realms of power. As O'Faolain later does more fully, Joyce exposes a colonial-sexual matrix, including one of its ancient and abiding myths: that of the disloyal, sexual Irish woman.

In explaining his theory that 'england is in the hands of the jews', the schoolteacher Deasy in *Ulysses* attributes the supposed problem to the sins of 'Woman': 'A woman brought sin into the world... A faithless wife first brought strangers to our shores here... A woman brought Parnell low too' (2.390-94). The Citizen echoes Deasy's accusation: 'A dishonoured wife...that's what's the cause of all our misfortunes...The adultress and her paramour brought the Saxon robbers here...the strangers' (12.1156). As I have noted elsewhere, in his mocking invocations of the contemporary discourse of eugenics, Joyce again implicitly critiques the racial-patriarchal logic of some key versions of nationalism (Doyle 1994, 113-17). At the same time in, for example, Stephen's tale of the two virgins who climb Nelson's pillar, Joyce parodies the counternarrative of the nation, in which Ireland is an old or young virgin woman, the Colleen or Kathleen ni Houlihan, who embodies the pure and 'virgin' state of the nation. If the downfall of the nation occurs through sexual transgression, clearly sexual purity must lie at the heart of national integrity.

Yet Joyce exposes how this counter-narrative of the virgin at the heart of Ireland actually contributes to the crippling of the nation. It disembodies it. It founds its identity on a refusal of the fullness of the very body it struggles to liberate. Above all, he dramatizes, in ways I have explored fully elsewhere (Doyle 1994, 117-22), how Stephen's search for identity is blocked by this contradictory ideology of the body, as mythologized in women's sexuality: for there is a contradiction between Stephen's powerful sense of bodily connection to his mother and her desire for him to honour an Irish Catholic tradition that dishonours her body as one 'made not in God's likeness' (1.420-22). Whether he chooses or rejects this tradition that demonizes woman's sexual body, Stephen betrays his physical connection to his mother's body, and in turn to the material ontology of Ireland's communal life (including for instance its enclosure by the 'snotgreen sea').

O'Faolain's female characters struggle with the same anti-colonialist yet patriarchal myth that Joyce parodies. In a distinct echo of the story the Citizen invokes in *Ulysses*, Judith Clancy learns in her convent school that 'women bore inherited guilt' because it was 'an Irishwoman's frail morals which led to the English coming here in 1169' (34). Meanwhile, O'Faolain bestows the name 'Grainne' on her other main female character, a name borrowed from one of the stories in which a woman's sexual desire brings destruction to the nation, the legend of Fionn MacCumhal.[1] As we will see, the lesson of this story comes back to haunt the modern Grainne in 1979 when she has an affair with an Irish-American.

What we see at work in this myth of the faithless Irish woman who allows the invasion of strangers is what can be called a kin-patriarchal logic. As I have argued in *Bordering on the Body*, the patriarchal economy is most often also a kinship economy, defined within blood lines that in the West are typically extended to racial or ethnic and national boundaries. The control and exchange of women's bodies in marriage occurs within or across these boundaries, so that the reproductive woman is a maker and marker of kin-group boundaries: she is forced across a kin border (in exogamous kin-patriarchal communities) or she is prohibited from crossing a border (as in Ireland and the endogamous forms of kin-patriarchy that dominate in the West). In either case, her function is to reproduce, through offspring, the life of that border. Her sexuality and her mothering are always already racialized or nationalized.

The mythologies that develop within colonized countries often reflect this racial-patriarchal schema, but in highly defensive form, in that women are blamed for the 'invasion of strangers'. In *No Country for Young Men,* O'Faolain scrutinizes the contemporary sexual body politics that derive from the myth of the sexually pure, nationalist woman who preserves—but also potentially betrays—the integrity of the colonized nation. At the same time she writes a story of how the bodies' 'material reciprocity' operates to trouble the constraints of this mythology, and she pursues a body-attentive narrative method in which the body as site of sexual-colonial repression may also become the vehicle of sexual-national transformation. As Joyce does through Molly Bloom, O'Faolain promises a breaking-open of history and memory through the activities of the sexualized woman, in this case Grainne, even while she also reveals how memory returns in the guise of a virgin body to condemn that attempt and reclaim the wayward female.

―――――――――

No Country for Young Men weaves two parallel plots, involving the lives of two different generations of a prominent Irish Republican family. The elder patriarch Owen O'Malley, and decades later his nephew Owen Roe, are involved in sensitive subversive political activities and as a consequence carefully guard their intentions and their public images. In the early generation of the 1920's, Owen O'Malley is engaged to marry one Kathleen Clancy. While he is in prison, however, she becomes attracted to the Irish-American Sparky Driscoll who is in Ireland as a representative of sympathetic Irish Americans. Here already O'Faolain inserts an anomolous middle term into the Irish-English binary in the form of an Irish-American who is a Republican sympathizer but still a moderate and, moreover, an 'outsider' who arouses distrust. This is especially so since Sparky's mission is to gather information about which elements of the Republican cause American money should support, as well as to track down leads on the whereabouts of a large sum that has already been funnelled to the cause, the latter of which puts his Irish associates on the defensive. In fact that money is buried in the yard of the family of Kathleen Clancy in anticipation of a split in the resistance between those who will accept a separate Northern Ireland and those, including Kathleen's fiancé Owen O'Malley, who will not.

As a treaty is signed which partitions Ireland, tension among the Republican factions rises and suddenly Sparky Driscoll is killed. But crucially it is neither Owen O'Malley nor his associates who kill Sparky; no, instead we learn that this men's battle has pulled a woman into its current, specifically the virgin figure embodied in Kathleen's convent-educated sister, Judith.

Importantly, Judith's denial of her sexuality and distrust of her sister Kathleen's sexuality are exactly what lead her to kill Sparky. The protected youngest of the family and more fully under the influence of the convent nuns, Judith has 'carefully kept herself from knowing about soppy things like love and courting' (232). But when one night Sparky kisses her, she discovers sensations that provoke her fear and desire: she feels his 'tongue sliding [dementedly] between her lips…[and] she wanted to laugh and push him away and instead she felt her lips parting. She felt as though a warm current of water or some unknown, insidious element had taken hold of her. Her body was behaving wildly' (260). Judith's body has begun to spill beyond the bounds of the ideology she has, with much encouragement, adopted for it. When Kathleen later tells Judith why she likes Sparky, Judith can only respond lamely, 'You're cracked!' because 'Memory of the treacherous way her own body had responded to Sparky's kiss undermined argument. No wonder they spent so much time instilling morality into girls, my goodness!' (280).

Several weeks later, Kathleen confides to Judith that she intends to break her engagement with Owen and leave the country with Sparky; Judith shows shocked disapproval. When Sparky comes to meet Kathleen, Judith leads him astray but in the process ends up alone with him in one of the big houses. The substitution here of the virgin body of the Irish woman for the one who flirts with strangers issues in a final irony. Sparky once more arouses Judith's desire by stroking her neck as they talk. She leaps away from him and simultaneously begins to argue against his support of political compromise. He hints at his knowledge of the hidden money and the thought occurs to Judith that 'maybe Kathleen was his source' (341). Here is the old myth surfacing: Judith's suspicion springs from the notion that a woman's sexual desire leads her to associate with 'strangers' and betray the nation.

Sparky meanwhile points to Judith's innocence as the basis for her view of politics: 'Kathleen', he says, 'has seen dead men. She had to smuggle your brother's corpse out of the police morgue. That's why she's digusted with war. *You* haven't seen anything of the war. It's all in your head. Abstract. I don't believe you would kill a rabbit' (342). He might be right about Judith's support for fighting being the effect of her innocence; but he is wrong about her ability to kill. Sparky takes an old bayonet down from the wall (the use of this old landlord's weapon is itself an irony) and says to Judith, 'Here, feel it. Weigh it. Imagine you're driving it into the guts of a real man. You wouldn't do it'. But in the next moment she does. She murders Sparky himself.

Judith commits violence precisely according to the logic of the innocent ideology she has been bred to: she purges from their midst the stranger who threatened to intrude upon the bond between her sister and her sister's republican fiancé Owen, and by extension to violate the pure purpose of the Irish nation. By revealing at the end of her novel that the virgin nun Judith is after all the murderous actor in the plot of colonial intrigue, O'Faolain exposes the deadly underside of the virgin myth. That is, Judith's resistance to her sexuality ignites a violence whose murderousness is a measure of her repressed desire. The body that is apparently most removed from and impervious to colonial infection—the convent woman's body—actually carries within it the effects of that history, including a smothered sexuality, in a way that joins it to the violence. (As we will see, the character Patsy Flynn embodies this same connection between constricted sexuality and colonial violence.) Judith's innocent body is thus the final and hidden preserve of a violence—and a sexuality—it apparently opposes.

This moment of the murder becomes a memory that Judith loses hold of for fifty-seven years. It is one the reader does not learn of until the final pages of the book, and in this sense O'Faolain places her readers as well as her characters at the mercy of a legacy whose violence sometimes operates invisibly, without our understanding, via the circuitous paths of repressed memory. The novel opens in 1979 with Judith, now a senile nun, trying to remember something. The interval between the killing in 1922 and her remembering of it in 1979 is recreated in the distance between the novel's opening and its close. In the intervening years, as we slowly learn in the intervening pages, Judith is at first catatonic, then receives shock treatment, then is for most of her life committed to a nunnery. When the novel opens, she is largely incoherent, but through her fragmented memories we learn that Owen O'Malley—who did after all marry her sister Kathleen after Sparky died—had a political stake in Judith *not* remembering what she did—for it would discredit his sect of the Republicans. He therefore had a hand, it seems, in the decision to give her shock treatment and to keep her in the convent even when she wanted to leave.

If the suppression of Judith's memory is in effect the suppression of her sexuality (the deeper cause, as the novel suggests, of her murder of Sparky), then this plot implies that the suppression of her sexuality serves the nationalist cause. Her murderous act and suppressed memory sustain the nationalist resistance, protecting its duplicities, even as nationalist resistance sustains the myth of women's necessary sexual (and political) innocence. Yet this innocence turns out to be enforced with a violence and a captivity that makes republicanism complicit with the colonialism it struggles against. The myths of sexual innocence and colonial guilt—which might have seemed 'ideologically exclusive'—turn out in several ways to be materially reciprocal, to merge materially in the body of Sister Judith.

Perhaps most interesting for our understanding of the way there exists a 'material reciprocity within ideological exclusion', the more modern woman and the sexual mother, Grainne, becomes midwife to the cultural memory aborted within the body of Sister Judith. Not only do nationalism and myths of virginity intertwine at their cores in this novel, but also virginity and promiscuity turn out to have interests and a history in common, in the persons of Grainne and Judith. Again O'Faolain throws colonial-sexual oppositions off-center and traces instead the threads binding them to one another.

To clarify the point, I must once more recapitulate the plot. At the opening of the novel when the convent shuts down and she must leave, Sister Judith comes to live with her nephew Michael and his wife Grainne. Grainne at first resents Judith's presence, seeing it as a ploy on her husband's part to win her back (she and Michael have recently been separated); but she eventually comes to care, physically and emotionally, for this old woman who is clearly entangled in a web of troubled memories. (In one scene in which Judith mimics a jabbing motion that dates unconsciously from the murder scene, she tells Grainne, 'I'm seeking a memory'. Grainne in turn 'stared in fascination. A sensuous apathy had come over her' [92].) At the same time, in this 1979 phase of the plot, an Irish-American man, James Duffy, comes to Dublin to research a film which will garner American support for the Republican cause. He comes home by chance one drunken night with Grainne's husband, is greeted at the door by Judith lunging about with an umbrella as if it were a bayonet, and meets Grainne, toward whom he feels a strong attraction. On learning that Judith is the surviving sister-in-law of the famous republican Owen O'Malley, he becomes intrigued by the possibility of hearing her version of the past, in particular of the Sparky Driscoll murder, which was reported as a British act. In the process of pursuing this possibility, he becomes involved sexually with Grainne, and, both for James's sake and out of her own sympathy for Judith, Grainne encourages her great-aunt to recover her memories. This begins a process of what Sethe in Toni Morrison's *Beloved* calls 'rememory', by which Proustian bodily experiences and clues—specifically linked in this novel to the sexuality of Grainne—provoke Judith's recall of the traumatic event. O'Faolain sets up this process in several ways.

First of all O'Faolain abundantly uses metaphor to suggest the link between memory and physicality, showing how unwanted memory becomes lodged in the physical, in the flesh. Thus Judith describes her apprehension of a lost memory as troubling 'the edge of her mind like a speck at the corner of your eye or fluff in your nostril' (37). At the same time, as hinted in this latter image, O'Faolain's body metaphors often partake of the farcical, the deflationary, the grotesque—as when her narrator describes a character's bottom lip which captures overflowing drops of beer as 'shooting forward like an anteater's proboscis to scoop up prey' (70). The grotesque aspect of her imagery is connected, I suggest, to her sense that the repression and violence—or more precisely the handling of a legacy of violation through a repressive myth of sexual innocence—surfaces in the bodies of Dubliners. This is what her character James Duffy recognizes when he guesses that 'the scar-tissue faces he'd seen on the streets were the result of ways of living which would have left less visible scars' (171).

At the same time, O'Faolain tells a tale of embodiment that reveals a slippery underside which frustrates the sexual-colonial hold on the body. Both Judith and Grainne are particularly sensitive to the power of a body to exert a subversive influence. In an early encounter with Sparky, for example, Judith looks him 'straight in the eye as she never did look, and had been taught in the convent never to look, at men. He looked straight back and she felt a series of small shocks ripple through her. She didn't like Sparky Driscoll's interfering ways, his pushiness or his opinions, but this sensation was a binding thrilling one' (335). Thus does the body follow a movement of its own, sometimes against the grain of virginal political intentions.

Grainne's lover James believes, as she puts it, that 'you could break up one order and found another on the body's anarchy. That she could leave Michael and marry him' (295). Although Grainne doubts this when she first notes it, she does in effect come to believe it and attempt it. Meanwhile O'Faolain goes even further. By building her fiction in part on the logic of bodies and rememory, O'Faolain suggests that its order may not simply be anarchic. On the contrary, the body operates as a guide for her female characters, a signal beckoning attention to neglected knowledge such as when Sister Judith is pushed to recall one of her memories by the painful 'tension in her stomach and in the back of her neck'. Most important, Judith's bodily sensations form a bridge between the past and present, in effect generating a kind of narrative phenomenology of potential cultural tranformation.

For instance, when the narrator at one point tells us 'she was sweating' the description refers simultaneously to the young and the old Judith: 'Both Judiths were clammy and terrified inside their clothes' (9). Her body is the hinge by which the narrative swings between past and present and urges the reader as well as Judith toward a revelatory future. In this way, attention to the corporeal ground of being, sensitivity to the sweating body, far from introducing a principle of anarchy, actually undergirds O'Faolain's narrative order, wherein the corporeal is the meeting point of past and present, the pivot by which the narrative moves from one to the other—and in the process offers hope for another, more corporeally integrated future. The body—while not fixed in its meaning or essence, or in fact exactly *because* it is not fixed—serves as a vehicle of the movement through history.

O'Faolain particularly links sexuality and memory, most lyrically in Judith's comparison of her memory to the bog that bordered the convent school of her youth.

> Topiaried trees and slices of lawn contrasted with the surrounding landscape which was a bog. This region was active as a compost heap and here the millenial process of matter recycling itself was as disturbing as decay in a carcass. Phosphorescent glowings, said to come from the chemical residues of bones, exhaled from its depths... Sometimes, in later life, Judith would say 'my memory is a bog', referring as much to its power of suction as to its unfathomable layers (12).

The clue here is that for the nuns of the convent 'the bog was pagan and [they] saw in it an image of fallen nature. It signified mortality, they said, and the sadness of the flesh' (12). If Judith's memory is a bog, this passage points to the fact that part of what is buried there is her 'flesh', though not so much *its* sadness as the sadness of its loss in 'unfathomable depths'. Meanwhile, by creating a close narrative parallel between the developing sexual relationship of James and Grainne, on the one hand, and the recovery of Judith's memory, on the other, O'Faolain links memory and the sexual body not only imagistically but structurally, as a narrative catalyst.

Unfortunately, however, just as Judith's memory of her part in the murder (and implicitly of the sexuality that helped to provoke it) reaches the surface, teased forth by her, Grainne's, and James's attention to bodily memory cues (they present her with familiar places and things to prompt her memory); James Duffy, the Irish-American outsider who has loved Grainne and might record Judith's memory, is killed. Again, in this second case, it is not directly the patriarchal politician Owen Roe who murders the sexually dangerous outsider, but rather a sexually repressed and colonially-abused underling named Patsy Flynn.

Patsy Flynn is a man who blushes at the mention of sex and 'had never touched a female' (265). Like Stephen Dedalus, Patsy is an asocial creature who traces his problems back to betrayal by his mother (265). Like the Citizen, he considers women 'security leaks' (184) in the national struggle. At the same time, Patsy's very physicality carries the intertwined effects of colonialism and this sexual constriction. He has been in prison himself and his body still lives that history. Ever since 'they force-fed me one time we were on hunger strike', he has a tendency to splutter and choke when he eats (184). O'Faolain dwells on this eating after purposefully framing it within this history; we watch him rub 'a fat dollop of fried bread into the yolk of his egg. The skin of the yolk swelled, erupted, and the projectile of bread slid into the yellow well' (183). Meanwhile for fear of catching cold after his experiences of deprivation, he never washes and chews eucalyptus cough drops all winter, which leaves him smelling unpleasantly of two kinds of pungency at once. It is this body that spies suspiciously on Judith, James, and Grainne (worried about the past Republican secrets they might uncover) and finally discovers Grainne and James making love—after which, like Judith, in horror at his own sexual arousal, he is driven to kill James. The colonized body again effects the murder of the sexualized body. Colonial intimacy, as lived by the force-fed body of a prisoner, issues once more in a fatally colonized intimacy.

Through a Dickensian labyrinth of connections, then, Grainne's sympathy with the colonized and sexually repressed body of Judith in turn brings into play the equally colonized and repressed Patsy Flynn who in turn kills *her* American lover, thus thwarting her subversive desire, which might have evaded this cycle of violent bodily history. And yet, although within a tenacious colonial logic the repressed body returns to reclaim the sexualized body of Grainne, nonetheless Grainne—the sexual, transgressive mother figure[2]—fosters the de-virginalization of memory in prompting the return of Judith's past. O'Faolain's narration stages its own act of embodied resistance by abandoning all reifying 'allegories of otherness', to borrow another of Suleri's phrases, and embracing instead narrative allegories of physical entanglement; she choreographs another version, perhaps a healing version, of the fraught dialectical dance of colonial intimacy.

With this story, O'Faolain unsettles easy oppositions between innocent and guilty, pure and impure, dominant and disempowered, by minding the gender drama intertwined with the nationalist drama at its roots, and specifically by focusing on how bodies play out the contradictions which ideologies generate. Her novel makes clear that binary models of power, while constitutive of the colonial problematic, are pitifully inadequate for the task of understanding the complex internalizations, repressions, deformations, and reversals acted out by these bodies. Like the virgins who climb Nelson's pillar in *Ulysses*, the virgin embodiment of a pure Ireland veils an ignorant underside as productive of repression as the colonialism it supposedly resists.

Although Grainne is after all defeated by the power of physically-embedded repressions—via Patsy—she does decide to leave her husband

Michael before she knows about the death of James. She may well return to her husband, but her physical act of walking away from him, with which the book ends, signifies one more small step away from the colonization of intimacy—if not in Grainne's life, then in our lives as readers of this story in which the body as site of repressed cultural violences also functions as the site of new corporeal intimacies which sometimes slip the hold of colonization.

'In history as in matter', says one of O'Faolain's characters, 'nothing is lost. It comes back in another form' (164). What O'Faolain's novel also suggests is that it is in fact thanks to matter that in history and memory nothing is lost. History, and the memory of it, are *preserved* in matter, in touching or scarred or hungry bodies—and this phenomenological reservoir is both crippling and enabling. Through matter, through the body's processes of rememory and resistance, colonial history unfolds. But to tell those memories through the bodies in which they are lodged, to acknowledge the desire the body carries in it side by side with pain, is to feel a series of small shocks that may signal the transition into a post-colonial future.

Notes

1. For discussion of the Mac Cumhal legend in relation to O'Faolain's novel, see Ann Weekes, 'Diarmuid and Grainne Again: Julia O'Faolain's *No Country For Young Men*', *Éire-Ireland* (Spring 1986), 21: 89-102; Thomas Moore, 'Triangles and Entrapment in Julia O'Faolain's *No Country For Young Men*', *Colby Quarterly* March 1991; (27)1: 9-16; and Laura B. Vandale, 'Woman Across Time: Sister Judith Remembers', *Colby Quarterly* March 1991; (27)1: 17-26.

2. Although I have not focused on it here, part of Grainne's supposed transgressiveness as perceived by other characters is as an unconventional mother, including the suggestion (on the part of her husband and Owen Roe) that she has neglected or not sufficiently guided her son Cormac. As O'Faolain creates her, she is a wonderfully transgressive combination of the actively sexual (with Owen Roe and James Duffy) and the maternal (towards her son and Judith).

Works Cited

Doyle, Laura. (1994) *Bordering on the Body: The Racial Matrix of Modern Fiction and Culture.* New York: Oxford UP.

Feldman, Allen. (1991) *Formations of Violence: The Narrative of the Body and Political Terror in Northern Ireland.* Chicago: U of Chicago Press.

Joyce, James. (1986) *Ulysses*, ed. Hans Walter Gabler. New York: Random House.

Moore, Thomas. (1991) 'Triangles and Entrapment in Julia O'Faolain's *No Country For Young Men*'. *Colby Quarterly* 27.i: 9-16.

O'Faolain, Julia. (1987) *No Country for Young Men.* New York: Carroll & Graf.

Suleri, Sara. (1992) *The Rhetoric of English India.* Chicago: U of Chicago Press.

Vandale, Laura B. (1991) 'Woman Across Time: Sister Judith Remembers', *Colby Quarterly* 27.i: 17-26.

Weekes, Ann. (1986) 'Diarmuid and Grainne Again: Julia O'Faolain's *No Country For Young Men*', *Éire-Ireland* 21: 89-102.

FROM THE SPECTRE TO THE SPECULAR:

Imaging the Colonial Body in Post/Modern Times

Janet Harbord

This paper seeks to explicate the relation between 'racial' difference and the corporal in an historical context, in particular to focus the question through a reading of modern and postmodern frameworks. Two questions in particular inform the paper which are worth setting out here. First, is it a modernist sensibility that informs the present readings of cultural difference and the body, or does the postmodern signify a shift in understanding? And second, what particular significance does the body have in the imaging and understanding of cultural difference? As the form of this paper imposes limits on the detail of the answers, the intention here is to draw some continuities between modernism and postmodernism, and to argue that the history of bodies is crucial to understanding notions of cultural and 'racial' difference today.

Post/modern 'Others'

While she was being massaged she told me only that the children's governess had brought her an ethnographic atlas and that some of the pictures in it of American Indians dressed up as animals had given her a great shock. "Only think, if they came to life!" (Freud, *Studies on Hysteria*, 1893, 109-10).

Here, in the emerging moments of the period that has become known as modernism, two types of bodies are the focus of the analyst's attention: the body of the hysteric and, within the hysteric's discourse, the bodies of American Indians. The task of the analyst is to bring the white European female body back into the disciplined confines of European thought to harness it to reason, to produce the effective subjugation of the corporal. This was of course what psychoanalytic practice was to achieve, a shoring up of the fragile divisions produced over many centuries in European culture. But what is significant about this particular moment in Freud's *Studies on Hysteria* is that the cost of this division is made to signify; the American Indians precisely must not come to life, but remain within the static confines of the image, fixed and life-less, signs marking the distance between civilization and its 'primitive' counter-parts.

Psychoanalysis was to become known as the theory of the unconscious and, later through Lacan's work, sexual difference, but the notion of 'race' as a structuring principle operating within the discourse of the meanings of bodies was to become a less publicized principle in this duration. Interestingly, the connection that Frau Emmy made between her own body and racial difference provides an historical framework for psychoanalysis and unconscious processes, a subject that has all too often been charged with a universal ahistoricism. To say that the emergence of racial otherness in the (imperial) discourse of hysteria is the return of the (colonial) repressed is perhaps a useful, if simple, paradigm. What is more significant is the way that the notion of 'race' emerges out of a European conceptualization of the corporal. This is the Cartesian tradition of philosophy that divides the mind from the body, the abstract from the corporal, and places one term as the dominant, positioning our bodies as the inferior part of our (divided) selves. In other words, the body itself is othered in the tradition of European discourse that has privileged the abstract as the force of reason, rationality. It is precisely this division of body from mind that has facilitated the reading of other types of bodies as inferior. Bodies in general become the subservient term of a binary, made docile to the rational mind, and are then arranged in a hierarchy.

Moreover, another binary opposition, of culture/nature, contributed to the paradigm of reading bodies as racialized. If all bodies are nature to the mind's culture, then all bodies need harnessing, controlling, ordering in the same way that nature is harnessed by 'civilization'. Given that the white European body had, at the turn of the century and through the regimes of Victorian propriety in particular, been made docile through practices of clothing and behavioural policing, other bodies, particularly bodies on display in public spaces, like the images of the red Indians, were signs of a primitive, chaotic culture. The body then played a significant part in the history of imperialism, providing a rationale for colonial reform 'abroad', returning to the centre of modernist Europe as an abject spectacle erupting in the discourse of the hysteric.

Whilst I would agree with Stuart Hall's comments, in the interview 'On postmodernism and articulation', that there is no clear distinction that separates modernism and the postmodern but rather a combination of ruptures and continuities, this paper uses these terms in order to talk about change, to historicize discourses of 'race'. I argue here that certain notions of the 'other' in contemporary critical discourse paradoxically reinvoke, or keep in play, many of the modernist oppositions outlined above. The othering of 'the other' in postmodern discourse, which ostensibly practices a deconstruction of the structures of difference, ironically often has the effect of making this difference concrete. As Diana Fuss argues in a recent essay on the politics of identification, there are limits to the usage of the term 'other': 'To invoke "the Other" as an ontological or existential category paradoxically risks eliding the very range and play of cultural differences that the designation is intended to represent' (Fuss 1995). In an argument that claims the need to historicize identifications, she returns to the work of Frantz Fanon to reconstruct a notion of alterity and difference, citing Fanon's critique of the term 'otherness'. For Fanon, according to Fuss, the discourse of otherness fails on two counts, first because it lacks historical specificity which registers how others are in fact different from each other. Second, it does not acknowledge that the dialectic of the binary is located (originates from) the economy of the same, meaning that both parts of the dialectic are constructed in and through the colonial subject. Nowhere has this become more apparent than in the discipline of anthropology, where an interplay of self-other has problematized the foundations of the discipline, the study of cultural difference, and brought the disciplines of anthropology and cultural studies into congruence.

The impact of this insight, and of poststructuralism generally, on the discipline of anthropology is evidenced in several ways which have been addressed in the work of James Clifford (1988), Paul Rabinow (1977) and Marie Louise Pratt (1986). Clifford in particular is influenced by poststructuralist accounts of language, and in *Writing Culture*, provides a convincing account of the way in which the cultural and linguistic structures that precede each of us determine what we speak, and indeed become. In other words, we are already 'spoken' when we enter language as subjects. The positions are already determined, including, importantly, the positions of the colonial encounter. This produces the seeming paradox for anthropology that in order to discover 'difference', we need to have a notion of what it is in order to recognize it. Clifford's point is that no encounter is an origin, a new day or horizon, but the accumulative text of all previous encounters.

This has broader implications for the acquisition of knowledge more generally, for it discredits the practice of anthropological fieldwork as nothing more than the projection of our own desires and meanings onto the 'native' subject; in other words, anthropology performs a type of mirroring. For Clifford, the discrediting of fieldwork as 'objective evidence' is tied to the broader collapse of science as a legitimate narrative, a collapse described initially by Lyotard in his *Report on the Condition of Knowledge* (in Lyotard 1984). According to Clifford, the legitimacy of the anthropological account was historically derived from aligning two contradictory accounts. First, the experiential account of fieldwork, a description authenticated through the presence and immediacy of the encounter. Second, the suppression of the presence of the writer-as-observer in the translation of experience into knowledge, or from ontology to epistemology. Thus, the subjective is erased by the claims to objectivity in the final account.

But there is another act of translation, and a transition, that takes place in the anthropological encounter, again noted by Clifford and also emerging in Homi Bhabha's work on the postcolonial (Bhabha 1994). This is a transition that in its first stage is concerned with noting ethnic/racial difference, the 'shock' encounter of the anthropologist and the indigenous subject. This encounter qualifies the practice of anthropology as the investigation and annotation of cultural differences; thus, the greater the differences 'found', the better, as a justification of the expedition. The second stage, however, recuperates the 'other' from the object of enquiry to the subject through a process of discovering similarity, or 'they really are like us after all' which, Clifford notes, closes many anthropological narratives. In particular Clifford critiques the work of feminist anthropologists whose fieldwork exemplifies this staging of objectification and subsequent reincorporation of the 'other' within the fold of a universal humanism. This humanism, which focuses on the common plight of women across cultures, is critiqued by him as masking the different balance of power underpinning the western anthropologist's position (career and economic status) against the poverty of the indigenous women ('Introduction: Partial Truths' in Clifford 1986).

The implications of this transition, which depends on a reversal of identification practices, are drawn out in Bhabha's work where this process of noting difference and sameness is reconfigured as a double demand made (historically) by the colonial master, to simultaneously be and not be 'like me'.[1] It signifies the disjunction between identification as an imaginary act which can seemingly 'overcome' differences, and the location of difference physically, as a barrier to this identification. In other words, the corporal enters the symbolic in a way that erases the imaginary. The black subject can 'pretend' to be white, and this is what is demanded by the colonial master, yet his/her difference will always be read off the surface of his/her body. Bhabha, however, uses the trope of mimicry to signify the instability of this demand, mimicry being a practice that can be read in (at least) two ways, as either a mimicry of subversion or a mimicry of subjugation. The elusiveness of the act leaves the question open: is imitation mockery of another, or conversely identification with them? The value of mimicry for Bhabha is the degree to which the practice remains open, ambivalent, sliding somewhere along the scale of acquiescence and ridicule. He contends that the double signification of the body, 'dressed' as white but retaining the mark (colour) of 'racial' difference, is able to destabilize white identity both ways round.

The significance of Bhabha's work on mimicry has been that its concern is not with the way in which imperialism produces the 'other', but with how 'other' subjects destabilize the terms of that production. Bhabha's work provides the account with a notion of agency on the part of the colonized subject, a notion that Clifford's work shares. Both of these accounts intervene and challenge the use of the dialectic self/other in academic discourse as a complacent binary that effectively contains all cultural difference under one sign. This containment also alleviates the anxiety around difference, in that the recognition of the dialectic itself produces a conclusion. Certainly in postmodern critical discourse this 'othering' has been both descriptive and proscriptive, keeping the simplistic duality in place rather than opening up the plurality of differences and recognising agency on the part of others. This has been the consequence of focusing somewhat exclusively on the process of othering (which remains historically and geographically unspecified), rather than unpacking that term.

The summative affect of postmodern critical attention has then reinstated the modernist dialectic of self/other through the recognition that there can be no knowledge of difference which is not circumscribed by what we already know. This takes us back to the anthropologist's dilemma of how to speak of ethnic difference without merely reproducing the self's own fantasies of that difference. What I am arguing is that this postmodern reflexivity concerning the practice of 'othering' unwittingly reinscribes it through an emphasis on the temporal to the exclusion of the spatial and the geographic. This reflexive account of the present suggests that postmodernism has impacted on 'the west' in a homogenous way, and conversely that 'the third world' has largely remained outside of this.[2] The binary remains in place. According to postmodernists such as Jameson (1985), only recently have the effects of modernity trespassed on the 'primitive' sites of other cultures (he describes the third world as the last bastion of a pre-multinational conquest). In opposition to this, Appiah argues that postmodernists demand of Africans what modernism did, that is, a 'primitive authenticity' passively awaiting multinational domination (Appiah 1993). For him, the binaristic thinking that characterized modernity continues in the present formulations of a homogenous west versus a unified Africa. Like Clifford, he suggests that there are no pockets of authenticity, but an infinite range of cultural relations characterized by dynamic histories of importation and exportation, effecting forms of cultural translation that are never simply characterized by inscriber/ inscribed.

In/Authentic Bodies

The body as the site of authenticity then continues to present a focus for these debates on how we understand cultural difference in postmodern times. Bodies carry that weight of 'the natural' versus the rational, and indeed part of the recent trend in Britain of tattooing, scarification and piercing might be regarded as the transgressing of this binary; through these practices the body does not just perform in the transient sense of dressing up, but rather the body (nature) is actively inscribed and made to signify through culture.[3] The nature/culture divide is troubled through this practice. In the second part of this paper I want to turn to a photographic image that suggests a similar re-inscription of a 'primitive' (Brazilian) body which transgresses the binary of post/modernist thought. It is not only the image that is of interest in this discussion, but the contexts of its circulation.

The photograph, 'Adrianna, Transvestite, Brazil', taken by Polly Borland, is an image of a transvestite standing naked, facing the camera, located in what appears (from the sparse interior) to be a hotel room. Adrianna has bleached blond hair and is wearing make-up, and, having hidden the penis from view, appears inititially (at first glance) to be female. The photograph appeared first in the *Independent on Sunday's Review* section, having won the John Kobal Portrait Award, a prize sponsored in part by the newspaper. It was then featured in an exhibition of the portrait award winners at the National Portrait Gallery, London, and reproduced in an exhibition catalogue. The editorial comment suggested that the common theme of the entries for that year (1994) had been the problematic of sex/gender identity.

Two weeks later the image appeared in the *Independent on Sunday* again, this time in a feature on multinational companies selling silicon to Brazilian transvestites who wished to transform (feminise) their bodies. The feature was an exposé of multinational exploitation, disclosing that the silicon had adverse effects, leaving bodies ill-shaped and pock-marked. The editorial and photography represented the story as one of western domination of indigenous, 'primitive' peoples. Whilst this piece of documentary journalism effectively 'uncovers' a story, the focus of the critique is so generalized by its referent, 'multinationals', that it compounds the reported sense of non-agency. If, in other words, multinationals are at once everywhere and nowhere in particular, there can be no response. The critique of multinationals as the agent of exploitation is then far safer than a critique of their predecessor, the nation-state; the latter was at least locatable. A critique of multinationals cannot target the source of exploitation, distancing the subject from any sense of responsibility.

The image interests me particularly for the way in which the circumstances of its circulation testify to a complex range of relations with Brazilian culture that are potentially both binaristic and also more complex than this. The most obvious of these is perhaps the primitivist relation, which establishes Adrianna as the 'native' body corrupted through its dealings with 'civilization', which the newspaper report might suggest. This would be substantiated by the notion of the image of Brazilian transvestism as 'primitive art', part of the western fantasy of racial and sexual excess. Yet these readings suggest a certain ease and simplicity with which the text can be categorized, placed on one side of a dividing line, as 'bad' (primitivist) representation, effectively 'othered'. What this image might also suggest is a culture in which sexuality figures in a complex way, where perhaps gender norms and sexual practices have a greater degree of variance than in Britain, one of the contexts of the image's circulation. What the image certainly does suggest, through the use of bleached hair (a western signifier? American starlet?) and transforming body shape, is that the idea of a racial 'essence' is not appropriate here; multinationals may have provided exploitative chemicals, but the desire to transform the 'natural' body, to complexify gender signification across the body, pre-existed this particular encounter. What the image might suggest in a different reading context is the notion of cultural hybridity, a mixing of signs of 'race' and gender as styles, evidence precisely of the history of cultural importation-exportation referred to by Clifford.

Images, of course, do not essentially mean anything; rather their interpretation depends on the circumstances of production, circulation and consumption. 'Adrianna' testifies to the range of interpretations that can befall an image, signifying anything from multinational exploitation to a celebratory hybridity. But this is not the point. The point here is precisely that academic contexts of interpretation can be just as prescriptive and regressive as any other contexts. Postmodernism in particular, through collapsing the legitimacy of knowledge, has perpetuated a complacency in its theorization of difference as self/other. This readily supplies a frame-work, the same framework, of interpretation for all cultural encounters.

This also reproduces the earlier modernist sense of absolute differences that remain polarized, unable to read each other except through their own fantasies of difference. Whilst fantasy has a significant part to play in reading cultural difference, I want to suggest that the dynamics of exchange, of the indigenization of global effects, or the making local of broader events, needs greater critical attention. If the local/global is to replace the model of cultural imperialism as a way of understanding a range of relationships between groups of varying power and capital, then the understanding of the local needs to be developed further. As Doreen Massey has pointed out (1991; 1992), it is not appropriate to think of the imposition of one culture on the bounded space of another; rather we need to think of local identities which are variously constructed out of resources which may not be 'local' in origin, but are reconfigured in this space. In this framework, the notion of 'origin', either as the root of an imposing power, or as a local 'authentic' culture, is challenged.

The body, I would argue, has a specific place in the history of the debate about cultural imperialism. For the body, as I have noted above, has served as a key term and object in European modernist thought; indeed, Turner (1992) has gone as far as describing the history of the West as 'not so much a transformation of culture under the impact of rationality as the transformation of the human body'. The somewhat generalized category of 'the body' has become a subject of great interest in recent Cultural Studies debates, but it is only a white western body that is seemingly capable of transgressing the categories of nature/culture. The discourses of nomadic cyborgs abound in the landscape of the postmodern, but the transformation of these particular (white) bodies is associated with the technological proficiency of the west, albeit an expertise leading to an apocalyptic end.[4] This Eurocentric notion of the transformative body needs to be challenged. In a way the image of Adrianna can be seen to do exactly that, to suggest the plasticity of the (other) body, capable of transformation, reinscription, reconfiguration not at the hands of an imperial power, but at the nexus of a web of discourses and influences that travel in both directions, inwards and outwards.

Otherwise one of the most distinctive continuities between modernism and postmodernism will be the reproduction of the notion of alterity, of cultural difference as absolute. As Suleri has noted (1992), the theoretical reiteration of the self/other binary also entrenches these positions in a 'fallacy of the totality of otherness'. Only if 'cultural difference' in all of its manifestations is allowed to 'come to life', for subjects to emerge as agents, to exist in localities that are at once different from one another and also connected diversely to the global, only then will Frau Emmy's Indians leap out of the European atlas book that has mapped them for so long.

Notes

1. See Bhabha's accounts of an ambivalence at the heart of colonial identification processes (1985, 1986).
2. For a discussion of the effects of a global postmodern mapping, see Gayatri Spivak (1987).

3. For interesting coverage of these practices see V. Val and Andrea Juno (1989).
4. Whilst technology has provided an escape from essentialism for feminism, the implications of bodies radically reconfigured have not been worked through so convincingly in relation to 'race'. Donna Haraway's work (1989) is perhaps the most interesting explication of this, for example.

Works Cited

Appadurai, A. (1988) 'Putting Hierarchy in its place', *Cultural Anthropology* 3.i: 36-49.

Appiah, K.A. (1993) *In My Father's House: What Does it Mean to Be an African Today?* London: Methuen.

Bhabha, Homi K. (1985) 'Sly Civility', *October* 34.

Bhabha, Homi K. (1986) 'Of Mimicry and Man: The Ambivalence of Colonial Discourse', in James Donald and Stuart Hall, eds. *Politics and Ideology*. Milton Keynes: Open University Press.

Bhabha, Homi K. (1994) *The Location of Culture*. London & New York: Routledge.

Clifford, James & George E. Marcus, eds. (1986) *Writing Culture: the Poetics and Politics of Ethnography*. Berkeley: University of California Press.

Clifford, James. (1988) *The Predicament of Culture: Twentieth Century Ethnography, Literature and Art*. Cambridge, Mass.: Harvard UP.

Freud, Sigmund. (1893) 'Studies on Hysteria', in A. Richards, ed. *Pelican Freud Library 3* (trans. J. Strachey and A. Strachey). Harmondsworth: Penguin, 1974.

Freud, Sigmund & Joseph Breuer. (1895) *Studies on Hysteria*. New York: Avon, 1956.

Fuss, Diana. (1995) *Identification Papers: Readings on Psychoanalysis, Sexuality and Culture*. New York and London: Routledge.

Hall, Stuart and Martin Jacques, eds. (1989) *New Times: The Changing Face of Politics in the 1990s*. London: Lawrence & Wishart.

Hall, Stuart. (1996) 'On postmodernism and articulation: An Interview with Stuart Hall', ed. Lawrence Grossberg, in *Stuart Hall: Critical Dialogues in Cultural Studies*, eds. David Morley and Kuan-Hsing Chen. London and New York: Routledge: 131-50.

Haraway, Donna. (1989) *Primate Visions: Gender, Race and Nature in the World of Modern Science*. New York: Routledge.

Jameson, Frederic. (1984) 'Postmodernism, or the cultural logic of late capitalism', *New Left Review* 146: 53-92.

Lyotard, Jean Francois. (1984) *The Postmodern Condition*, trans. Geoff Bennington and Brian Massumi. Manchester: Manchester UP.

Massey, Doreen. (1991) 'A Global Sense of Place', *Marxism Today*.

Massey, Doreen. (1992) 'A Place Called Home', *New Formations* 17.

Pratt, Mary Louise. (1986) 'Fieldwork in Common Places', in James Clifford and George E. Marcus, eds. *Writing Culture: The Poetics and Politics of Ethnography*. Berkeley, California: University of California Press.

Rabinow, Paul. (1977) *Reflections on Fieldwork in Morocco.* Berkeley, California: University of California Press.

Spivak, Gayatri. (1987) *In Other Worlds: Essays in Cultural Politics.* London: Methuen.

Suleri, Sara. (1992) *Meatless Days.* Chicago: University of Chicago Press.

Turner, Bryan S. (1992) *Regulating Bodies: Essays in Medical Sociology.* London and New York: Routledge.

Val, V. and Andrea Juno, eds. (1989) *Research: Modern Primitives.* Hong Kong: Research Publications.

FRAMING THE MEXICAN BODY

Andrea Noble

A 1993 article in *Vogue* magazine tells the story of how the Museum of Modern Art in New York came to be in receipt of a series of prints by the Italian-American photographer Tina Modotti:[1] 'In the early fifties…a man appeared at the front desk, put a large brown paper parcel on it, declared that he wished to give this 'anonymous gift' to the institution—and rushed out of the building' (Cunliffe 210). I am interested in this anecdote for a number of reasons. The historical moment of the donation of the parcel containing the prints is of vital importance here. I would suggest that, at this particular juncture in the 1950s, the Modotti prints were not concealed inside the brown paper parcel because of their subject matter, because of what they depicted. Sarah M. Lowe's *Tina Modotti: Photographs* offers a representative selection of those images included in the anonymous donation; significantly, none of Modotti's so-called sloganistic and overtly Communist photographs, such as the 1927 *Hammer and Sickle*, appears to have formed part of the parcel. Instead, what was at stake was the signature inscribed on the surface of the prints. To be found in possession of a 'Modotti', that is to say, a photograph signed by a card-carrying Communist at the height of McCarthyism in the USA, posed a potential danger. Hence the anonymous donation. The trace of the signature 'Tina Modotti', on the surface of the prints, ultimately leads back to the inscribing body. The containment of the Modotti prints within the parcel, therefore, represents a brief and significant moment of disembodiment. The prints become detached from the body that produced them in order to sever their link with another body, that of the donor.

However, the image of the anonymous donation does not only raise issues around bodies and signatures. It also has further resonances which depend upon the fact that the anonymous donation is essentially an act of disavowal. The donor's actions are motivated by the need to deny his connection with some element of the parcel in his possession: the signature/body. Disavowal, of course, is central to a particular concept of fetishism. My aim in this essay is to explore Modotti's *Roses* in the light of the issues of signature and bodies outlined above which, in turn, can be theorized through an understanding of two concepts of fetishism. The first is a Marxian notion of commodity fetishism which accounts for the way in which, under capitalism, objects become invested with economic value in a system of circulation and exchange;[2] and the second is a Freudian notion of

195

psychic fetishism which accounts for the way in which objects become invested with sexual value, in a process whereby the fetish-object comes to stand in for the female genitalia in a gesture that basically bespeaks castration anxiety.[3]

As Naomi Shor points out, the association between the two concepts of fetishism is nothing new:

> The convergence of Freud's theorization of psychic fetishism with Marx's theory of commodity fetishism in the nineteenth century points up the historicity of the concept and the phenomenon, both of which seem bound up with the history of capitalism in its ascending and triumphant phases (116).

This essay, however, will focus specifically on the association of these dual concepts of fetishism as they are played out both within and beyond the physical frame of Modotti's photograph Roses. This particular photograph, and the events that took place at the time of its sale in 1991, are prime sites for an understanding of the workings of commodity fetishism. This is because, without an intrinsic use-value, the photograph and the signature etched on its surface were to be injected with economic exchange-value through a set of complex cultural processes. These processes will be the subject of the first section of the essay. In the second section, in which I develop a reading of *Roses*, I shall argue that a notion of psychic fetishism is a key element for a formal analysis of the photograph. *Roses* is a photograph that effectively plays on and ultimately subverts the kind of psychic dramas that are perpetually reenacted within conventional images of the female body.

I

Some forty years after the clandestine donation of the prints in the 1950s, Modotti's *Roses* fetched the (then) record sum of $165,000 at auction at Sotheby's, New York. In what follows, I will trace the way in which this particular Modotti photograph becomes marked with the invisible inscription of value within capitalist culture. I will draw especially on Laura Mulvey's recent analysis of commodity fetishism, where she states:

> Fetishism of the commodity…is a political symptom particular to capitalism and those societies that come under its sway. Commodity fetishism also bears witness to the persistent allure that images and things have for the human imagination and the pleasure to be gained from belief in phantasmagorias and imaginary systems of

representation. Objects and images, in their spectacular manifestations, are central to the process of disavowal, soaking up semiotic significance and setting up elisions of affect. Most of all, they are easily sexualised (Mulvey 1996, 5).

Mulvey's notion of the easy sexualization of objects and images within a Capitalist system of circulation and exchange, and the way in which this sexualization adds to the allure and therefore value of the commodity, will be particularly crucial to my argument. If, earlier, I emphasized a moment of disembodiment in the trajectory of a number of Modotti's photographic prints, it is because it is atypical. Modotti, I will now contend, has come to represent the iconic female body which has been manifestly eroticized and exoticized. Indeed, the iconic body is a key factor in the record sum fetched by *Roses*.

Despite the fact that the body is (apparently) not represented within the frame of the photograph, I want to trace the links between the female body and the inflated commodity value of *Roses*. Focusing on the literature and events surrounding the 1991 sale of *Roses*, and the cultural conditions under which the image was produced in 1920s Mexico, I will argue not only that Modotti's body is a key factor in the record sum fetched by *Roses*, but that this body has been codified as specifically Mexican and Communist. Modotti's sexualized body now circulates as a commodity in a marketplace that ascribes value to images made by 'exotic' women in 'exotic' locations. Furthermore, I will argue that the process of commodification which Modotti's Mexican body has undergone is a form of colonization which makes it difficult to plot either Modotti or Mexico onto the cultural map as anything but paradigms of exotic Otherness.

It is unlikely that the anonymous donor of the Modotti prints to the Museum of Modern Art will ever be identified. The identity of the current owner of *Roses*, however, is well and truly in the public domain. The image was purchased by the San Francisco based Suzie Tomkins:

> [She] gained business fame as the spirit behind Esprit sportswear, but her claim to photographic glory was her...acquisition of Tina Modotti's blockbuster photo, Roses, Mexico. Now Tomkins is combining her art with her commerce: She's reproducing the Modotti image (albeit sideways) on the handtags of her Suzie Tomkins line of clothing (Squiers 16).

Tomkins's interest in *Roses* is based only indirectly on the image itself. She purchases the image, I would suggest, because of the symbolic associations that the signature 'Modotti' evokes. There are two factors worth underlining as far as the symbolic associations of Modotti's signature for Tomkins are concerned. First, Modotti was a woman photographer and, second, she was politically radical. It is important to note that not only is Tomkins a successful business woman, she also considers herself something of a connoisseur of art. These two activities, of course, are not unrelated. Tomkins was looking to invest in a signature whose cultural capital would complement her own status as a woman entrepreneur (i.e. she, like Modotti, is a woman who operates in a man's world). She is attracted to Modotti's signature because, through its Mexican and Communist associations, it has come to represent the ultimate in radical chic—glamorous, gutsy, exotic, sexy and with just a hint of danger. However, these attributes have little to do with any photograph that Modotti might have made. Instead, these attributes are predicated on Modotti's status as an iconic body.

It is likely that, on making her purchase, Tomkins would have been aware of Modotti's role as the model and muse of the North-American photographer, Edward Weston. It is in Weston's photographic images of her that Modotti's body assumes its iconic status. His series of images, *Tina on the Azotea*, precedes any photograph that Modotti herself made.[4] And it is Weston's photograph that is responsible for another factor that contributes to the elevated commodity value of *Roses*. That factor is evoked in the title of Modotti's *Roses*, which significantly, in the Sotheby's catalogue, gains the appendage, *Mexico*.[5] Despite the fact that Modotti was Italian-American there has been a great deal of emphasis placed on the Mexican context. This is due, not so much to the fact that Modotti produced the bulk of her photographs in Mexico—a country in which she lived from 1923 until 1930—as to the prior location of her body as a Mexican object in Weston's *Azotea* series.[6] This objectification functions on two levels. Firstly, on the level of the visual sign, although the nude is a trope borrowed from a painterly tradition, what distinguishes the photographic representation of the nude from that tradition is what Abigail Solomon-Godeau terms 'photography's ostensible purchase on the real' (249). Weston's image functions as an apparently transparent representation of Modotti's body which is located within a specifically Mexican context, as the Spanish word *Azotea* (or rooftop) within the English title indicates. It is this conjunction of image and text that leads to the objectification of Modotti's Mexican body. Secondly, this photograph of Modotti-as-Mexican-Body exists alongside a series of other images of Mexican objects, such as the *pulquerías* and toys that so fascinated Weston during his fabled stay in Mexico. Modotti's Mexican status, therefore, has nothing to do with any sense of a 'real' national identity, but is predicated on having been photographed as a Mexican object. Furthermore, her objectification as Mexican is ultimately a question of bodily identity.

That Tomkins's investment in the signature 'Modotti' hinges on its bodily and Mexican connotations is confirmed by the events surrounding the sale of *Roses*. On the successful purchase of *Roses*, Tomkins's 'photographic consultant', Merrily Page, delivered a press communiqué in which she revealed the identity of the other bidders for the image, including the pop icon Madonna. Page exultantly declared that she understood that Madonna was bidding for the image because she 'had an intense interest in feisty women' (Squiers 16). Madonna's drive to possess *Roses* is significant on a number of counts, and underscores the way in which the codified body figures at the centre of a complex promotional web. Firstly, as a popular artist working within the global public arena, Madonna herself 'has come to represent the perfect post-modern body in both theoretical and popular discourse' (Schwichtenberg 10). Both women signify the body in what is effectively a two-way interchange, insofar as Modotti's signature is replete with cultural capital for Madonna, just as the conjunction of Madonna's and Modotti's is for Suzie Tomkins. Secondly, Madonna is believed to have an interest *not* in the *images* made by 'feisty' women, but in the 'feisty' women themselves, where 'feisty' connotes a particular kind of sexual/sexy female body.

Modotti, like Madonna, was Italian-American. Yet this link is nowhere made evident. Madonna's interest in feisty Mexican women, however, is well-documented. She is said to own a number of paintings by the Mexican painter Frida Kahlo and 'to have purchased the rights to the artist's life-story' (Franco 226). During the sale of *Roses*, the Mexican context becomes a key selling-point, as is borne out in the short fragment of text that appears below the reproduction of *Roses* in the Sotheby's catalogue:

In 1926 Diego Rivera captured the essence of Modotti's work in the following words: 'Tina Modotti has done marvels in sensibility on a plane, perhaps more abstract, more aerial, even more intellectual, as is natural for an Italian temperament. Her work flowers perfectly in Mexico and harmonizes with our passion'.

The quotation selected for the catalogue entry significantly omits any mention of Modotti's North-American connections, either in the form of her immigration from Italy to California in 1913 or in the form of the influence of her teacher, Edward Weston. On one level, the exclusion of

Weston might appear liberating: his presence problematizes any critical approach to Modotti's photographs informed by feminist theories of representation. However, the argument that Weston's exclusion from the catalogue is the outcome of some sort of feminist strategy is difficult to sustain—although feminism in the guise of radical chic does have something to do with the sale price. This, after all, is the world of dealers and speculation. There is more at stake in the exclusion. On the one hand, the Rivera quotation *does* acknowledge Modotti's Italian roots. But on the other, the catalogue entry prioritizes her location within a specifically Mexican cultural context, both in terms of its content and also in terms of what Rivera himself represents. Rivera's voice functions as another signifier in the chain of celebrity endorsements surrounding the image and its sale. For the kind of consumer who would frequent Sotheby's sales, Rivera would be a household name with specific connotations of 'Mexicanness'. In turn, 'Mexicanness' would be imbued with a particular set of cultural and historical associations for this consumer.

In *Raiding the Icebox*, Peter Wollen states: 'the Mexican Renaissance [in the 1920s] is the one recent Third World art movement that has had a significant impact on the metropolis' (194). This impact was felt particularly in the USA. All three of the major proponents of muralism, Diego Rivera, José Clemente Orozco and David Alfaro Siqueiros, travelled north to paint in the USA, where California represented a specific point of entry. Furthermore, it should noted that California, until relatively recently, *was* Mexico: California, New Mexico, Arizona and Texas were 'sold' to the United States in 1848 under the Treaty of Guadalupe Hidalgo. California is also home-base to Suzie Tomkins's international company, Esprit.

The invocation of an historically-specific and implicitly romanticized notion of 'Mexicanness', embodied in the figure of Rivera himself, is coupled with the Muralist's words, which feed into the worst kind of stereotypes of Mexican exoticism: 'Modotti's work flowers perfectly and harmonizes with our passion'. And, above the quotation, the photograph seems literally to illustrate this flowering passion. The catalogue entry, therefore, promotes the notion of Mexico as a mythical and exotic space. It omits to mention Modotti's significant collaboration with Edward Weston. It aligns her, instead, with the Mexican Rivera, because in an economy of desire, his 'Otherness' as opposed to Weston's 'Self' is simply more valuable. Ironically, California today is also home to a sizeable Mexican-American community and 'Mexicaness' is loaded with negative connotations. However, Rivera belongs comfortably to a distant past. He belongs to an era when Mexico existed in the popular imagination as a glamorous playground where North Americans, Weston amongst many others, could find themselves in confrontation with the 'Other'.

Just as the Mexican context inhabited by Modotti and Rivera exists at a sufficiently safe distance in the past to be glamorous, so too does another factor they share in common and which would be tacitly understood by Sotheby's clientele. Both were committed Communists. But there is a fundamental difference in how the political activity of both is interpreted. Whereas Rivera is constructed as an artist whose radical ideals are manifest in the murals he painted across Mexico and the USA, Modotti's status as a Communist is interpreted in terms of the sexual relationships that she had with prominent Communist men, amongst them, it was rumoured, Diego Rivera.

This association between Modotti's Communist lovers and her political convictions is made emphatically by the Mexican poet and Nobel prize winner Octavio Paz. In 1983, a major retrospective of the work of Tina Modotti and Frida Kahlo went on show at the Museo Nacional de Arte, Mexico City. The exhibition was conceived of and curated by the British critics Laura Mulvey and Peter Wollen, and had originally opened at the Whitechapel Gallery in London earlier that same year. The exhibition was accompanied by a catalogue, including an essay by Mulvey and Wollen in which they reconsidered the work of Kahlo and Modotti in the light of developments in feminist visual theory.[7] The exhibition and its accompanying essay were effectively to relaunch Kahlo and Modotti, and to spark both critical and commercial interest in the two women. In response to the exhibition's overtly feminist agenda, during its showing in Mexico City, Octavio Paz published an article in the influential cultural magazine *Vuelta*, in which he stated:

[E]n algo se parecen Frida y Tina: ninguna de las dos tuvo pensamiento político propio. Al seguir una causa, siguieron a sus maridos y amantes. Nos interesan no como militantes sino como personas complejas y pasionales. Sus figuras pertenecen más a la historia de las pasiones que a la de las ideologías (48).

Frida and Tina do have something in common: neither of them had their own political thought. By following a cause they simply followed their husbands and lovers. They do not interest us as militants but as complex and passionate people. They belong more to the history of passion than to the history of ideology [translation mine].

201

Although I would most certainly not endorse Octavio Paz's point, he is not entirely wrong. Despite Modotti's overtly Communist images such as *Hammer and Sickle*, despite her involvement in organisations such as International Red Aid, she *does* belong more to the history of 'passion'. But this is because critics like Paz choose to consign her to that place, conflating the ideological with the bodily, thereby denying Modotti any political agency whatsoever. Positioned as it is within the safe space of a by-gone age; ironically, Modotti's Communist body circulates in the post-cold-war era as a commodity in a market in which it signifies the ultimate in radical chic. Commenting on the political dimension of the sale of *Roses* and its latter-day location on Tomkins's handtags, Sotheby's photography expert Beth Gates-Warren is quoted as saying: 'Tina Modotti, who was a communist, would probably have loved it—everyone will have access to the image now' (Squiers 16).

Yet she could not have been further from the truth. The sale of *Roses* represents a moment at which the signature 'Modotti' becomes excessively over-determined with bodily connotations and the image itself becomes elided. By investing in Modotti's signature, Tomkins was investing in an iconic body to promote herself and thereby enhance the saleability of her products. Modotti's body becomes a site at which a number of key signatures converge: Modotti's, Madonna's and Rivera's. These signatures in turn become appended to Tomkins's own signature. This is graphically illustrated by the handtag on which the image comes to function as a logotype for Tomkins's company. *Roses* occupies the top quarter of the handtag, on which it appears sideways. Below the image there is a brief section of typewritten text by Tomkins herself in which she explains the premise of her collection. Below the text the bottom quarter of the handtag is occupied by the flamboyant signature 'Susie Tomkins'. It is perhaps a sign of the times that once the body/signature had served its purpose Suzie Tomkins simply discarded it. She is quoted in *Vogue*: 'actually, we don't credit the picture which we're using as icon material. Though we use big blow-ups of it in the shops, we're not celebrating Tina Modotti' (Cunliffe 275).

The erasure of the signature at this point in the 1990s represents a second moment of disembodiment, mirroring that other moment back in the 1950s with which I opened this essay. The signature and the very real danger that it represented in the 50s, I would suggest, has been co-opted by the fashion industry and its charge of danger has been defused. The processes of commodity fetishism, whereby *Roses* becomes inscribed with the mark of value through the over-determination of the sexualized female body, have had serious implications for an understanding of the image. Once commodified and in the marketplace, *Roses* loses its significance as a cultural statement. However, beyond recapitulating and thereby to some degree exposing the processes and consequences of commodity fetishism, what more can be done to reappropriate Modotti's photograph and reinfuse it with cultural meaning?

II

Having described a range of paradoxes underpinning the sale of Modotti's *Roses* which have proscribed readings of the photograph, I propose now to re-evaluate the photograph, taking my cue from the feminist art historian Griselda Pollock, who has stated that in 'a visual system which recruits the image of woman as a fixed object …feminine desire will figure itself or find forms of representation as that which exceeds fixing, picturing, framing, containing, objectifying' (130). What especially interests me about Pollock's formulation is this notion of exceeding the frame, because *Roses* is precisely an image which pushes issues of framing and excess to the fore.

In terms of the formal composition of Modotti's image, the focus is on the irregular curved shapes of the arrangement of the rose petals that saturate the photographic frame. However, what at first sight seems to be an image about irregularity is in fact organized around strictly geometrical principles. The right-hand corner is occupied by the largest, most open rose, thereby creating an off-centre centre. This central rose is framed above and to the left by three smaller and less open roses. The bottom right-hand corner forms a square which is encased neatly by the inverted L-shape composed of the three surrounding roses. The image, therefore, is full of frames within frames. However, if a frame is that which separates inside from outside, then this image is also full of transgressed frames: the irregular, round shapes of the petals overspill the straight horizontal and vertical lines within the main frame which, in turn, is transgressed. The petals overspill the edges of the photographic frame. What are we to make of these transgressed frames within frames? Just how significant the 'discourse of the frame' is becomes apparent when we consider it: first, in the light of the viewer's relationship with the image; second, in terms of the subject matter itself; and third, as a specifically photographic representation of its subject matter.

In an article on feminism and photography theory, Lindsay Smith describes the way in which geometrical perspective 'assumes an established linear relationship between a vantage-point (the eye of the subject looking) and the vanishing-point (the culmination of the look upon an object) according to the eventual convergence of lines of geometral projection' (238). The linear relationship between viewer and image is established partly by perspective, and partly by the frame. The frame is that which instructs the viewer how to position himself (*sic*) in relationship to the image. *Roses* is, therefore, an image that lacks clear instructions as to the viewer's positionality. The image at once acknowledges a straightforward relationship between the viewer and the image through its play on the notion of framing. At the same time, this relationship is problematized, through the way in which frames within the image are constantly transgressed.

The relationship between the viewer and the photograph becomes even more complex when we address the question of subject matter. Lynda Nead, in her study of the female nude, explores the crucial role that the frame plays in constructing an 'acceptable' image of the female body within a visual economy grounded on the psychic need to project a flawless image of 'woman'. Nead describes the sets of values that subtend the categories of art and obscenity within this economy: 'Art is…defined in terms of the containing of form within limits; obscenity on the other hand, is defined in terms of excess, as form beyond limit, beyond the frame and representation' (20). Nead here is referring specifically to the *female* nude. By obscene, we are to understand those images of the female body that exist beyond the realm sanctioned as 'acceptable' within the prevalent visual economy, namely images that might conceivably provoke anxiety in the male viewer. Within the parameters of Nead's discussion, *Roses*, I would suggest, *is* obscene. Up until now my argument has focused on the bodily connotations surrounding Modotti's signature, despite the apparent absence of the represented body in *Roses*. Now, I would like to suggest that the body, or at least a part of it, *is* represented in the image. It is here that I would like to introduce the Freudian notion of fetishism into the discussion, for the fetish is precisely an object that stands in for that which would otherwise be considered obscene.

The bodily part to which Modotti's photograph alludes comes into focus if we read the image in conjunction with another image for which Modotti served as model. In *Temptation* (1920), by Modotti's first husband Roubaix de L'Abrie Richey, the rose figures as a familiar trope. The rose as fetish features as a recurrent motif in both art and literature which stands in for that which lies below it—which, according to Nead, lies beyond the frame of representation—the female genitalia. That the rose is such a familiar and recurrent trope indicates that what it stands in for is literally unrepresentable. In *Temptation*, the rose is contiguous to the female genitalia, which it masks, for to acknowledge what lies below the rose is to confront a potent symbol of lack. Significantly, the psychic anxiety that the sight of the genitalia would unleash in the male viewer is symbolically figured in de l'Abrie's image. In the bottom right-hand corner of the sketch, there is a skull. The skull, with its distinctive hairstyle, visually echoes the head of the female form representing the figure of Temptation. The female skull is shown devouring a snake. The Freudian connotations of the snake hardly need spelling out. In *Temptation*, a metonymical displacement takes place, from the castrating skull/mouth to the rose/cunt. However, while the anxiety that the sight/site of the genitalia would provoke is hinted at in the image, that anxiety is allayed on two levels. It does so, firstly, by replacing the genitalia by the rose and secondly, by the wholly conventional framing of the body. This is an 'acceptable' image of the female body. The framing of the body allows the viewer critical distance from which to contemplate it. This distance reinforces the viewer's objective mastery of the female form, and the rose-fetish attests to the viewer's desire to retain a belief in the phantasmagoric female phallus according to the classic formula: 'I know what lies below, but all the same...'.

Not so in Modotti's image which, by reference to de l'Abrie's sketch, plays on the notion of the rose as fetish, but sets up a radically different kind of viewing experience. *Roses* does not invoke the rose as fetish by reference to *Temptation* alone. Like many of Modotti's images, Roses is a photograph which creates a feeling of texture and tactility, inviting the viewer to touch it with the eye.[8] In particular, the frontal, saturated focus of the photograph serves to emphasize the silky, velvety texture of the petals. Velvet, it will be recalled, is the texture of fetish *par excellence*: 'the inquisitive boy peered at the woman's genitals from below, from her legs up; fur and velvet—as has long been suspected—are a fixation for the sight of the pubic hair' (Freud 155). However, whilst *Roses* plays with the conventional notion of the fetish, at the same time, it radically problematizes the experience of viewing.

Unlike *Temptation*, in *Roses*, the body that frames the genitalia is not represented. Conventionally, this body-frame would also be framed by the image's physical frame, offering the viewer double security. The stability that this double frame might have offered the viewer, is absent in *Roses*. It is, furthermore, undermined by the proliferation of frames contained within the image, as I have already outlined. As it is, bereft of the security of the frame, the viewer is left to contemplate an image saturated by roses, which represent a potent symbol of lack. This is where the importance of an understanding of the status of *Roses* as a photographic image lies. A reading of *Roses* as lack functions on two levels. Firstly, as I have argued, the roses as the subject matter of the photograph represent the female genitalia and therefore metonymically represent lack. Secondly, the proliferation of frames within frames in the photograph destabilize any kind of straight-forward relationship that the viewer might enjoy with the image. However, framing is also vitally important to an understanding of the way in which *Roses* plays on a notion of the rose as fetish in a further sense. The photographic frame, insofar as it is present, is formed by the layers of rose petals. Here it is possible to trace a link between the frame and lack. John Tagg, in his discussion of framing and discourse, articulates just such a relationship between the frame and lack: 'The frame is all show and yet it escapes visibility, like the labia which, to the infibulating eye Freud gives the little boy, already present the desolate spectacle of 'nothing' to be seen, enframing the sight of pure difference' (97).

Modotti's photograph, on both a thematic and compositional level, stages an encounter with alterity, with the 'sight of pure difference'. This encounter takes place in a space in which the viewer is not only denied the security of the frame, but this frame itself comes to figure lack, the sight of nothing (and everything) to see. On this level, *Roses* is an obscene, even a scandalous image. However, the factor that ultimately makes it utterly scandalous is the fact that this is a photographic image. That is to say, photography's ostensible purchase on the real—its apparent ability to offer a transparent, unmediated representation of reality—in the final analysis points towards the possibility of a direct reference between the signifier and the signified, the rose/cunt.

Post Script

In 1995, the Philadelphia Museum of Art staged a major retrospective of Modotti's photographs, curated by the critic Sarah M. Lowe. Sponsors of the show included the Pew Charitable Trusts and the National Endowment for the Arts. But the show's major sponsor, who brought with her publicity as well as money, was Madonna:

> While Madonna has quietly sponsored many exhibits over the years, she wanted to make this one a media event. 'Madonna doesn't want or need the press for everything she does,' explains her curator, Darlene Lutz. 'But she has strong feelings about Modotti's work and felt that publicity would bring more people into the gallery.' And so Madonna decided to pay her share by auctioning off her 1969 Mercedes convertible—the one you've seen in her video for *Deeper and Deeper*—bringing in twice its book value, $56,350, which she donated (Rubin 75).

The processes of commodity fetishism at work around the frames of Modotti's photographs, it would appear, are set to become ever more complex as 'Modotti' traverses the capitalist system of circulation and exchange. It remains to be seen, however, whether interest in the photographs as objects worthy of critical study will manage to keep apace of the overtly commercial interest that the signature/body 'Modotti' elicits.

Notes

1. Tina Modotti (1896-1942). For biographical information, see Hooks (1993).
2. Karl Marx, *Capital*, vol. 1, especially 'The Commodity' pp. 125-177 and 'The Process of Exchange', pp. 178-187.
3. Sigmund Freud, 'Fetishism', *Standard Edition of the Complete Psychological Works* vol. 21, pp. 147-158.
4. This is borne out in Cunliffe's Vogue article with which I opened this chapter. The article features a full-page reproduction of Weston's *Tina on the Azotea* which faces the title page of the article.
5. I have been unable to find any other source that lists the photograph's title as *Roses, Mexico* other than in the literature that appeared around the time of the sale.
6. The fact that Modotti produced the bulk of her photographs in Mexico is not insignificant, and critics have tended to claim her as a Mexican photographer. See Conger and Poniatowska (45), where Poniatowska declares that Modotti was Mexico's first woman photographer.
7. A full-length version of the catalogue essay is reproduced in Mulvey (1989, 81-107). It has also been published in abridged form in Betterton (211-16), and Frascina and Harris (145-159).
8. For a discussion of texture and tactility, see my 'Tina Modotti and the Politics of Signature'.

Works Cited

Betterton, Rosemary. (1987) *Looking On: Images of Femininity and the Visual Arts and Media*. London: Pandora.

Conger, Amy and Elena Poniatowska. (1990) *Compañeras de México: Women Photograph Women*. Riverside: The University of California.

Cunliffe, Lesley. (1993) 'Guns and Roses', *Vogue*. September: 210-13, 275.

Franco, Jean. (1993) '"Manhattan will be more exotic this fall": the Iconisation of Frida Kahlo', *Women: a Cultural Review* 2: 220-7.

Frascina, Francis and Jonathan Harris. (1992) *Art in Modern Culture: An Anthology of Critical Texts*. London: Phaidon.

Freud, Sigmund. (1961) 'Fetishism', in *Standard Edition of the Complete Psychological Works*. vol 21. London: Hogarth Press and the Institute of Psychoanalysis.

Hooks, Margaret. (1993) *Tina Modotti: Photographer and Revolutionary*. London: Pandora.

Lowe, Sarah M. (1995) *Tina Modotti: Photographs.* New York: Abrams.

Marx, Karl. (1976) *Capital.* London: Penguin.

Mulvey, Laura. (1989) *Visual and Other Pleasures.* London: Macmillan.

Mulvey, Laura. (1996) *Fetishism and Curiosity.* Bloomington and Indianapolis: Indiana UP; London: BFI.

Nead, Lynda. (1992) *The Female Nude: Art, Obscenity and Sexuality.* London: Routledge.

Noble, Andrea. (1995) 'Tina Modotti and the Politics of Signature', *Women: A Cultural Review* 6: 286-95.

Paz, Octavio. (1983) 'Frida y Tina: Vidas no Paralelas', *Vuelta* September: 48.

Pollock, Griselda. (1992) 'The Gaze and The Look: Women with Binoculars—A Question of Difference', in *Dealing with Degas: Representations of Women and the Politics of Vision*, ed. Richard Kendall and Griselda Pollock. London: Pandora, 106-30.

Rubin, Sabrina. (1995) 'Lucky Star', *Philadelphia* September: 75.

Schwichtenberg, Cathy, ed. (1993) *The Madonna Connection: Representational Politics, Subcultural Identities, and Cultural Theory.* Oxford: Westview Press.

Shor, Naomi. (1992) 'Fetishism', in *Feminism and Psychoanalysis: A Critical Dictionary*, ed. Elizabeth Wright. Oxford: Blackwell, 113-17.

Smith, Lindsay. (1992) 'The Politics of Focus: Feminism and Photography Theory', in *New Feminist Discourses: Critical Essays on Theories and Texts*, ed. Isobel Armstrong. London: Routledge, 238-62.

Solomon-Godeau, Abigail. (1991) *Photography at the Dock: Essays on Photographic History, Institutions, and Practices.* Minneapolis: University of Minnesota Press.

Sotheby's Catalogue: sale date 17 April 1991.

Squiers, Carol. (1993) 'Suzie Tomkins Markets Modotti', *American Photo* 4: 16.

Tagg, John. (1995) 'A Discourse (With the Shape of Reason Missing)', in *Vision and Textuality*, ed. Stephen Melville and Bill Readings. London: Macmillan, 90-114.

Wollen, Peter. (1993) *Raiding the Icebox: Reflections on Twentieth-Century Culture.* London: Verso.

AFRICAN REMAINS OF THE DAY:

Art and Object at the American Museum of Natural History

Lisa Botshon

> This is a weekend for the African explorer, and you don't have to go
> by way of the Cape of Good Hope, either... [T]he many cultures and
> esthetics of the big continent on the downtown side of the
> Mediterranean will be making a splash in Manhattan.
>
> *The New York Times,* June 8, 1990

As a venerable institution of New York City, the American Museum of
Natural History is a place of cultural memory for many New Yorkers, and
has fascinated generations of children with everything from beetle wings to
dinosaur bones, from birchbark canoes to the great blue whale that takes up
the entire ceiling of a huge museum hall. In 1995 the Museum celebrated its
125th anniversary, provoking waves of nostalgia among many who
remember the required stop for all city elementary school children. During
the celebration the *New Yorker* published an extensive article in which James
Traube quotes a salient passage from J.D. Salinger's *Catcher in the Rye*:

> The best thing...in that museum was that everything always stayed
> right where it was. Nobody'd move. You could go there a hundred
> thousand times and that Eskimo would still be just finished catching
> those two fish, the birds would still be on their way south, the deers
> would still be drinking out of that water hole... The only thing that
> would be different would be *you* (48).

Holden Caulfield's affirmation of the Museum's constancy seems
appropriate for the anniversary. When I went back to the Museum several
years ago, for the first time since childhood, it initially looked more or less
the way I remembered it. At first, the only thing that seemed different was
me. The blue whale still threatened from its ceiling perch, the enlarged cross-
section of the forest floor still loomed with giant beetles and grubs.

I have come to realize, however, that the Museum, far from having settled
into a comfortable stasis, has most definitely undergone change, much for
the better. For example, in 1990, the Museum curated a breakthrough
exhibit entitled 'African Reflections: Art From Northeastern Zaire', which
ran for about a year before it went on tour around the USA and was

eventually dismantled. This exhibit was a new approach for the Museum of Natural History, an institution that has been, for many reasons, resistant to showing its treasures as 'art'. But this exhibit, which was quite courageous in ways I will discuss below, also led me to seek out the museum's permant exhibition of African objects, displayed in traditional ethnographic formats; the viewing of these two exhibits together caused me to consider more deeply the responsibilities of a museum of natural history to both its holdings and its constituencies. This essay is an attempt to think through some of the problems inherent in the American Museum of Natural History's traditions and new approaches to display from the perspective of someone who gets both misty-eyed in the hall of invertebrates and distraught in the gallery of African Peoples.[1]

First, a little historical background. The American Museum of Natural History was founded by a group of wealthy denizens of New York in 1869 to encourage both beginning and professional study of the 'natural sciences'. One of these, ethnography, was a budding science and, by the end of the nineteenth century, was operating almost solely in conjunction with museums (many connected to universities) which housed the collections brought back for further examination.[2] The Museum helped fund expeditions all over the world and was a site at which ethnographers could collect and categorize materials which were then put on display for the public.

The Museum, though meant for public education, was first geared primarily towards supporting professional scientists. It sent tentacles in the form of safari-suited men (and occasionally women) throughout the world in search of objects to bring back, order and display. In an anecdotal history of the American Museum of Natural History, Douglas Preston writes, 'More than anything, natural scientists of the late nineteenth century believed deeply in the value of *collections*. To them, collections were *facts*. They held secrets about the world, secrets that could be extracted through careful study' (24).[3] Collecting is what has traditionally defined the Museum's ideology, and it is historically associated with the way in which the West has regarded the rest of the world as its own property. When the Museum sent out its Congo Expedition in 1909, for example, to explore, acquire and bring back parts of what was later known as Zaire, it was participating in a realm of action intricately connected to colonialism.

Significantly, the fruits of Europe's colonial past, objects marked by the discourse of Western power, are now housed in museums around the world, and displayed with little or no reference to their many contexts. This is especially true of older ethnographic exhibits. The hall of African Peoples in the American Museum of Natural History is a classic case. First conceived in

1961, the exhibit (originally called 'Men of Africa') took years to complete; outside experts were called in to help, and it was finally installed in 1968. The exhibit, one of nine of the Museum's permanent 'Peoples' exhibits, is located on the second floor, handily near the hall of African mammals, which includes a still-stunning display of African elephants trumpeting down the center, the brainchild of scientist and hunter Carl Akeley.[4]

Its proximity to the animal displays aside, African Peoples is both fascinating and disturbing. Let me dwell on the fascinating first. A visit in 1995, during the Museum's ongoing anniversary celebration, revealed scores of beautiful objects, many of which looked better than they did even a few years earlier: clearly the museum had invested in cleaning the formerly dusty display cases. There was an impressive array of dance costumes from all over the continent, including a Yoruba costume made of snail shells that was of particular interest. There was also some terrific beadwork, carved ivory, and intricate textiles. One could easily spend a good deal of time here examining the objects individually but, ultimately, the presentation is unsettling.

One of the most noticeable items is a large map of Africa on the wall, arranged by tribe; no national boundaries grace this illustration. Indeed, in each of my many visits to this hall I have been struck by the paucity of information about modern nations. It is far too easy to walk through these rooms, look at the displays, and forget that these objects come from real people who lived or live in places like Kenya, Cameroon, and Zaire, countries that have political, economic, and cultural fluctuations of global importance. And, although most of the objects displayed were collected in this century, the rhetoric of the accompanying explanations encourages ahistorical readings of the people who created them. Utterly absent from the signage and display is the sense of the development of cross-cultural communities, the exploitation of imperialism, and the painful and violent processes of nation formation that most African countries went through even before 1968, when this exhibition was put together.[5] In the hall of African Peoples, life is presented as almost pre-lapsarian. Some spears and such are shown—these, we are informed, are for occasional raids, which allow tribes like the Masai to 'blow off steam'.

As might be expected, most of the general information presented about Africa relies on archaic anthropological description. For example, there are little molecular-type models of 'The African Family', and confusing signage about clans and tribes; these serve mainly to impart a scientific rhetoric and render the displayed artifacts as fragments of primitive peoples who are best understood in distanced, timeless, ethnographic terms.[6] The objects displayed are mostly suspended in glass cases. They are strangely disembodied, disassociated from their functions, with little reference to how they are or were used, or who made or used them. They are largely categorized by ecosystem, of which there are four: River Valley, Grasslands, Desert, and Forest, implying that geography has been one of the greatest factors in determining the African culture. Significantly, the animals across the hall are represented similarly.

The objects are accompanied by ethnographic data which provide little insight into the original dynamics between the object and its creator or user. It is also unclear where the objects came from or, especially, how the Museum procured them. Donald Horne explains that this kind of worship of the object-in-itself does not 'tell its history; we are confronted by objects without social process. It is as if relics of human society were dropped on us like meteors from outer space' (249). The displays have been designed by a few Western scientists who have decided what best represents a multitude of African people, and in doing so have appropriated particular objects that once belonged to others.[7] The small print of certain labels is equally revealing, as the 'original' ownership of an object or collection is usually attributed to the Western collector, rather than the African producer.

When it comes right down to it, the politics underlying this exhibit are pretty bankrupt. Here, as James Clifford would say, history has been airbrushed out (202). The thoughtful visitor cannot help but see how the continent of Africa is sterilized, categorized and homogenized in response to the dictates of an antiquated American anthropology. The beauty and intrinsic interest of the objects presented are counterbalanced by the idea of all Africans as primitives, living close to nature, guided by the kinship patterns of their ancient ancestors, weaving baskets, and providing the Museum visitor with the dark half of the mirror by which we see ourselves.[8]

It becomes more apparent, then, why it was so important for the museum to develop the temporary exhibit: 'African Reflections: Art from Northeastern Zaire'. This exhibit was initially conceived when a professor of history and political science, Curtis Keim, came to the museum and, according to his collaborator on the exhibit, Enid Schildkrout, claimed 'the Mangbetu [a tribe in what is now Zaire] didn't have anthropomorphic art in the 19th century and they don't have it today'. Dr. Schildkrout says that they 'debated this for several years and [they] finally concluded that something happened in the colonial period, from the 1890's to the 1920's, that made anthropomorphic art flourish as an art style among the Mangbetu' (quoted in the *New York Times* July 1, 1990). It turns out that what influenced the Mangbetu art was in fact Europeans—both the colonial presence of the Belgians, and the European market for African art. The Mangbetu figured out what would sell and made to order.

This, I must admit, is a compelling story. And it has many of the elements missing in the Hall of African Peoples: greater focus, fuller history, the inclusion of colonial encounters, an understanding of market pressures, and the celebration of individual craftspeople (now called artists). 'African Reflections' successfully broadened the visitor's perspective of the objects, which were from the same expeditions as some of the objects downstairs. Noteworthy too is that this exhibit attemped to portray the Museum's own interaction with the people of northeastern Zaire by incorporating narrative relating the history of the two Museum-funded zoologists who went there on a six-year scientific expedition in 1909.

The introductory panel explained that the exhibit meant to trace 'the origin of the Mangbetu-style art from the mid-19th century to the present'. Looking around the gallery, however, it was difficult to find any objects that did not originate in the early part of the century. In fact, the fine print at the bottom of the introduction revealed that most of the objects came from the Congo Expedition of 1909–15. Thus, the 'tracing through the century' mission was somewhat misleading. It was interesting, though, that similar objects downstairs in 'African Peoples' were called 'ethnographic artifacts', whereas here everything was under the umbrella term 'art'. Also significant is that the display of these objects was more or less the same as downstairs, with a few more tasteful neutral tones at the bases and backboards of display cases. Here objects were divided, not by ecosystem, but by use genre (Musical Instuments, Pottery, etc.), with few forays outside these categories. While I appreciated the radical step the museum took in portraying these objects in a different way, I wondered whether labelling these objects as art was progress in representation.

The re-assessing of these objects as art did, however, accomplish several things. It was eye-opening to think of the same objects as in the Hall of African Peoples as the creations of individual artisans. This lessened the dehumanization of the creative process and brought the individual artist into contemplation. Additionally, the objects acquired more value as art than as artifact, although this is a problematic transformation.[9] There is at present a large market for primitive art, and this, as Sally Price says, 'is customarily heralded with warmth and pride. Here, too, the pride...emerges from the same limited presence that such events [as the incorporation of primitive art into Western institutions] come about through an enormous commendable broadmindedness and largesse on the part of the host culture' (25).[10] This paternalistic quality of Western institutions is inherent in both African exhibitions, where the Museum, as Price argues, relishes its own 'enlightened appreciation of cultural diversity' (25).

One of the more courageous aspects of 'African Reflections' was the assignation of a good deal of space to a discussion of the two zoologists who, in 1909, went forth into the Congo to collect mostly animal specimens in the name of the American Museum of Natural History. The twenty-seven year old Herbert Lang and eighteen year old James Chapin (who, incidentally, interrupted his studies at Columbia University for this trip) spent six years in a region now known as Zaire primarily to study wildlife. Their main mission, in fact, was to document and bring back okapis, an animal related to the giraffe. Their okapi is still on display in the hall of African mammals. But along the way the two men documented their hosts as well, and traded for and were given gifts of many Mangbetu crafts. Lang and Chapin, who had intended to stay in Zaire for only two years, returned to New York in 1915, on the eve of World War I, with reams of field notes and photographs as well as over 4000 Mangbetu objects among their 54 tons of cargo. The story of Lang and Chapin is incredible, and evokes a thrill similar to that found in the novels of Rider Haggard.[11] It is amazing to think the museum was able to keep alive and make real the boys' adventure tales so popular during the apex of colonialism.

The narrative of 'African Reflections' seemed to play off this adventurers' tale with a twist of multiculturalism, which lent the project, as one *New York Times* reviewer noticed, 'an idyllic aura of cross-cultural cooperation that may be a little inaccurate' (August 3, 1990, C23). The signage attempted to distinguish the 'great explorers' from their preceding 'marauding slavetraders', in order to preserve their men from being associated with Western 'atrocities', and to prevent the Museum from being implicated in foreign 'disruption'. But the Museum reverted to its old ways when it insisted on attaching Lang and Chapin's names to all of their 'found' objects. Although the African artist was given more room than usual here ultimately the collectors achieved prominence.

Although the Museum incorporated the word 'colonialism' in its representation of foreign forces in Africa, a word that is deftly hidden in the permanent exhibit downstairs, most of the narrative in the section entitled 'Colonialism in the Congo' involved the relationship between King Leopold II and the Belgian government. A discussion of Leopold's reign over the Congo Free Estate was distancing and abstract, as the text read that *some* felt that he had committed 'atrocities'. Neither the exhibit nor the much more extensive exhibition catalogue adequately explore the relationship between Leopold and the Museum. But the story of this relationship, and of the carving up of the African continent in general, seems critical to understanding how these objects reached their New York City destination, and what they mean in an international context.

214

In their catalogue Schildkrout and Keim do provide some explanation of the Berlin Conference of 1884–85 that basically authorized a 'land rush for the major parts of the continent of Africa' among the European nations, during which Leopold acquired what he called the 'Etat indépendant du Congo', the Congo Free State (36).[12] But the author/curators gloss over the violence and greed (forced labour, heavy taxation, and reports of cruelty) associated with his regime, and instead choose to concentrate on his 'humanitarian goals and an interest in scientific exploration', which, of course, was of great help to the Museum (48). In brief, King Leopold II had a connection with the financier J.P. Morgan, who was a trustee of the Museum, and in 1907 Leopold presented the Museum with a gift of 3500 objects collected in the Congo Free State. During this period the Belgian king was harshly criticized for his administration of this parcel of African property; the Museum—which was interested in expanding its collection of African artifacts, and had negotiated with Leopold about their expedition plans—was drawn into this debate. Nonetheless, not only was this information erased from the exhibit, the catalogue, too, skirts over this overt connection between the Museum and exploitative imperial practices.

While it is understandable why Schildkrout and Keim leave out these details, it is compelling to think about what one might have learned and the connections one might have made if they had been incorporated into the exhibit. The Mangbetu associated with the production of the objects on display might have been the same Mangbetu who mutinied against colonial rule. The king who generously bequeathed many objects to the Museum in the name of science and education was the same king who extracted rubber and ivory from his African subjects. These parallel histories were hinted at in the exhibit and are nervously sketched in the catalogue, but they were never fully accessible to the Museum visitor.

Moreover, the signage displayed open admiration for the 'civilizing' Belgian administration, which had taken over from Leopold in 1908, and 'continued to export rubber and minerals, introduced new crops for export, and built railroads, roads, and commercial centers'. In addition, the catalogue maintains: 'Although Lang and Chapin attempted to be apolitical, in the end they both came to view the Belgian regime as beneficent' (57). The Belgian government was quite cooperative with the Museum's mission and even provided some funding for the expedition. Hence, Lang and Chapin were in no position to criticize in public the new colonial administration, regardless of its activities.

Nonetheless, Lang's black and white photographs added an element to the exhibit that was otherwise lacking. One photo depicts a few European men hanging around a train, one shows the home of a colonial administrator, another is a portrait of a group of Africans and Europeans standing in front of a chapel, and the last portrays a trial in which a European man dressed in a white suit sits behind a desk giving orders to his barefoot African assistant, also dressed in a white suit. To the rear is a lineup of four African men chained together. They are the only ones looking at the camera. No external narrative accompanied these photographs. The main theme here seems to be how Belgium civilized the primitives through industry, religion, the courts, and so on. The rhetoric of violence is omitted, save through the last photograph: the chained men's gaze defies the Museum's passive voice and insists that the viewer think about the conflict involved.

Lang's vision of Africa dominated the entire exhibit as his photographs of the people of Northeastern Zaire were displayed throughout. Ultimately though, 'African Reflections' severely limited the potential of this African gaze, and the vision of Africa that it could reflect. Lang, a prolific photographer, rejected many photographs from his finished ethnographic albums, because, as Schildkrout and Keim contend, 'they revealed aspects of daily life that [he] felt were not African or sufficiently traditional. For example, people sometimes wore imported European clothes, but the more formal portraits show them dressed in raffia, bark cloth and feathers' (1990b: 75). The authors are careful to mention that Lang was an untrained ethnographer and a man limited by the ideology of his time. But this fact is not that interesting in and of itself, particularly given the lack of detail concerning the cross-cultural relationships that must have occurred between the Museum zoologists and their Congo porters, assistants, and hosts.[13] The expedition of 1909 must have been heavily reliant upon a spirit of cooperation, but it was also influenced by economic conditions whereby Lang and Chapin had a great deal more power than the men they employed. In addition, Lang and Chapin were in the Belgian Congo for a total of six years, enough time for them to have learned local languages and for them to have been intimately acquainted with more than a few individuals. We can only speculate on the complexity of relations that existed between the zoologists and the Congolese during the height of the colonial era.

A more contemporary addition to this exhibit was a video entitled 'Mangbetu in the Modern World'. This was the only part of the exhibit that attempted to show the Mangbetu as participants in contemporary society. In something of a breakthrough compared to 'African Peoples', several Mangbetu talked about what the objects displayed in the Museum meant to them, but in traditional ethnographic documentary fashion, their voices were often overridden by the disembodied voice of the English-speaking narrator. However, I noticed that after going through the whole gallery, many visitors passed over the film completely, thereby missing the only effort at providing a contemporary African perspective.

It was the very last display that seemed to interest visitors most. This was an installment of the Museum Shop. Here one could purchase everything from a replica of a Mangbetu-style vessel displayed in this exhibit, to an Ethiopian mason basket similar to one displayed in 'African Peoples'. The shop acutely reminded me that the exhibiton was reduced without its market value stuck on a price tag. I wondered if the objects on display were more valuable after they were reproduced in the shop, or was it the other way around?

I am critical of 'African Reflections', not because I think it was a poor exhibit, but because I think it was an important one. Despite its failings, this exhibit provided the most complete and honest representation of African objects that I have ever seen in a museum of natural history and, in many way, it far exceeds even recent art exhibits of similar objects.[14] Perhaps the greatest flaw of 'African Reflections' was its temporality. After its national tour it was disbanded, leaving the much less progressive hall of African Peoples as the only site in which one might see and think about African objects.

Additionally, the Museum seemed to regress in its anniversary activities. In 1995 the Museum designed a new self-guided tour called 'Expedition: Treasures from 125 Years of Discovery'. Children were given guides and locator maps with which they could find particular 'treasures' on each floor. The Museum designed 'base camps' and 'field stations' in selected areas, which featured early 20th-century photographs of Museum scientists out in the field, fuzzy film footage of old jeep trips through central Asia, ancient Remington typewriters, and rusty canteens. These sites evoked Ralph Lauren-type safari nostalgia and, together with the maps and guides, they mimicked adventures associated only with colonial situations. The 125th anniversary might have given the Museum a reason to pause and think about how better to represent its many artifacts, especially those belonging to the 'peoples' exhibits. The 'Expedition' guide, however, demonstrated the Museum's resistance to certain kinds of change, and its heavy investment in the colonial adventure story.

Recently the American Museum of Natural History revamped its entire dinosaur exhibit for $12 million, in hopes of drawing more visitors to its ageing halls. The new exhibit features a completely refurbished space with robotic dinosaur heads, computer stations and a skeletal tyrannosaurus rex that has been repositioned to reflect the latest hypotheses concerning its movement. The new space is bright, user-friendly and wildly popular. But repositioning dinosaur bones only accomplishes so much. I would like to see the museum put its money where its anthropology is, and help visitors see that Africa is a continent of varied nations and cultures that have moved and shifted as modern nations and cultures do, and that it is not, and never was, a blank space on the map of a little boy's imagination. Although the temporary 'African Reflections' was certainly a step in the right direction, the Museum would do well to investigate and invest in display that avoids the dehumanization of traditional anthropology and the commodification of artifact as art. Ultimately, I must remain loyal to this institution, which so inspired me as a child, but I will relish the day when I walk into the Hall of African Peoples and find that I am not the only one to have changed.

Notes

1. In the last decade or so, studies devoted to the exploration of museum activity have mushroomed. Comprehensive volumes of collected essays include Ivan Karp and Steven D. Lavine's *Exhibiting Cultures*, Karp and Christine Mullen Kreamer's *Museums and Communities*, and Flora Kaplan's *Museums and the Making of 'Ourselves'*. This essay owes some of its sense of direction to these earlier studies.

2. See George Stocking's *The Ethnographer's Magic* for an excellent collection of essays on the history of anthropology. Several chapters, including one on Franz Boas's career and one on philanthropic funding, are of particular relevance to the American Museum of Natural History.

3. Mieke Bal aptly notes, 'Collecting is what scholars, pioneers, art lovers, colonialists, and museums do; gathering is what primitive folk do' (47).

4. While the stuffed animals still draw millions of visitors each year, the politics behind these displays are disturbing. Donna Haraway's important essay, 'Teddy Bear Patriarchy: Taxidermy in the Garden of Eden, New York City, 1908–36', historicizes the creation of this hall and links Akeley's vision of a hall of dead African mammals to the eugenicist pursuit of white racial purity.

5. An exception to this presentation is a sign placed *outside* the hall that conveys a sense that the objects of Africa's past might help gain a better understanding of the present. In addition, during a visit in 1990, I noticed a photomural entitled 'Africa Today', which included some shots of urban scenes and industrial agriculture. However, this work, like all the others in the gallery, was not really historicized or contextualized.

6. The labels still utilize the 'ethnographic present', aptly described by Sally Price as 'a device that abstracts cultural expression from the flow of historical time and hence collapses individuals and whole generations into a composite figure alleged to represent his fellows past and present' (57). This is evident in the line about the Masai blowing off steam, quoted above. One is provoked to ask: Have

the Masai always needed to 'blow off steam'? Do they still? Do all the Masai need to do this?

7. Douglas Preston comments that 'although the Museum exhibits cover 700,000 square feet of floor space, only about one or two percent of the collection is on display' (xi).

8. See Marianne Torgovnick and James Clifford, among others, for now-classic discussions on the discourse of primitivism and how it has been used in Western culture.

9. Barbara Kirshenblatt-Gimblett argues, 'Ethnographic objects move from curio to specimen to art, although not necessarily in that order' (392). Depending on the exhibition, then, it is also possible to conceive of art objects 'reclassified for scientific purposes' (393). Objects are mutable, mobile, and reclassifiable according to the exhibitor's purpose and the viewer's perspective.

10. Another problem in the reclassification of African objects as art is a competitive market that makes it difficult for African nations to buy or buy back what are considered to be national treasures. See Ekpo Eyo for a partial list of colonial plunderings that left cities, palaces and tombs bereft of important works. Eyo also comments on the current market for African art and the legislation that impedes reparation of much African cultural heritage.

11. In a transcribed interview recorded in 1960 and published in 1990, James Chapin recalls imbibing regular doses of quinine, tramping through woods with a caravan of local men as porters and assistants, Mangbetu dances, European administrators, making nails for packing crates out of confiscated guns, and, of course, hunting down animal specimens for the Museum. What more could one ask for from an adventure story?

12. Leopold ruled the Congo Free State and Belgium, for which he was constitutional monarch, as separate entities. The Congo Free State belonged to Leopold as private property; however, the two were financially linked. The inhabitants of the Congo Free State resisted both occupation and taxation, and staged various mutinies until Belgium took over the state in 1908. See Stengers and Vansina's concise entry in the *Cambridge History of Africa* and Emerson's volume on Leopold for more detailed investigations of his rule.

13. We do know that the Congo Expedition employed over 38,000 porters over the course of six years, and trained eighteen men as field assistants. Lang and Chapin were thus, at overlapping times, employers, scientists, adventurers, and maybe even friends to the people they met and worked with.

14. The 1996 exhibit of African art at the Guggenheim, for example, rivals the Museum of Natural History's Hall of African Peoples in its lack of focus and abject politics.

Works Cited

Bal, Mieke. (1996) *Double Exposures: The Subject of Cultural Analysis*. New York: Routledge.

Chapin, James. (1990) 'Pictures from an Exhibition', trans. Thomas Gilliard. *Natural History*, November 1990: 18-33.

Clifford, James. (1988) *The Predicament of Culture: Twentieth Century Ethnography, Literature and Art.* Cambridge: Harvard UP.

Emerson, Barbara. (1979) *Leopold II of the Belgians: King of Colonialism.* London: Weidenfeld and Nicolson.

Eyo, Ekpo. (1994) 'Reparation of Cultural Heritage: The African Experience', in *Museums and the Making of 'Ourselves': The Role of Objects in National Identity*, ed. Flora E.S. Kaplan. London: Leicester UP.

Haraway, Donna. (1989) *Primate Visions: Gender, Race, and Nature in the World of Modern Science.* New York: Routledge.

Horne, Donald. (1984) *The Great Museum: The Re-Presentation of History.* London: Pluto Press.

Kaplan, Flora E.S. (1994) *Museums and the Making of 'Ourselves': The Role of Objects in National Identity.* London: Leicester UP.

Karp, Ivan and Steven Lavine, eds. (1991) *Exhibiting Cultures: The Poetics and Politics of Museum Display.* Washington: Smithsonian Institution Press.

Karp, Ivan and Christine Mullen Kreamer, eds. (1992) *Museums and Communities: The Politics of Public Culture.* Washington: Smithsonian Institution Press.

Keim, Curtis and Enid Schildkrout. (1990a) *African Reflections: Art from Northeastern Zaire.* Seattle: University of Washington Press.

Keim, Curtis and Enid Schildkrout. (1990b) 'Art of Africa', *Natural History* June 1990: 72-7.

Kirshenblatt-Gimblett, Barbara. (1991) 'Objects of Ethnography', in *Exhibiting Cultures: The Poetics and Politics of Museum Display*, eds. Ivan Karp and Steven Lavine. Washington: Smithsonian Institution Press.

Preston, Douglas. (1986) *Dinosaurs in the Attic: An Excursion into the American Museum of Natural History.* New York: St. Martin's Press.

Price, Sally. (1989) *Primitive Art in Civilized Places.* Chicago: University of Chicago Press.

Shepard, Richard F. (1990) 'Out of Black Africa: Varied Perspectives of Life and the Arts', *New York Times* June 8, 1990: C1, 17.

Smith, Roberta. (1990) 'The Genius and Panache of Africa's "Parisians"', *New York Times* August 3, 1990: C1, 23.

Stengers, Jean and Jan Vansina. (1985) 'King Leopold's Congo, 1886–1908', in *The Cambridge History of Africa* vol 6, eds. Roland Oliver and G.N. Sanderson. Cambridge: Cambridge UP.

Stocking, George W. (1992) *The Ethnographer's Magic and Other Essays in the History of Anthropology.* Madison: University of Wisconsin Press.

Torgovnick, Marianna. (1990) *Gone Primitive: Savage Intellects, Modern Lives.* Chicago: University of Chicago Press.

Traube, James. (1995) 'Shake Them Bones', *New Yorker* March 13, 1995: 48-62.

INDEX

221